Samuel Johns(
Journey into vvui uɔ

Popular readings of Johnson as a dictionary-maker often see him as a writer who both laments and attempts to control the state of the language. Lynda Mugglestone looks at the range of Johnson's writings on, and the complexity of his thinking about language and lexicography. She shows how these reveal him probing problems not just of meaning and use but what he considered the related issues of control, obedience, and justice, as well as the difficulties of power when exerted over the 'sea of words'. She examines his attitudes to language change, loan words, spelling, history, and authority, describing, too, the evolution of his ideas about the nature, purpose, and methods of lexicography, and shows how these reflect his own wider thinking about politics, culture, and society. The book offers a careful reassessment of Johnson's lexicographical practice, examining in detail his commitment to evidence, and the uses to which this might be put.

Dictionary-making, for Johnson, came to be seen as a long and difficult voyage round the world of the English language. While such images play their own role in lexicographical tradition, Johnson would, as this volume explores, also make them very much his own in a range of distinctive, and illuminating, ways. Johnson's metaphors invite us to consider—and reconsider—the processes by which a dictionary might be made and the kind of destination it might seek, as well as the state of language that might be reached by such endeavours. For Johnson, where the dictionary-maker might go, and what should be accomplished along the way, can raise pertinent and perhaps troubling questions.

Lynda Mugglestone's generous, wide-ranging account casts new light on Johnson's life in language and provides an engaging reassessment of his impact on English culture, the making of dictionaries, and their role in a nation's identity.

Lynda Mugglestone is Professor of the History of English at the University of Oxford and Fellow and Tutor in English at Pembroke College, Oxford.

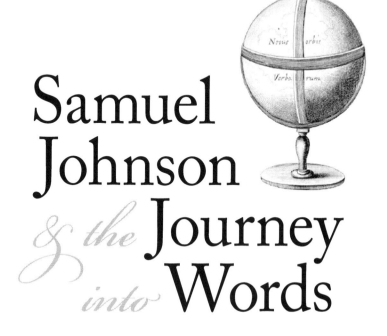

Samuel Johnson & the Journey into Words

LYNDA MUGGLESTONE

OXFORD
UNIVERSITY PRESS

OXFORD
UNIVERSITY PRESS

Great Clarendon Street, Oxford, OX2 6DP,
United Kingdom

Oxford University Press is a department of the University of Oxford.
It furthers the University's objective of excellence in research, scholarship,
and education by publishing worldwide. Oxford is a registered trade mark of
Oxford University Press in the UK and in certain other countries

© Lynda Mugglestone 2015

The moral rights of the author have been asserted

First published 2015
First published in paperback 2018

Published in the United States of America by Oxford University Press
198 Madison Avenue, New York, NY 10016, United States of America

British Library Cataloguing in Publication Data
Data available

Library of Congress Cataloging in Publication Data
Data available

ISBN 978-0-19-967990-4 (Hbk.)
ISBN 978-0-19-883068-9 (Pbk.)

Contents

Preface

In a good introduction, Johnson wrote in *Rambler* 158, 'something
... must be discovered, and something concealed'. The 'intellectual
appetite' must be stimulated but not satiated: 'He that reveals too
much, or promises too little... equally defeats his own purpose.'[1]
Johnson's maxims offer a challenge for all prefaces in an image of
perfection that this particular Preface will undoubtedly fail to reach.
A sense of the productive tension which must exist between what
is—or is not—concealed resonates widely within Johnson's own
work. As for Lawrence Lipking, Johnson often occupies an intri-
guing 'double register' in ways which unite the exploration of
dissonant perspectives and approaches.[2] Johnson, writes Fussell, is
characterized by his 'all but simultaneous embrace of antithetical
opposites'.[3] This book, too, was prompted by similar forms of
antithesis and contiguity in terms of Johnson's role as dictionary-
maker between 1746 and 1755. 'Opposites' and 'contradictions', in
Fussell's terms, abound.

The nature of Johnson's lexicographical achievement can, of
course, contribute to a sense of the, quite literally, 'monumental',
whether in Boswell's image of Johnson as 'literary Colossus'[4] or, as
for Christopher Smart, in envisaging the *Dictionary* as the linguistic
equivalent of St. Paul's Cathedral. For Smart, Johnson as architect of
English has—like Wren—constructed an edifice which should
endure for all time. Johnson's *Dictionary* was a 'monument of
English philology', he extolled:[5] it is 'a work I look upon with
equal pleasure and amazement, as I do upon St. *Paul's* Cathedral;
each the work of *one* man, each the work of an *Englishman*'.[6]
Johnson's stated ambitions to 'fix the English language', explored
in his *Plan of a Dictionary of the English Language* of 1747,[7] are
symbolically rendered in stone in ways which resolve other well-

established tropes of the problematic materiality of English. We need, Swift had urged, words 'more durable than brass'.[8] Johnson's *Dictionary*, as we will see, came into being against a complex background of both cultural and linguistic expectation in which immutability had long been constructed as a particular object of desire.

Yet, against such ambitions for stasis and control, Johnson can, throughout the dictionary years, construct a very different set of images for the enterprise in which he is engaged. Fixity, for example, exists against his iterated imaging of language as the sea, and lexicography as a voyage, in which ambitions to constrain the 'intumescence of the tide' are doomed to failure (*Yale* XVIII.106). As he writes to Thomas Warton in 1755, the dictionary as journey is almost at an end. In his imaging, the *Dictionary* is not a monument but a ship—undoubtedly 'vasta mole superbus' ['proud in its great bulk']—but defined, too, by its mobility and, in the days of sail, its inevitable responsiveness to external conditions.[9] Johnson embraces, too, as Chapter 1 explores, a set of antithetical identities in which power and powerlessness co-exist. As lexicographical drudge, he must trudge the 'track of the alphabet' (*Yale* XVIII.25). As a writer who intends to rule a 'new world' of words, his power might have to be absolute, involving—here in ventures of a very different kind—the processes of 'subjection' and attack (*Yale* XVIII.58). Thomas Tickell's image of the kind of linguistic enslavement which the proper regulation of English should enforce ('in happy Chains our daring Language bound, / Shall sport no more in arbitrary Sound') can, for Johnson, inform other conflicts of this kind.[10] In Johnson's 'new world' of words, the subjects might be quelled in colonial metaphors in which power is prime. Yet, in still other images, power is reversed. Johnson, as 'slave of science' (*Yale* XVIII.73), must simply follow where knowledge leads.

While lexicography, as other dictionary-makers confirm, can easily be figured as a journey into words,[11] Johnson's handling of this trope—and the reality of what he does in his own ventures in this respect—can offer therefore a range of fruitful directions for exploration. For Johnson, the different directions the dictionary-maker might pursue, as well as the state of language that might be reached—and ruled—by such endeavours, form composite parts of what he described in 1755 as the 'long and painful voyage' which he had taken 'round the world of the English language'.[12]

The different chapters of this book, as Chapter 1 details, map the course of the first edition of the *Dictionary*, situating it within the lexicographic landscape of its time, as well as within Johnson's wider writing both during and after the dictionary years. The structure is loosely chronological, spanning the years of lexicographical composition from 1746 to 1755, though individual chapters often engage with a thematic core—probing the problems (and polysemies) of ordering the world of words in Chapter 4, for example, or focussing on the border territories of language in Chapter 6 where expectations of Johnson as border guard, defending English from incursion, are placed alongside his exploration in the liminal zones where English is still being formed. Close attention is given to the *Dictionary* itself, and the nuances of Johnson's evidence and approach—not least in his treatment of variation and change in a language which was, as he reminded readers in 1755, all too alive.

'Both the advantage and the difficulty' of writing about Johnson, as Walter Jackson Bate has memorably stressed, 'is that almost every aspect of his thought is so intimately connected with all the others'. The result, he adds, is that 'as soon as we pick up one corner of the blanket, we suddenly find the whole of it brought into our arms'.[13] While the *Dictionary* has often remained outside considerations of this kind, Johnson's work in his wider life as writer will, in fact, frequently illuminate the nexus of ideas which informed lexicography in Johnson's hands. Power and powerlessness, dictatorship and suffrage, human desire and aspiration (in language as all else), the problems of hope and the difficulty of perfection and truth, alongside the conflicted domains of doubt and certainty, as well as the exigencies (and problems) of collection, all emerge as recurrent themes. These add a complex backdrop to the *Dictionary*, and the directions that Johnson—as writer and lexicographer—might take.

In language, as Johnson found out, there is, of course, always more to be said, while the constraints of what can be included in a single work impose their own tensions between what is 'omitted' as well as 'performed' (*Yale* XVIII.111). As Johnson wrote of the *Dictionary* in 1755, it was, if ended, by no means 'completed' (*Yale* XVIII.101). The same applies, if in more pervasive ways, to this book: Johnson as writer on language can encompass a range of topics to which a single volume can scarcely do justice. Individual chapters could easily have been written on the fourth edition, as well as on Johnson's ventures into regional Englishes and other varieties, or into the language of science, trade, and commerce. Johnson's engagement with what 'we' do in language set against what 'they do', in referring to the Scots, offers, for example, some productive lines of further enquiry. As we will see, who 'we' are in the *Dictionary* often raises interesting aspects of English, and English in use. Examples, too, could have been multiplied at a range of points, illuminating and extending what Johnson does. For Johnson's treatment of Scottish, and the patterns that can be observed, I instead refer the reader to Marina Dossena's interesting article '"The Cinic Scotomastic"? Johnson, His Commentators, Scots, French, and the Story of English' in another book which explores the eighteenth-century world of words,[14] and, for the fourth edition, to Allen Reddick's detailed study in *The Making of Johnson's Dictionary, 1746–1773* as well as his exploration of the Sneyd–Gimbel materials.[15] Johnson is much 'too profuse in his quotations', Thomas Edwards expostulated in 1755 on the abundance of illustrative examples which the *Dictionary* contained.[16] It is perhaps just as well that some of those once included in this volume have not made the final cut.

Johnson's thinking on the life of words is wide-ranging and often surprising. Certainly, students and colleagues, as well as family and friends, may have been surprised over the last five years at just how often Johnson can be made to appear in conversation, or in discussion of topics that are ostensibly far removed from dictionaries. My children too seem to have gained an unexpected familiarity with the routes of eighteenth-century English, though, as a number of friends have observed, the fact that I have in recent months inadvertently addressed my youngest son as 'Johnson' on several occasions probably means that it is time to stop. I would, however, like to thank Bob DeMaria and Jim McLaverty for answering a range of queries, and Bob in particular for allowing early access to the Yale Digital Johnson which has undoubtedly expedited completion of this work. Linda Loder has usefully handled my queries on classical writing; while discussions with colleagues at a range of conferences, at which some of this material received an early outing, have invariably proved both useful and rewarding.

I would also like to thank the John Fell Oxford University Press Fund which supported research for this book at a critical stage. Thanks are also due to the The Bodleian Libraries, The University of Oxford, for permission to reproduce p. 2 of Matthew Hale's *The Primitive Origination of Mankind* (Dep c.25/2), the frontispiece to Edward Phillips's *New World of English Words* (Vet. A3 d. 196), and the frontispiece to *The Gentleman's Magazine* for 1752 (Per. Bibl.2), and to the National Portrait Gallery, London, for permission to reproduce John Hall's engraving of Samuel Johnson.

Lynda Mugglestone

October 2014

List of figures

1

Journeys into words

Lexicographer: 'A writer of dictionaries; a harmless drudge, that busies himself in tracing the original, and detailing the signification of words.' Inserted between the entry for *lewis d'or*, defined as 'a golden French coin, in value twelve livres', and that for *lexicography*, 'The art or practice of writing dictionaries', Samuel Johnson's definition has become one of the canonical images of his own role in writing his *Dictionary of the English Language* of 1755.[1] Drudges, as other entries in the *Dictionary* confirm, are scarcely to be envied. Oppression, and a clear absence of autonomy, characterize their lot. The *drudge*, writes Johnson, is 'One employed in mean labour; a slave; one doomed to servile occupation'. As a verb, *drudge* fares no better. Four lines from Thomas Otway's 1682 play *Venice Preserv'd* deftly illuminate the fate of those who, as in Johnson's accompanying definition, must 'labour in mean offices' and 'toil without honour or dignity': 'The poor sleep little: we must learn to watch / Our labours late, and early every morning, / Mid'st Winter frosts; then clad and fed with sparing / Rise to our toils, and *drudge* away the day.'

Dictionary-making, in such conceptions, can seem both uninviting and unrewarding. '*To make dictionaries is* dull *work*', as Johnson famously noted under sense 8 of *dull* in the *Dictionary*. Dullness of this kind, as he further explained, is 'Not exhilaterating; not

Samuel Johnson and the Journey into Words. Lynda Mugglestone
© Lynda Mugglestone 2015. First published 2015 by Oxford University Press.

delightful'. Johnson is, as his *Plan of a Dictionary of the English Language* (1747) suggests, merely compelled to beat 'the track of the alphabet with sluggish resolution' (*Yale* XVIII.25). His path is depicted as linear and tedious, narrow and circumscribed. Lexicography is 'drudgery for the blind' which, as he adds, requires little more than the ability to bear 'burthens with dull patience' (*Yale* XVIII.25).

Johnson's language seems relentlessly negative. Engaged in the 'toil of artless industry', the dictionary-maker is, as the 1755 'Preface' confirms, merely 'the slave of science' (*Yale* XVIII.73). As in the 'Short Scheme for Compiling a New Dictionary of the English Language', which Johnson drafted in April 1746, oppression can be rendered still more evident by the 'Shackles' of his trade which he must bear (*Yale* XVIII.461). Even metaphorically, the terrain which the lexicographer occupies is limited, its horizons low. 'It appeared that the province allotted me was of all the regions of learning generally confessed to be the least delightful, that it was believed to produce neither fruits nor flowers', Johnson writes in his *Plan* (*Yale* XVIII.26–7). Such, at least, is common 'opinion', he observes, of the lexicographer's role.

Other aspects of Johnson's self-figuration during these dictionary years are nevertheless somewhat different. 'I have', he stated to David Garrick, 'sailed a long and painful voyage round the world of the English language'.[2] He used another version of the same words to the playwright and writer Edward Moore, as the early biography of Johnson by William Shaw records. 'The true state of the fact', as Johnson stressed to Moore of the lexicographic ventures on which he had been engaged, is that of a 'hazardous and fatiguing voyage round the literary world'.[3] If difficulty remains, dictionary-making is removed to a strikingly protean space. It is a 'voyage' which, by definition, takes the lexicographer far away from the fixed and linear path on land. Circumnavigation suggests not drudgery but an imaginative and wide-ranging geography of words on which the dictionary-maker has embarked. As in Shakespeare's

The Winter's Tale, the sea is, by its very nature, 'unpathed'.[4] 'Untracked; unmarked by passage', as Johnson elaborates in his entry for this word. Johnson's journey, as he writes to Thomas Warton in February 1755, has been across a 'vast Sea of words' (*Letters* I.92).

Prototypically, we tend, of course, to imagine lexicography as something which is, almost by definition, devoid of literary device. The dictionary is a work of reference, dominated by factual information on words and meaning, spelling, and etymological derivation. In dictionary-making, the 'poet' is 'doomed at last to wake a lexicographer', as Johnson wrote of his own processes of transformation between 1746 and 1755 (*Yale* XVIII.100). Creativity and the literary imagination are, he suggests, inevitably left behind in employment of this kind. Johnson, at work on the *Dictionary* and immured in his attic in Gough Square from late 1747,[5] is by the same token habitually seen as static and enclosed. Characterized, as by Clifford, by his 'huge bulk', he seems quite literally hemmed in;[6] the attic, reached by a narrow and winding staircase, was 'a shambles, with piles of books, papers, and rickety furniture' and 'with massive oak beams', as Clifford adds. As in the 1787 engraving by John Hall (see Figure 1) or E. M. Ward's later portrait of Johnson reading Goldsmith's *Vicar of Wakefield*, Johnson is envisaged as peering, myopically, at the pages before him in ways that seem remote from the wide vistas of circumnavigation, or the varying prospects of a voyage.

Nevertheless, how lexicographers see their work or conceptualize what they aim to do—as well as what they have achieved—is, in contrast, often very different. They can, in this respect, prove markedly inventive, drawing on images and ideas which, at least on the surface, are far removed from the exigencies of definition or the scrutiny of words. Quests, watches, hives, storehouses, geology, and archaeology all appear across the history of English dictionaries. John Baret in his *Alvearie* saw the dictionary as a bee-hive in which collective industry might gather the lexical 'nectar' that his pages

Figure 1. Samuel Johnson by John Hall, after Sir Joshua Reynolds (line engraving, published 1787). © National Portrait Gallery, London.

stored,[7] while the *Gazophylacium Anglicanum*, which was published anonymously by Stephen Skinner in 1689, was, as its title indicates, a *gazophylacium* or 'treasure-chest'.[8] For the later *Oxford English Dictionary (OED)*, the dictionary-maker was a biographer, detailing the life-history of words.[9] Journeys prove no different. That dictionary-making can be seen as a journey into words has a history that spans the Renaissance to the twenty-first century.[10]

Ephraim Chambers, whose work Johnson studied as he set about his own *Dictionary*, had, for example, depicted knowledge as a landscape which the dictionary-maker must traverse. Chambers's lexicographer is, in essence, a cartographer of words. Careful mapping was essential, he had warned; the routes which could be taken must be made transparent lest 'the Sciences become canton'd out into so many separate Districts, and the due Communication between them cut off'.[11] Chambers's *Cyclopaedia* of 1728 had used metaphors similar in kind. Definition, and the accuracy on which a dictionary must depend required exploration within a 'Commonwealth of Learning'—a 'Land of Knowledge' in which, as Chambers stressed, 'provinces' extend in countless different directions.[12] The dictionary must act as a guide, providing directions and clearing unnecessary difficulties in ways which are seen as central to any work of reference.

Still earlier precedents for the venture into words can, however, also be located. Exploration, and the image of the dictionary-maker as Renaissance discoverer in a new—and hitherto unknown—realm underpins, for instance, both Thomas Blount's *Glossographia* of 1656 and Edward Phillips's dictionary of two years later. As Blount stressed, his work was the result of over twenty years' endeavour within a *'new world of Words'*.[13] The new-world ventures of more literal explorers are appropriated; the *Glossographia* ranges across the expanses of a lexicon newly transformed by the English Renaissance. Further individual journeys into knowledge are, Blount indicates, to be facilitated by the information on words and meaning which he has slowly gathered up. His aim was to provide clarity for those who might find themselves, as he had been, 'gravelled in English Books' by the unfamiliar words and senses which English now contained.[14] Gravel: 'To stick in the sand', Johnson's Dictionary would later explain.[15] As Blount's metaphor warned, without the dictionary, the individual reader might easily run aground, the flow of words impeded and comprehension brought to a halt.

Phillips appropriated Blount's phrase as the title of his own New World of English Words of 1658—though, as Blount contended, Phillips's acts of appropriation had, in reality, been far more extensive. Exploration seemed to have been restricted to considerable portions of Blount's own work: 'Twelve Months had not passed, but there appeared in Print this New World of Words...extracted almost wholly out of mine.'[16] Nevertheless, in what was indeed a new addition, Phillips's accompanying frontispiece (see Figure 2) provided a vivid imaging of the 'novis orbis verborum' that the good dictionary-maker must cover. Language, as here, is a globe which the lexicographer can survey; it evokes too the breadth of those territories that readers might, courtesy of lexicography, now also acquire with ease.

It was, however, John Florio's earlier Worlde of Words, first published in 1598, which had perhaps made these connections most explicit. For Florio, dictionary-makers are indeed like 'Seafaring men', adventurers who are set sail upon a realm that is both 'deepe, and dangerous'. Drudgery is displaced by danger and a form of heroism, which is, in terms of lexicography, often forgotten. As in Florio's opening address 'To the Reader', he describes a 'new voyage' in a 'paper-sea' in which 'discouerie', as befits a dictionary, 'may happily profit other men'. The loneliness of lexicography is clear; Florio contrasts the course which he must take with that adopted by other lexicographic projects, such as those in which the academicians of the Académie Française or Accademia della Crusca were engaged. Such collective enterprises, he stresses, are remote from the solitary and hazardous endeavours to which he had instead been bound. Writing the Worlde of Words, he had, he states, been 'but

Figure 2. Edward Phillips, frontispiece: *The New World of English Words*, 1658. The Bodleian Libraries, The University of Oxford (Vet. A3 d. 196).

one to turne and winde the sailes, to vse the oare, to sit at sterne' or *'to watch vpon the upper decke'*. The solitary lexicographer, Florio stresses, must in this respect be *'boute-swain, pilot, mate, and master'*. Bound on a journey across *'a sea more diuers, more dangerous, more stormie, and more comfortlesse then any Ocean'*, he alone must hold *'all offices in one, and that in a more vnruly, more vnweildie, and more roome-some vessell, than the biggest hulke on Thames'*.[17]

Florio would, in fact, assume an unexpected prominence in the eighteenth century. William Warburton's edition of Shakespeare, published in 1747 as Johnson was in the first stages of composing his own 'unweildie vessell', identified Florio as the potential model for Holofernes in *Love's Labours Lost*. 'By *Holofernes'*, Warburton stated, 'is designed a particular character, a pedant and schoolmaster of our author's time, one *John Florio* ... who has given us a small dictionary ... under the title of *A world of words'*.[18] Warburton read Florio with care. His 'Preface', importantly, hence came to engage not only with Shakespeare as dramatist but also to incorporate a lament for the deficts of contemporary English lexicography. 'We have', Warburton wrote, 'neither GRAMMAR nor DICTIONARY, neither Chart nor Compass, to guide us through this wide sea of Words'.[19] Florio's metaphorical legacy is plain. For Warburton, the 'paper-sea' required new endeavours; Chamber's mapping of English had, in this view, proved inadequate. Users of English still lacked sufficient guidance on the use and meaning of words.

Johnson had also been paying close attention to Warburton's lament and the images he deploys. As Johnson indicates, for example, it is Warburton's use of Florio to which he himself returns as his own *Dictionary* nears completion. 'I now begin to see land, after having wandered, according to Mr Warburtons phrase, in this vast Sea of words', as he wrote to Thomas Warton in 1755 (*Letters* I.92). Johnson echoes, too, Florio's images of exile, danger, and return. The limited sphere which the dictionary-maker occupied in the 1747 *Plan* has, by this point, apparently been displaced. 'As it was low, it likewise would be safe', as Johnson had, for example, consoled himself, describing the course to which he was henceforth bent (*Yale* XVIII.27). Florio provided a firm corrective for such views. His world of words is an Odyssean quest in which conflict, as well as endurance, might be required. Rather than safety, Florio evokes the '*Lande-Critikes, monsters of men*' who wait, with anticipation, on the shore to which the dictionary-maker must return. Their capacity for violence—and attack—is plain. Their '*teeth are Canibals, their toongs adder-forkes, their lips aspes-poyson, their eyes basiliskes*', he states with carefully cumulative detail. '*Their words*', he adds, are '*like swordes of Turkes, that striue which shall diue deepest into a Christian lying bound before them. But for these barking and biting dogs, they are as well-knowne as* Scylla *and* Charybdis'.[20] Dictionary-making is, in this light, fraught with difficulty from beginning to end.

Contemplating his own return from the various exigencies of lexicography in 1755, Johnson would confess similar fears to Warton. 'What reception I shall meet with on the Shore, I know not', he acknowledged: 'Whether I shall find ... a Calypso that will court or a Polypheme that will eat me' was, he admitted, unknown (*Letters* I.92). He is, he suggests, prepared for conflict, as well as stalwart defence of what he has performed. As for Odysseus, 'Ithaca' nevertheless served to lure him back to the sense of home, and his wider life as writer. 'Hail, Ithaca! After many labours, after bitter suffering, / Gladly I touch your shore', as Johnson had declared in another image of journeys and return, and the difficulties that these might encompass in terms of lexicography. Embedded in his entry for *Grubstreet*, and placed almost mid-way through the *Dictionary*, Johnson envisages his return from the 'stormie seas' of lexicography to what is, as Kernan stresses, a very different world of words.[21] *Grubstreet*: 'Originally the name of a street in Moorfields in London, much inhabited by writers of small histories, dictionaries, and temporary poems; whence any mean production is called *grub-street*', the accompanying definition explains.[22]

Writing the world of words

Journeys could, as this suggests, assume a particular resonance for those who, in various ways, find themselves ranging across the world of words. That similar patterns of metaphorical thinking pervade Johnson's accounts of the *Dictionary* should not therefore surprise. As in his echoing of Florio, the legacy of earlier lexicographers is often clear. Lexicography, as a range of writers emphasize, is rarely an entirely independent venture but instead often draws on a sense of tradition and established precedent.[23] Johnson's figuration of his task is, in some ways, no different. As in the *Plan*, his imaging of the path the 'drudge' must follow offers clear correlations with Chambers's work. Similar images of mapping appear in Johnson's comments on his ambitions to 'discover the coast' in ways that might facilitate the passage of later lexicographers (*Yale* XVIII.58). He draws, too, on the 'province' which can be 'enter'd', as well as that which is, by convention, allotted to those who must toil in search of words and meaning (*Yale* XVIII.27). For Johnson and Chambers alike, the 'lacrimae lexicographi' [the tears of the lexicographer] would, in another well-established trope, firmly remind the reader of the difficulty, and demands, of what must be performed.[24]

Johnson's familiarity with Phillips is equally clear, attested at a range of points across the *Dictionary*. The *World of Words* hence verifies Johnson's entries for *burrock* and *chafery*, informing the meanings which the *Dictionary* provides.[25] Similar evidence appears under *burton* and *deplumation*. Phillips's distinction between words and things, as Kolb and DeMaria suggest (*Yale* XVIII.xxix), influences Johnson's similar considerations in the 1747 *Plan*. Johnson can, of course, draw on Phillips's earlier enterprise in other ways, hailing the 'shore' of the native language as that of a 'new world' which the dictionary-maker must, in various ways, record (*Yale* XVIII.58).

Other dictionary-makers are, however, usually content to adduce a single journey type as they explore the nature of their task. Chambers, as we have seen, is a cartographer of information, mapping knowledge on land in the diatopic spaces of 'cantons' and 'provinces'. Florio, Blount, and Phillips—as well as Warburton—all posit a journey by sea. Johnson can, in contrast, present a diverse—and often dissonant—set of narratives. Janus-like, Johnson's lexicographic journeys can instead take place on land and at sea, involving discourses of power and powerlessness, and movement as well as intended stasis. They probe, too, questions of governance in the state of language which is thereby to be reached, and in which 'suffrage', 'liberty', and oppression are variously to be imposed or denied by the course the dictionary-maker might take.

Across Johnson's 'Scheme' of 1746, the various versions of the *Plan of a Dictionary* of 1747, and the *Dictionary* itself, as well as in other comments which Johnson made on the subject of lexicography, a range of journeys and journey types, as well as conflicted—and conflicting—images of identity will, for example, repeatedly intervene. Johnson, as we will see, can be adventurer and invader, soldier and sailor, colonialist, conqueror, and explorer. He can depart on 'excursions' and circumnavigate the literary world; he can trudge a well-established path and envisage ransacking 'the obscure recesses of northern learning' (*Yale* XVIII.100). The dictionary can be figured as a ship or rowing boat, its return to a harbour, port, as well as to a shore. As in his return to 'Ithaca', Johnson can be Odysseus as well as drudge. In his 'wandering', too, as Johnson suggests to Warton (*Letters* I.92), he has, in a range of ways, departed from the course which was initially envisaged. *Wander*: 'To rove; to ramble here and there; to go, without any certain course', as the relevant entry in the *Dictionary* explains: 'It has always an ill sense'. As for Odysseus, the journey undertaken has been far larger in scope and scale than had been hoped,[26] as well as marked by indirection and the lack of steady advance. Looking back across his years of lexicography, Johnson's diction suggests a clear sense of departure from the apparent certainties, and limited range, with which he began.

'It's always wise to take metaphors seriously', Jack Lynch warns, noting that this is, perhaps 'doubly so with so careful a writer as Johnson'. 'It's trebly so in the *Dictionary*', he adds.[27] There are, Howard Weinbrot affirms, 'few prose writers with a more metaphorical style than Johnson's'.[28] The *Dictionary*, in this light, proves no exception. Johnson's metaphors can, in a range of ways, invite us to consider (and reconsider) the processes by which a dictionary might be made and the kind of destination it might seek, as well as the state of language that might be reached by such endeavours. For Johnson, where the dictionary-maker might go, and what should be accomplished along the way, can often seem to raise pertinent and perhaps troubling questions.

As in the *Plan*, Johnson's figuration, as we have seen, neatly outlines the expected predictability of what the dictionary-maker should do. A *track*, as the *Dictionary* confirms, is, the 'beaten path'—one which is already well-known and can, in this light, merely be followed to its expected destination.[29] In terms of textual pragmatics, the 'track of the alphabet' is, after all, perhaps non-negotiable. Dictionary-makers in the eighteenth century admittedly possess slightly more latitude than their modern counterparts; the alphabet can contain twenty-four or twenty-six divisions, depending on whether I and J, and U and V are seen, as for Johnson, as the 'same' letter, or are rendered distinct, as by Anne Fisher in her *Accurate New Spelling Dictionary*.[30] Nevertheless, the sequence to be followed is otherwise fixed; the dictionary-maker is constrained to move in certain directions, gathering evidence accordingly.

Yet, as Johnson confirms, the means by which the lexicographer might, in any sense, move from A to Z can remain open to careful scrutiny. So, too, can the negotiations which might need to take place between expectation and actuality, or the desire for stability as set against the complex truths of a living tongue. The expected passivity of the drudge, as the 1747 *Plan* makes plain, can, for example, sit uneasily against the kind of discourses of intended power which popular prescriptivism across the eighteenth century repeatedly advanced in terms of lexicography, and the models of correctness which might thereby be both instituted and imposed. As Chapter 2 will further explore, expectations that Johnson's *Dictionary* would play a prominent role in this respect are clear. 'You know [Johnson] is writing a Dictionary, that will be an Attempt to bring the English Language to somewhat of a Standard', as Samuel Richardson wrote to Thomas Edwards in 1753.[31] 'One great end of this undertaking is to fix the English language', as Johnson had declared of the course which he was, intentionally, to follow (*Yale* XVIII.38). Johnson's honorary degree—the M.A. which he received in 1755 just before the *Dictionary* was published and which was displayed, after his name, on its title-page[32]—was awarded in anticipation, and approbation, of ambitions of this kind. Johnson 'is even now labouring at a work of the greatest usefulness in adorning and fixing our native tongue', the terms of his conferment proclaimed.[33] Against the mutability which English so clearly revealed, stasis was depicted as an incontestable object of desire.

Johnson's metaphors can both reflect—and problematize—this remit of intended control, and the agency it requires. If the drudge is left to trudge the track of the alphabet, other images serve, simultaneously, to foreground the power which lexicography, in popular configurations of this kind, must require. As we have seen, Johnson can evoke Phillips's 'new world' in one of many images of the 'shore' to which the dictionary-maker is bound. Yet Johnson's 'new world' denotes, at least at this point, a realm of British words which is, by implication, about to be assailed. He is, he notes, like a 'soldier', despatched by his patron Lord Chesterfield and intent on incursion.[34] 'When I survey the plan which I have laid before you, I cannot, my Lord, but confess, that I am frighted at its extent, and, like the soldiers of Cæsar, look on Britain as a new world, which it is almost madness to invade', as Johnson states (*Yale* XVIII.58).

The state of English, in figurations of this kind, awaits the exercise of the dictionary-maker's rule. Lexicography, surprisingly, can be a battle in which dictionary-maker is assailant and language a territory to be vanquished. The fabled 'harmlessness' of the drudge ('Innocence; freedom from injury or hurt', as the *Dictionary* later explains) can seem remote. If, like Florio and Blount, Johnson voyages, he does so with what can seem a very different intent. The metaphorical 'shore' is peopled not by Florio's 'Lande-Critikes' but by the native tongue. 'I hope, that though I should not complete the conquest, I shall at least discover the coast, civilize part of the inhabitants, and make it easy for some other adventurer to proceed farther, to reduce them wholly to subjection', as Johnson continues (*Yale* XVIII.58). Civilization as an image of linguistic amelioration can, as Barrell observes, veer uncomfortably towards colonial process, bringing other aspects of 'new' and 'old' world into play.[35] 'The inhabitants he intends to civilise are the nation's words', Sorensen confirms.[36]

'Hope' nevertheless already problematizes what might be achieved, undercutting the apparent confidence—and resolve—of what is otherwise claimed, and placing the intended outcome in doubt. If *hope*, as the *Dictionary* explains, is 'to expect with desire', it is a process which, across Johnson's writing, is often scrutinized for the fallibilities it reveals, whether in terms of human aspiration or the dubious prospects of expectation. As in 'The Vanity of Human Wishes' which Johnson would write one year after completing the *Plan*,[37] hope is not necessarily to be encouraged. Instead, coupled with 'desire' (as well as 'fear' and 'hate'), it can 'O'er spread with snares the clouded maze of fate' where, in other images of the difficult journey, 'wav'ring man, betray'd by vent'rous pride' must 'tread the dreary paths without a guide'. 'How rarely reason guides the stubborn choice', Johnson notes, or, indeed, 'Rules the bold hand, or prompts the suppliant voice' (*Yale* VI.92).

While, as we will see, expectation—and the extent to which this is to be indulged—will often provide a further element in Johnson's critical reading of his lexicographic enterprise, what Johnson 'hopes' in the 1747 *Plan* can therefore already introduce its own complexities into what, precisely, he intends to do. Johnson can, simultaneously, seem to advance and retreat from the agency one might expect. Conquests which remain incomplete are not, of course, conquests, while references to adventure and adventurers likewise serve, in the semantics of eighteenth-century English, to render victory in the world of words a matter of marked uncertainty. As Johnson confirms, an *adventure* is 'an event of which we have no direction'; it is, he adds under sense 3, 'The occasion of casual events; an enterprise in which something must be left to hazard'. By definition, as the *Dictionary* makes plain, adventurers cannot know where they will go, or the outcome of their endeavours. The endeavour can, of course, be made, but—for Johnson and his successors alike—the result can equally remain in doubt.

The diction of discovery can project a different course again, even if one in which Johnson might perhaps seem more confident of what may be achieved. '*A higher Degree of Reputation is due to* Discoverers *than to the* Teachers *of* speculative Doctrines, *nay even to* Conquerors *themselves*',[38] as Sprat had earlier exclaimed in terms of the Royal Society, commending the beneficial consequences that journeys might, in this respect, entail.[39] A *discoverer*, as the *Dictionary* confirms, is 'one that finds anything not known before; a finder out'. Figured as explorer-traveller, Johnson might therefore, like Chambers, simply map new information about the realm of words in a lexicographical correlate of, say, Sir Francis Drake whose 'new world' explorations (and heroic 'endeavour to depart from the beaten track') Johnson had patriotically described in *The Gentleman's Magazine* in 1740.[40] George Anson's recent 'circumnavigation' of the world, also serialized in *The Gentleman's Magazine* (probably with Johnson's editorial help) offers other parallels;[41] 'discovering the coast' had been one of its achievements, mapping, for example, the 'whole coast, from the Streights of *Magellan* to Streights *le Maire*' in a diction in which the concerns of knowledge, independent observation, and truth are often prominent.[42] Johnson, as Thomas Curley confirms, regularly drew on Anson in the dictionary years, evoking aspects of Anson's journey, and the difficulties it brought, in the *Rambler* essays which he began writing in 1750.[43]

Johnson's journeys on land and sea offer, of necessity, other oppositions. Johnson's metaphors can jostle uncomfortably, offering conflicted—and conflicting—patterns of identity and intent. '*Ground* the *earth* (generally as opposed to the water)', as Johnson had noted in 1746, illustrating the process of definition by antonym (*Yale* XVIII.407). 'The ocean; the water as opposed to the land', the *Dictionary* likewise confirmed, here under *sea*. The entry for *land* simply reverses this divide: 'Earth; distinct from water'.[44] 'It is necessary . . . to explain many words by their opposition to others; for contraries are best seen when they stand together', as Johnson commented in the *Plan* of methods of this kind (*Yale* XVIII.50). Such 'contraries' are nevertheless marked across Johnson's writing on the *Dictionary* and the course he might pursue, as well as the methods he would adopt. English, as we have seen, is variously a territory to be conquered, and a terrain to be laboriously traversed. Yet, for the dictionary-maker to make the sea a locus of exploration is, of necessity, to foreground instability rather than containment, and potential dislocation rather than expected triumph. As Johnson states in the *Dictionary*, the *sea* as metaphor denotes 'any thing rough and tempestuous', foregrounding the kind of difficulty and danger which Florio eloquently laments.[45] It is, as Auden later observes, an iconic image of chaos and lack of regulation— representing not stasis and solidity but 'the primordial undiffer- entiated flux'.[46] Voyages, as Varney warns, can 'virtually be seen as an enactment of ambivalence' in their use in eighteenth-century literature. As he adds, 'the form of the voyage account' was often deployed as 'a vehicle ideally suited to the representation of a subtle, multifold and often ambiguous response' to what is encountered along the way.[47]

Language and lexicography, as Johnson realized, offered similar potential. If the sea suggests disorder and, by extension, the complex challenge behind what the lexicographer sets out to do, it can, in equal measure, also suggest the fallibility of such aims. As Canute had long ago confirmed, turning the tide is not within what human power can achieve. The 'Sea of words' will therefore prove quite literally disturbing for a dictionary-maker who should aim to stabilize usage in a remit of correction and prescriptive control. While a path can be followed—even if it might, as Johnson suggests, need to be renewed by new endeavours[48]—water offers no such certainties within the remit of 'ascertainment' in which Johnson's work was popularly placed.[49] As in 'The Vanity of Human Wishes', attempts to impose power over the waves are made to evoke the folly of unreasoned ambition rather than a sense of realistic endeavour. 'The waves he lashes, and enchains the wind; / New pow'rs are claim'd', as Johnson notes of Xerxes's journey, and his desire to control the seas on which he sails (*Yale* VI.103). Emulation is not encouraged; 'Great Xerxes' (*Yale* VI.102) does not become an exemplar of either wise or rational thinking. Instead, as Johnson writes, he must learn 'humbler thoughts' before he can continue on his way. The 'pow'rs … claim'd' do not, in reality, exist.[50]

By 1755, Johnson's examination of lexicographical ambition—and its equally unsound premises in this respect—would draw on closely similar terms. 'Sounds are too volatile and subtle for legal restraints; to enchain syllables, and to lash the wind, are equally the undertakings of pride, unwilling to measure its desires by its strength', as Johnson declares in the 'Preface' (*Yale* XVIII.105). If Johnson evokes Tickell's 'Prospect of Peace', by which 'our daring Language' is to be bound in 'happy Chains' by legislative decree, it is in terms which serve therefore to revise and redress, such assumptions.[51] Here, too, power is critically reassessed, as in the capacity of the dictionary-maker to enslave words to do his bidding.

The journey as device

Johnson's habit of 'thinking in images', as Greene explores, is by no means merely rhetorical.[52] Instead, across his writing, it provides a highly effective way of structuring ideas, of exploring—and perhaps uniting—dissonant perspectives. It serves, too, as a way of probing—and unpicking—received wisdom, as well as exposing perhaps unwelcome truths. Journeys, in this light, offered considerable potential. That writers negotiate a path in the very act of writing was, of course, a common trope. Journeys are, in this sense, both familiar, and familiarized. Johnson could, for example, be convicted as being too predictable in this respect by Elizabeth Montagu, here with reference to the essays which he would publish while he worked on the *Dictionary*. 'The *Rambler* is certainly a strong misnomer', she declared: 'He allwais plods in the beaten road of his Predecessors.'[53] Bacon and Locke were, conversely, commended by Alexander Pope for the new directions they had advanced. 'Bacon and Locke did not follow the common path but beat out new ones, and you see what good they have done', as Pope informed Joseph Spence in 1743.[54] 'He that will know the truth of things, must leave the common and beaten track', as Locke advised, here in a citation which Johnson carefully inserted under *path* in the *Dictionary* itself.[55]

Ephraim Chambers, importantly, had made a similar argument in terms of lexicography. 'When a Path is once made, Men are naturally disposed to follow it; even tho it be not the most convenient', he wrote in his *Cyclopaedia* of 1728: 'Numbers will enlarge, and widen, or even make it straighter and easier; but 'tis odds they don't alter its Course.' Yet, as Chambers also pointed out, 'Alteration' and 'Improvements made in the several Arts' can, in this respect, derive only from those who are prepared to move beyond where others had gone.[56] Tradition and innovation are placed in careful apposition. Just as in Johnson's *Plan*, if the 'track' that the dictionary-maker beats will, by convention, lead in one direction (*Yale* XVIII.26), it does not mean that this should or will always be followed. Departure, Chambers suggests, might be necessary in more ways than one.

Johnson's own interest in travel has, of course, been widely documented, even if the *Dictionary* has habitually tended to remain outside comment of this kind. Thomas Curley, Thomas Jemility, and

Thursten Moore have, among others, engaged in detail with Johnson's reading—and writing—in this respect.[57] As DeMaria observes, of the three books to which Johnson wished were longer, all are books of travel.[58] Travel spans Johnson's published work, whether in his engagement with Lobo's *Voyage to Abyssinia* of 1735 or in the account of his own *Journey to the Western Isles of Scotland* in 1775. In another 'Scheme' of the dictionary years, Johnson planned, for example, 'a collection of Travels, Voyages, Adventures, and Descriptions of Countries' (*Life* IV.382n), while his detailed introduction to John Newbery's *The World Displayed*—in which exploration and colonialism, circumnavigation and slavery are subject to further critical scrutiny of their own—appeared in 1759.[59] He remained, too, a regular, and meticulous, reviewer of travel books, publishing reviews of, say, Patrick Browne's *History of Jamaica*, and William Borlase's *History of the Isles of Scilly* in the *Literary Magazine* shortly after finishing the *Dictionary*.[60] *Travels*, as Johnson notes in another new sense-division that he registered in his *Dictionary*, are: 'Accounts of occurrences and observations of a journey into foreign parts.'[61]

Nevertheless, as in Johnson's own journeys to the Western Isles or in his fictional narratives by which *Rasselas* (1759) ventures outside the Happy Valley,[62] or in which, during the *Dictionary* years, various protagonists in the *Rambler* essays change their physical location or find out for themselves the deficits of received wisdom or the fallibilities of expectation, travel in Johnson's hands can repeatedly reveal not what is expected but instead something that is both more complex, as well as more truthful.[63] As in his 'Preface' to Lobo, it demands, and embodies, a change of perspective in which 'the diligent and impartial enquirer' who 'describe[s] things as he saw them' is commended over those who purvey 'romantick absurdities' and 'incredible fictions'.[64] That the writer should indulge in traveller's tales, with the hyperbole and exaggeration which these comport, is not advised. As Fred Parker notes, such patterns underpin what he sees as the quintessential properties of Johnsonian scepticism per se, and in which travel as device is often central, placing expectation against experience, theory against the complexity of human existence in all its forms.[65] 'The use of travelling is to regulate imagination by reality', as Johnson later stressed to Hester Thrale. It is a means by which 'instead of thinking of how things may be', we can 'see them as they are' (*Letters* II.78).

Seeing language as it is can, in this light, likewise emerge as one of the great enterprises of the *Dictionary* in which, for Johnson, travel as device can be put to good—and critical—use, along with the changes of perspective (and representation) that this will, by convention, demand. As Johnson, for example, already explores in the *Plan*, even the routes we imagine for the harmless drudge can, in this light, be made to suggest the salience of separating what we might conceive about the dictionary-maker's journey from its more complex realities. Johnson's diction deliberately engages with popular ideas what the dictionary-maker is 'believed' to be, not with what dictionary-makers are—or indeed what Johnson might be as he forges his own route through the world of words. Johnson's epistemic modalities are, we might note, marked. 'Believed'—like Johnson's use of 'appeared' in detailing other aspects of such imaging in the *Plan* (*Yale* XVIII.26), or, indeed, his equally sceptical 'supposed' when engaging with other aspects of opinion in the *Dictionary*[66]— should alert the reader, setting the stage for critical revision.

As Johnson makes plain, it is, in reality, expectations of this kind which likewise generate images of the narrow 'track' which must be followed with 'sluggish resolution' (*Yale* XVIII.25). It is from a similar perspective that the dictionary-maker is assumed to journey in a realm which, as Johnson adds, is 'believed to produce neither fruits nor flowers'. Such images, as Johnson indicates, draw on prevailing language attitudes, and on common assumption and 'opinion' about dictionaries and the nature of dictionary-making. Yet if 'opinion' of this kind is, as Johnson states, both 'long transmitted' and 'widely propagated' (*Yale* XVIII.26), this does not, of course, guarantee either its truth or its rational foundations. Opinion, as DeMaria confirms, is 'throughout the *Dictionary* . . . the name for conviction or belief when it is uncontrolled or unadjusted to the findings of judgement'.[67] It is, as Johnson explains, 'Perswasion of the mind'—and devoid thereby of the 'proof or certain knowledge' which experiential reality will, in contrast, bring.[68]

What we might imagine about dictionaries and dictionary-making, or envisage in terms of the relationships of power, control, and language which the dictionary-maker might institute, can, in this respect, also come to demand a surer and more realistic reassessment. Against what Kolb and Sledd describe as 'the congenital inertia of lexicographers',[69] Johnson's dissonant metaphors can therefore eloquently convey the challenges he faced, and the genuine difficulties which might surround the attempt to get from A to Z in terms of lexicography. Seeing the dictionary as journey places useful emphasis on process alongside finished product, as well as on the changes of direction which experience, as we will see, will necessarily bring along the way. Lexicography is, in Johnson's hands, revealed as an enterprise in which the dictionary-maker was expected to be both drudge and dictator, to obey and to secure obedience, to fix yet also to represent a language which was, as Johnson stressed, 'yet living' and, as such, 'variable by the caprice of every tongue that speaks it' (*Yale* XVIII.89). As for Xerxes, some readjustment will, as we will see, prove necessary before the end is reached.

For Johnson, nine years in the sea of words will, after all, separate *Plan* and 'Preface'. Material must be collected and ordered, senses separated, and headwords chosen. The 'maze of variation' will, as we will see, involve other journeys which can frustrate as well as bewilder, adding, too, still other difficulties to Johnson's intended mission of control (*Yale* XVIII.89). The ideological divides of prescriptive rule or descriptive process must likewise be resolved, together with the wider problems of inclusion (and exclusion) in the state of English. As Donald Greene notes, Johnson habitually both extended and revivified the images he deployed.[70] The journey into words would, in this respect, prove no exception.

21

The various chapters across this volume approach Johnson's journeys into words, and the state of language which results, from a variety of perspectives. Chapter 2, 'Writing the *Dictionary*: Departures and destinations', traces, in detail, the early history of the *Dictionary*, and the patterns of direction and redirection which appear between Johnson's 'Scheme' of 1746, the *Plan* of the following year (and its various iterations), as well as the 'Preface' which accompanies the completed *Dictionary* of 1755. 'The scheme, the plan, and the preface are not consistent, nor do they always clarify the book', writes Lipking: 'Each successive stage of making the *Dictionary* seems to represent a falling away.'[71] Yet to engage with the dictionary as journey and Johnson's iterated use of travel as device can, as we will see, offer a different—and productive—way of approaching this pattern, conceived not as decline but as a process of on-going movement and change.

Chapter 3 examines another aspect of the figuration by which Johnson depicts the process of lexicography—that of the 'excursions into books' (*Yale* XVIII.84) by which the information on words and usage would be collected for the *Dictionary*. Against the images of dictatorship and control which, at various points, inform the *Plan*, Johnson's 'excursions' are, as he admits, 'both fortuitous and unguided' (*Yale* XVIII.84). Aligned with the trope of the 'adventurer', they posit a series of empirical and experiential journeys into words as Johnson gathers up the illustrative raw material as evidence for his text. Extant copies of Johnson's marked-up books, moreover, allow such journeys to be recreated in ways which illuminate the nature of the resulting text, placing emphasis on the underlying processes by which the *Dictionary* gradually comes into being.

Johnson, as we have seen, repeatedly conceives the point at which the *Dictionary* is finished as a 'shore' or a 'coast' where 'land' is reached. Chapter 4, 'The ordered state: Power, authority, and the written word', considers the state of the written language that is established by means of the *Dictionary*, in both intention and actuality. A particular focus lies in the conflicting models of order which Johnson's writing on language reveals, as well as the political modelling of control by which Johnson was expected to assume dictatorship over an errant state of words. The nature—and limits—of power are, for Johnson, for his patron Lord Chesterfield, and for the booksellers who commissioned the text, of marked interest in terms of language. The chapter probes the nature of order, and its problematic imposition by means of a reference book, as well as Johnson's scepticism in terms of individual attempts to reform the ways in which words are used.

Chapter 5, 'Meaning, governance, and the colours of words', explores other aspects of intended control in the state of language, looking at the tensions which emerge between expected edicts and the common law of language. Against conquest, Johnson's engagement with style and variation emerges as particularly important, alongside the legitimate roles and responsibilities of the critic of words. The metalanguage of the *Dictionary*—and Johnson's labelling practices, dividing words into unmarked and marked territories—provides a particularly important focus, allowing other aspects of potential governance to come to the fore.

Chapter 6, 'Defending the citadel, patrolling the borders', turns to the border territories of language, and the nature of the 'coast' which is to be discovered. It examines the relationship of native and non-native words, as well as the ways in which citizenship might be conferred—or, indeed, denied to those who are already (at least in terms of language practice) inhabitants of the nation-state. Notions of purism and 'barbarism', as well as the question of invasion and settlement, can inform the desire to control (and patrol) the borders of the language/dictionary. The dualities of defence and protection likewise frame Johnson's changing positions on the dictionary-maker as border-guard. Johnson's categorization of loanwords into 'aliens' and 'denizens' (later appropriated by James Murray in the first edition of the *Oxford English Dictionary*) is equally significant, while multilingualism and Johnson's own brand of French resistance provide other points of reference.

Chapter 7, 'History and the flux of time', engages in detail with Johnson's reading of time in the *Dictionary*. If languages, for Johnson, are the real 'pedigrees of nation' (*Life* V.225), it is time that can appear as the true 'tyrant' in the national history which words record. Time, after all, will easily depose the lexicographer by forces that cannot be controlled. The chapter examines Johnson's engagement with the history of English, alongside the conflicting demands of etymology, semantic shift, and language practice, as well as obsolescence and lexical death. The interconnectedness of time and change emerges as a salient theme in Johnson's approach to language, poised between images of decay and mutability on one hand, and the natural and ineluctable on the other.

Chapter 8, 'The praise of perfection', looks, in conclusion, at Johnson's legacy as lexicographer and the problems of perfection and perfectibility as revealed in the *Dictionary* and its making. Returning to the image of destination, the chapter looks at the journey as educative experience, at discovery and self-discovery, examining, too, the lessons which are both learnt and forgotten in the endeavour to record the native tongue.

2

Writing the *Dictionary*: Departures and destinations

Far from being the 'father of the dictionary'—in what can still remain a popular configuration of his role[1]—Johnson worked in an era in which, as he noted, the 'zeal for ranging knowledge by the alphabet' was striking. Well over six hundred dictionaries, Lynch confirms, had been published in Britain by the mid-eighteenth century.[2] Lexicography had perhaps 'been carried too far by the force of fashion', as Johnson suggested one year after completing his own *Dictionary*; 'dictionaries of every kind of literature' were already in existence.[3] Providing an apt illustration of this general trend, it was the 'Preface' to Richard's Rolt's *New Dictionary of Trade and Commerce* of 1756 in which Johnson's words appear. If, as he admitted, he had neither read the book nor met the author, experience clearly brought its own qualifications. As Johnson confirms, by this point he 'knew very well what such a Dictionary should be, and wrote a preface accordingly' (*Life* I.359).

'Literature', which Johnson defined as 'Learning; skill in letters', here reflected a wide-ranging engagement with knowledge and its transmission rather than with the literary text alone. For booksellers, dictionaries were useful commodities, bringing, in many cases, a healthy return to those who published them.[4] The 'leading London

Samuel Johnson and the Journey into Words. Lynda Mugglestone
© Lynda Mugglestone 2015. First published 2015 by Oxford University Press.

booksellers were alert to investment in works that would have a popular sale, including dictionaries, encyclopaedias, and other texts', as Allen Reddick observes.[5] They are promoted, and advertised, assiduously; dictionary-making as genre was a fertile terrain in which the obsolescence of earlier works was ensured by the 'new' and 'improved' editions which appeared in their stead. Such works 'needed regular modernising and upgrading...providing a steady stream of sales', as Pittock observes.[6] Chambers's *Cyclopaedia* was, for example, in its 5th edition by 1742; Nathan Bailey's *Universal Etymological Dictionary*, first published in 1721, was in its thirteenth in 1747. Another version, as Philip Gove notes, was published in a head-to-head confrontation with Johnson's own work.[7] 'There was never from the earliest ages a time in which trade so much engaged the attention of mankind, or commercial gain was fought with such general emulation', Johnson affirmed in his 'Preface' to Rolt. Lexicography, as the history of eighteenth-century publishing suggests, easily played its own role in ambitions of this kind.

A number of significant developments would, in this respect, emerge. As in J. K.'s *New English Dictionary* of 1702 with its focus on 'Words, Commonly used in the Language',[8] the 'hard word' tradition of seventeenth-century lexicography—as evidenced by Blount and Phillips—was gradually to disappear. Dictionaries in the eighteenth century could display a striking comprehensiveness. The *Glossographia Anglicana Nova* of 1707 contained, for example, not only 'Such HARD WORDS of whatever Language, as are at present used in the English Tongue' but, as its title page promised, it also included 'the Terms of Divinity, Law, Physick, Mathematicks, History, Agriculture, Logick, Metaphysicks, Grammar, Poetry, Musick, Heraldry, Architecture, Painting, War, and all other Arts and Sciences'. John Kersey's *Dictionarium Anglo-Britannicum* (1708) comprised—in addition—the language of Pharmacy, Maritime Affairs, Military Discipline, Traffick, Gardening, and Husbandry, Handicrafts, Cookery, and Confectionary, as well as Horsemanship, Hunting, and Fowling. Bailey's work was similar, while the third edition of Dyche and Pardon's *New General English Dictionary* (1740) proclaimed its own distinctiveness by the 'ADDITION of the several MARKET-TOWNS in *England* and *Wales*'. Relevant entries, the title page explains, would give 'a general Description of the Places, their Situations, Market-Days, Government, [and] Manufactures'.

Johnson's *Dictionary* took shape alongside dominant patterns of this kind. From the beginning, however, a critical distance informed what he set out to do. The monolingual English dictionary, as it then existed—as Johnson comments in his *Plan*—conveyed 'a very miscellaneous idea'. Comprehensiveness had perhaps been carried too far, creating works in which readers were accustomed to seek 'the solution of almost every difficulty' (*Yale* XVIII.30). His own emphasis, as the *Plan* explains, would instead be on words not things, and the nuances of meaning and signification that words in English possess. Evidence would also be given greater prominence. Johnson's title page of 1755 exhibits, as a result, a striking— and forceful—economy. There are no extensive lists of assorted disciplines. Absent too is the proffered resolution of 'hard words', or the specification of local geography and habitation. Instead, as he indicates, this was *A Dictionary of the English Language: in which the Words are deduced from their Originals, and Illustrated in their Different Significations by Examples from the Best Writers*. This too, as we will see, represented another significant departure in the history of English lexicography.

Nevertheless, as Chapter 1 has explored, the legacy of other attitudes and expectations—especially with reference to what dictionary-making might achieve and the power it might wield— remained important in Johnson's allotted task. Language academies such as the Accademia della Crusca in Italy and, in France, the Académie Française (founded respectively in 1582 and 1635) had, for example, early integrated lexicography into intended processes of standardization and linguistic reform. Dictionary-making on this model was a means by which language would not merely be codified but also corrected and refined. In line with its designation as 'the academy of the bran', the Accademia della Crusca sought to sift and winnow existing usage. Its *Vocabulario*, first published in 1612, reflected a purified sphere of words and meaning; the contents were both select and selective. A fourth edition began publication, in six volumes, in 1729. The *Dictionnaire* of the French Academy, the first edition of which was published in 1694, followed a similar course, validating 'pur usage' in a remit of stabilization and normative control. As the Académie stressed, its ambition was to secure 'règles certaines' for the use of words.

As the educational writer George Snell confirms, an 'edict to ratifie and settle the English language' had long seemed equally desirable.[9] A dictionary written on this basis, he argued in 1649, would establish the boundaries of legitimate use, as well as operating as a *de facto* English academy. 'Everie word thenceforth to bee used, by anie native of *England*, contrariant to the edict for English language' might be 'adjudged and condemned for non-English', he exhorted. Given a reformed lexicography, it might be possible, Snell suggested, for English, like Latin, to transcend the vagaries of time and place. Control and stability are rendered evocative ideals. 'The language and the writing of it, and the signification of it will bee alwaies undoubted and certain', he postulated. English would be 'without variation and change, and held to an immutabilitie'.[10]

Snell's work on the *Right Teaching of Useful Knowledg* articulates with particular clarity a popular—and enduring—mythography in the history of English dictionaries. Across the seventeenth and eighteenth centuries, anxieties about linguistic variation—together with associated convictions about the remedial role that lexicography might play—remain prominent. The Royal Society, founded in 1660, had for example, established its own 'Committee for the Improvement of the English' some four years later. A 'Lexicon or collection of all the pure English Words' was swiftly proposed. Writing in June 1665 to Sir Peter Wyche (who acted as chair of the committee), the writer John Evelyn outlined ideals by which the 'prime, certain, and natural signification' of words, as well as a 'more certain Orthography' might be established. As for Snell, uncertainty and change are deemed highly problematic. As Evelyn suggested, 'no innovation might be used or favoured; at least till there should arise some necessity of providing a new edition, and of amplifying the old upon mature advice'.[11] Neologisms, rather than being introduced at the whim of the writer or speaker, were to be carefully evaluated before being legitimized by inclusion.

Yet, in reality, no such dictionary appeared, either under the aegis of the Royal Society or as a product of individual endeavour. Similar proposals were, for instance, made by Joseph Addison as well as the poet (and politician) Ambrose Philips in the early eighteenth century. A work for which the publisher Jacob Tonson reputedly offered the sum of £3,000,[12] Addison's projected emphasis on language standards and authority was clearly attractive. Philips's *Proposals for Printing an English Dictionary...explaining the Whole Language* (1724) likewise outlined his intention to establish 'The Distinction of Words, and Phrases, in relation to their *Propriety* and *Impropriety*', as well as 'the genuine and proper *Signification* of each Word' (and 'the proper Use and different Significations of the English *Particles*'). Yet, like Addison's work, this failed to materialize in print.[13] The native language remained unbound and unconfined.

Associated proposals for an academy of English also continued to be made. Swift's proposals to the Earl of Oxford were published as *A Proposal for Correcting, Improving and Ascertaining the English Tongue* in 1712, providing an influential model for later writers such as the orator John Henley, and the Earl of Orrery, who set out their own recommendations for linguistic reform.[14] Tobias Smollett engaged with similar issues, invoking a range of linguistic strictures and corrective ideals within the remit of the *Critical Review*.[15] A vernacular academy, as Swift had argued, might remedy that neglect by which 'our Language is less Refined than those of *Italy*, *Spain*, or *France*'.[16] Like Snell, he made good use of the spectre

of incomprehensibility. Just as Dryden in 1700 had found it necessary to translate Chaucer,[17] the same imperatives might, in time,
confront those desiring to read writers from the eighteenth century.
Unless appropriate measures to control change and variation were
introduced, Swift warns, the aspiring writer of history 'shall scarcely
be understood without an Interpreter' within 'an Age or two'.[18] 'As
I remember upon each return to my own country their old dialect
was so altered, that I could hardly understand the new', as Gulliver,
in Swift's *Gulliver's Travels* (1726) is likewise made to observe.
English is characterized not by refinement and polish but by a
potentially disorientating level of flux. Words in English change
almost every year, Gulliver notes, struggling to understand a language which no longer seems his own.[19] 'I would have our Language, after it is duly correct, always to last', Swift's *Proposal*
conversely exhorted: 'I see no absolute Necessity why any Language
should be perpetually changing.'[20]

Unsurprisingly, as Johnson's early biographer John Hawkins
confirms, the London booksellers had also 'long meditated the
publication of a dictionary, after the model of those of France and
the Accademia della Crusca'.[21] Here, too, the dictionary as commodity clearly played an important role. Given the self-evident gap
in the market, a work of this kind—prescriptive, regulative, and
which introduced similar models of control (and intended stasis) for
English—would, as the bookseller Robert Dodsley hypothesized,
undoubtedly 'be well received by the publick' (*Life* I.182). As Reddick
notes, recognition of the 'commercial potential of such an undertaking' firmly underpinned the dictionary enterprise which Johnson
was to undertake.[22] While a wide range of other dictionaries was, as
we have seen, in existence, a dictionary on this model, as Dodsley
recognized, was 'a Work which of all others we most want'.[23] *Want*
signals—and confirms—the sense of absence which Dodsley,
astutely, both identified and sought to remedy. As in Johnson's
Dictionary, to *want* is 'to be without something fit or necessary'; it
is 'to need; to have need of; to lack'—as well as 'to wish for; to long

for'. As Dodsley stresses, Johnson is to 'fix' English, not just 'propose to alter, or amend' it.[24]

It was this proposal—for a dictionary of a particular kind, and with a particular set of aims—with which Johnson was therefore approached in the mid-1740s. A popular narrative exists, of course, by which Johnson's ambition to act as linguistic legislator impelled, by itself, the course on which he sets out. As Hawkins stated, for example: 'Nor can we suppose but that he was in a great measure incited to the prosecution of this laborious work by a reflection on the state of our language at this time.' Hawkins adduces, too, Johnson's own sense of 'the imperfection of all English dictionaries then extant, and the great distance in point of improvement in this kind of literature between us and some of our neighbours'.[25] Johnson's criticism of existing works in the *Plan*, as in his comments on the problems of definition ('a task of which the extent and intricacy is sufficiently shewn by the miscarriage of those who have generally attempted it' (*Yale* XVIII.46)) certainly confirms his sense that there was, in lexicography, no room for complacency.

His interest in 'good' usage had likewise long been clear. Even as an undergraduate at Pembroke College, Oxford in 1728–9, Johnson had been attentive to idiom and attendant questions of acceptability. 'Sir, I remember you would not let us say *prodigious* at College', as his Oxford contemporary Oliver Edwards recalled in 1778 (*Life* 4.231n).[26] Johnson's letters to the young Samuel Ford in the mid-1730s are similarly telling.[27] A proper 'habit of expression' is important in Latin, Ford was informed. However, Johnson added, it was still 'more necessary in English'. In ways which already suggest certain consonances with his later work on the *Dictionary*, it was, Johnson states, only by 'a daily imitation of the best and correctest authors' that improvement in terms of English might be secured (*Letters* I.12).

In 1746 Johnson was nevertheless not a lexicographer but, as Hawkins stresses, an 'author by profession'—a professional writer who worked to realize the projects of others, and who, as a result, had long depended 'for a livelihood upon what he should be able, either in the way of original composition, or translation, or in editing the works of celebrated authors, to procure by his studies'.[28] 'No man but a blockhead ever wrote, except for money', as Johnson's often-quoted aphorism likewise proclaims (*Life* 3.19). The status of the *Dictionary* as a 'commissioned' text—one to which Johnson was contracted and directed to perform—is, in this light, apparent from the beginning (*Yale* XVIII.55). 'It was by [Dodsley's] recommendation that I was employed in the work' Johnson acknowledges (*Life* I.286). If 'works of learning' are to be written, 'it very often happens', that these 'are performed at the direction of those by whom they are to be rewarded', as he later comments in the *Rambler* (*Yale* III.119). Dodsley had already published Johnson's poem 'London' in May 1738 (paying him ten guineas for the copyright).[29] As Solomon confirms, by 1740 Dodsley 'was known internationally as "Pope's publisher" and . . . inundated with proposals from authors and other booksellers'. No other bookseller, he adds, 'approached Dodsley's fertility in imagining and executing literary projects'.[30]

It was, appropriately, in Dodsley's shop at Tully's Head in Pallmall in London that Johnson therefore first encountered the 'literary project' of the *Dictionary*, along with the suggestion that he might compile such a work. If he initially refused ('I believe I shall not undertake it', as the *Life* (I.182) records), the contract for the dictionary was nevertheless signed on 18 June 1746 with a sevenstrong consortium of London booksellers.[31] These, alongside Dodsley, included John and Paul Knapton, Thomas Longman (and his nephew, also called Thomas Longman), Charles Hitch, and Andrew Millar. Both Longman and the Knapton brothers were also responsible for other dictionaries at this time; Miller would likewise contract others during the *Dictionary*'s formation.[32] All nevertheless contributed to the substantial sum of £1,575 for Johnson's work and expenses in making what was, from the beginning, seen as a work of a very different kind.

As Johnson explains in the 1747 *Plan*: 'When first I undertook to write an English Dictionary, I had no expectation of any higher patronage than that of the proprietors of the copy, nor prospect of any other advantage than the price of my labour' (*Yale* XVIII.25). If Johnson is the writer, the 'proprietors' are the booksellers with whom the project originated and to whom the 'copy' belongs. The 'labour' is the dictionary which was to be written over the next eight years. As other comments confirm, Johnson had an astute grasp of the commercial realities which, behind the scenes, governed the production of books—including dictionaries. 'You may remember I have formerly talked with You about a military Dictionary', he wrote, for example, to the publisher (and magazine editor) Edward Cave in 1738. While this was not a project he contemplated for himself, Johnson set out its merits in firmly economic terms: 'The Eldest Mr. Macbean who was with Mr. Chambers has very good Materials for such a Work which I have seen, and will do it at a very low rate. I think the terms of War and Navigation might be comprised with good explanations in one 8vo pica which he is willing to do for twelve shillings a Sheet, to be made up a Guinea at the second impression' (*Letters* I.21–2). A similar consciousness informs Johnson's projections for the *Dictionary*. 'Its sale in other Countries', Johnson notes in the 1746 'Scheme', might perhaps be facilitated by the 'interpretation of the principal words in some other Languages' (*Yale* XVIII.407). Constructed on this model, he suggests, it might secure a multilingual, rather than monolingual, readership, crossing national borders in its role as commodity. As for other works in the eighteenth century, the 'interpenetration of market and writing' was a significant factor in both making and design.[33]

Planning the course

Johnson's planning for the *Dictionary*—for what it might perform, as well as what it might contain—exists in a range of versions, from the early (and now incomplete) 'Short Scheme for Compiling a new Dictionary of the English Language' to the *Plan of a Dictionary* which, published in August 1747, also exists in an earlier manuscript 'Fair Copy'. Across these versions, the details of the projected *Dictionary* gradually take shape. Potential directions are explored, and rejected. Others appear in their stead, clarifying the state of language which Johnson's endeavours are, ideally, to secure.

Schemes, as the *Dictionary* itself confirms, engage, of necessity, with the provisional. They set out a 'plan' or 'a combination of various things into one view', detailing 'design' and 'purpose', and intention rather than actuality.[34] As Fussell stresses, Johnson's preoccupation with 'schemes'—especially those that go awry—was to be a prominent feature of the dictionary years. Johnson's *Rambler* essays are, in this light, full of cautionary tales. 'Schemes, plans, and outlines all prove ironically deficient, defeated always by the surprising and unpleasant actualities of the *ad hoc*', Fussell notes.[35] Schemes reflect the 'inveterate disease of wishing', as Johnson notes (*Yale* IV.22) against which reality rarely measures up. 'Nothing is more subject to mistake and disappointment than anticipated judgment concerning the easiness or difficulty of any undertaking, whether we form our opinion from the performances of others, or from abstracted contemplation of the thing to be attempted', he likewise observed in May 1751 (*Yale* IV.286). More telling still perhaps is his comment in *Rambler* 14 (*Yale* III.75) that, while 'a man proposes his schemes of life in a state of abstraction and disengagement', he is, in so doing, 'in the same state with him that teaches upon land the art of navigation, to whom the sea is always smooth, and the wind always prosperous'. Metaphorical journeys, Johnson warns, by no means lead to the destination which might— at least in theory—have been envisaged. Schemes are, in this light, problematic from the outset.

In 1746 Johnson's popular identity as 'Mr. Rambler' lay, of course, in the future. Instead, in the 'Short Scheme for Compiling a new Dictionary', he was engaged in drafting his ideas, creating 'one view' from the various components which might, as we have seen, be brought into play in terms of eighteenth-century lexicography. Like the 'Fair Copy', the holograph manuscript of the 'Scheme' is usefully reproduced in facsimile in Volume XVIII of the Yale edition of *The Works of Samuel Johnson*.[36] Dated 30 April 1746, it is clearly a working version—a proposal on which the later contract for the *Dictionary* might be based. Most pages reveal both crossing out and rephrasing; Johnson's handwriting, and the limited punctuation he used, add further difficulties. It is, as Kolb and DeMaria note, a text which is 'unusually hard to decipher' (*Yale* XVIII.377).

It can nevertheless illuminatingly reveal the processes of Johnson's early engagement with his task, both in terms of his formulation—and reformulation—of what he was expected to do, as well as the conflicting routes which might, in fact, be taken. Given the 'want' which Dodsley identified, the diction of permanence and linguistic stability is, for example, marked. 'One great end of this undertaking is to fix the English Language', Johnson declares: 'Closely connected with orthography is <u>Pronunciation</u>, the stability of which is of great importance to the duration of a Language' (*Yale* XVIII.389). A set of confident past participles likewise project the linguistic stasis which lexicography might achieve. 'Thus may a Dictionary be compiled by which the pronunciation of the Language may be fixed, and the attainment of it facilitated, by which its purity may be preserved...and its duration lengthend [*sic*]', as Johnson states after surveying what he will attempt to do (*Yale* XVIII.423, 427).

Johnson's diction confirms the close alignment of the dictionary project with eighteenth-century prescriptive discourses, as well as with the stable state of language, which is, as for Snell and Swift, repeatedly posited as an object of desire. As in Swift's *Proposal*, English is, for Johnson, negatively positioned against 'more polished Languages'; its on-going variability and flux illustrates, by contrast, the remedial 'attention' with which French and Italian have already been provided (*Yale* XVIII.393). 'The accuracy of the French in stating the sounds of their letters is well known', as Johnson comments, for instance, of other precedents that are now to be observed for English too (*Yale* XVIII.395). English, conversely, is characterized by 'neglect' in what is, as we have seen, another long-standing topos of language comment (*Yale* XVIII.397). We lack 'certain rules', Johnson writes of pronunciation, here echoing the desiderata of the Académie itself (*Yale* XVIII.389).

Across the 'Scheme', the projected dictionary emerges as a means of normative instruction, as well as a work which might redirect and reform deleterious language change. As Johnson notes, a failure to distinguish active from neuter verbs 'has already introduced some barbarities into our conversation which may in time creep into our writings, if not obviated by just animadversions' (*Yale* XVIII.397). This, too, as he indicates, is to be part of the dictionary-maker's allotted task. *Animadversion*: 'Reproof; severe censure; blame', the relevant entry in the *Dictionary* later explains. The dictionary-maker's role is to evaluate existing practice and, when necessary, to tender appropriate reproof. Johnson's diction of obviation (*to obviate*: 'to meet in the way'; 'to prevent') emphasizes the salience of pre-emptive action. Proper language management should, Johnson suggests, ensure linguistic propriety for the speakers, and writers, of the future.

Johnson's hand is, however, not the only one which appears in the 'Scheme'. Instead, two sets of non-Johnsonian annotations are also in evidence. Both readers comment, and criticize, with relative freedom. Confirming the *Dictionary*'s intended place in a wider culture of correctness, they offer opinions and guidance, censure and advice, as well as models of correctness of their own. Providing the *Dictionary*'s first acts of reception history, they occur moreover at a stage in which the 'Scheme' was still malleable, as well as open to further redirection and change. As Kolb and DeMaria clarify (*Yale* XVIII.5), one of the readers was probably the clergyman John Taylor (1711–88) from Ashbourne in Derbyshire with whom Johnson had been at school.[37] The other still remains unknown.

That Johnson's engagement with his task might, in the opinion of his readers, be made more rigorous is a matter which swiftly becomes clear. Annotations on the drafted text repeatedly suggest further aspects for regulation and the imposition of corrective norms. With a certain irony, for example, Johnson's own prose—and the specific forms he uses in writing the 'Scheme'—become the subject of animadversion in their own right. Taylor, for example, firmly emends Johnson's preferred spelling of 'plow' to 'plough' (*Yale* XVIII.391). On one hand, this merely confirms the kind of variability which typified English usage in the mid-eighteenth century (and which Johnson was also expected to resolve in favour of a single corrected norm).[38] Yet, on the other, Taylor's emendation also serves to undermine—and negate—Johnson's framing argument, re-orientating what the dictionary-maker should do, and where he should go. 'It is to be remarked that many words written alike are differently pronounced', Johnson had stated (*Yale* XVIII.391), pointing out that 'Flow and Plow...may be thus registered Flow-Woe, Plow-now'. Taylor instead revises and rewrites, instituting norms of a different kind. 'Plough' in this emended reading should not be written 'plow', he points out. Nor, on this basis, should Johnson need to differentiate sound values which pertain to words which are only in error 'written alike'. It is 'plough' alone which should be 'registered', Taylor makes plain.

Johnson's account of the variant past participles used in English was subject to similar change. 'I Shook I have Shaken or Shook', Johnson had written in careful illustration of the vowel gradation which characterized strong verbs and their use (*Yale* XVIII.397). He exhibits marked neutrality at these alternative modes of construction. 'Shaken' and 'Shook' are placed in clear equivalence; either could be used. For a writer committed to fixity, he can, at times, seem strikingly tolerant. The early readers of Johnson's 'Scheme' again prove far more normative in both intent and practice. 'I have shook ought to be stigmatised', Taylor declares (*Yale* XVIII.399); such variation is seen as problematic—and profoundly inimical to what a dictionary of this kind ought to perform.[39] Even Johnson's use of 'animadversions' is, we might note, made subject to correction. Crossing it through, Taylor substitutes 'Censure' in its stead (*Yale* XVIII.397).

Johnson's use and selection of evidence prompts similar scrutiny. Commenting on the kind of phrasal structures which typically appear in English, Johnson had, for instance, reflected on the salience of usage and, in line with his expected remit, on what might be deemed 'inaccurate English' (*Yale* XVIII.401). Considerations of potential incorrectness hence frame his discussion of Addison's *to die for* ('And in the loaden Vineyard dies for thirst', taken from l. 118 of Addison's 'A Letter from Italy' (1701)). Yet, as subsequent comments in the 'Scheme' confirm, the validity of judgements of this kind can already emerge as an issue of some complexity. How was inaccuracy to be decided, and on what basis? In this instance, Johnson argued, the existence of other supporting evidence should surely make proscriptive condemnation untenable. It 'may be defended, and, I think justified by the authority of Sir John Davies', he states in conclusion. On this basis, 'to die for' is not 'inaccurate' but is, descriptively, a part of idiomatic English use.[40]

His readers did not agree. Annotations on the verso of this sheet firmly return attention to the issue of correctness. Johnson's conclusions, it seems, had failed to convince. Instead, the second (unknown) reader asks 'whether for [in the construction used by Addison] is not against Custom' (*Yale* XVIII.403).[41] As other annotations from Taylor confirm, the *Dictionary*'s intended role was not to observe and record. Instead, he stresses, it ought to offer wide-ranging regulation in this and other matters: 'At the Conclusion of each word there ought to be Examples ... of the Elegant uses of each Word & Phrase in which it is employed.' The proscriptive potential of the dictionary was, Taylor emphasizes, equally important. Entries should contain 'Examples of the Abuse of each Word &c wth Cautions how to correct & avoid it' (*Yale* XVIII.425). Like the 'Exercises in False Syntax' which start to appear in contemporary grammars,[42] the *Dictionary*, Taylor advises, ought set out a corrective model in which right and wrong are distinct, and the rules of 'proper' usage unambiguously delineated.

Johnson's role as lexicographer can, in a number of ways, already seem difficult. On one level, his rhetoric of correction and fixity accords due prominence to the kind of normativity which was, as we have seen, expected of a dictionary written on the models advanced by the academies of Italy and of France. Yet Johnson, at times, also exhibits striking latitude towards 'custom' and its concomitant variations. Significant, too, are early indications of a markedly rational engagement with evidence and what this might reveal. Johnson's early reading of scientists such as Herman Boerhaave had, as Schwartz argues, instilled in him a strong awareness of the values of empiricism and observation, and deduction rather than assertion.[43] In the 'Scheme', prescription and description can, it seems, already exist in uneasy symbiosis; if the *Dictionary*'s intended destination, in a remit of reform and control, is made plain, Johnson's tendency to explore and observe already seems to foreshadow some of the difficulties which practical lexicography would bring over the next nine years. Taylor's stance is far more uncompromising, repeatedly reminding Johnson of the obligations of his stated task.

Johnson's position on orthography is equally noteworthy. The initial drafting of his ideas is marked by its apparent latitude. As Johnson's comments on the variability of *plow* and *plough* indicate, the same word could indeed often assume different forms in contemporary usage (a pattern Johnson's own spelling also widely confirms).[44] Yet, while the extent of such variability had perhaps been problematic in earlier years, this was, the 'Scheme' suggests, surely no longer the case. Even if 'long vague and uncertain', eighteenth-century spelling is, in this view, now 'in many cases settled, and settled with such propriety that it may be generally received' (*Yale* XVIII.385). The absence of absolute norms does not prompt concern. Usage ('the Spelling in present Use') is given as the basis of the reference model that Johnson will provide. 'Received' English is based on what is used.

Nevertheless, as the surviving manuscript of the 'Scheme' testifies, this section—together with Johnson's preliminary conclusions on the nature of English orthography—was, in fact, to be firmly crossed through. In its stead, we find the first proof of intervention by Johnson's future patron, Lord Chesterfield, together with Johnson's reconsidered, and appropriately deferential, response. What is merely settled in 'many cases' is now seen as markedly inadequate. 'Your Lordship observes that there is still great uncertainty among the best writers', Johnson's revisions affirm; if spelling can in any sense be described as 'settled', it is now deemed settled merely 'by accident' (*Yale* XVIII.385).[45] Such variation as remains is, by the same token, no longer to be regarded as 'received' but as ripe for reform.

As other aspects of Johnson's on-going revision indicate, the 'Scheme' was, importantly, changing in other respects, too. Perhaps most significantly, it was evolving into the formal address to a patron which its later manifestation, the *Plan of a Dictionary*, would comprehensively reveal. Chesterfield, as Hedrick affirms, was not only a celebrated statesman but was also 'an enthusiastic devotee of language fixing', as well as being widely regarded as 'an authority on polite address and proper usage'.[46] As Dodsley recognized, with what Boswell described as 'the true feelings of trade' (*Life* I.264), Chesterfield made an ideal patron for a dictionary of this kind.[47] As the later 'Fair Copy' of the 'Plan' indicates, Johnson's projected 'design' had 'been thought by your Lordship of importance'. The text is now addressed directly to Chesterfield, setting out a work which, as Johnson confirms, had proved 'sufficient to attract your Favour' (and, indeed, as another now cancelled section stated, to 'excite your Curiosity' (*Yale* XVIII.430–1)).

Redirection: Writing the *Plan of a Dictionary*

By 1747, as the manuscript 'Fair Copy' of the *Plan* confirms, Lord Chesterfield—Philip Dormer Stanhope—was publically established as Johnson's patron.[48] Johnson, in an extensive new section, looks back in awe to an era 'in which Princes and Statesmen thought it part of their Honour to promote the improvement of their native Tongues' and in which 'Dictionaries were written under the protection of Greatness' (*Yale* XVIII.430). Such erstwhile patrons, Johnson observes, had been duly 'solicitous for the perpetuity of their Language'. Yet, as he now declares, Chesterfield, through 'unexpected Distinction', has—here in the mid-eighteenth century—become the patron of Johnson's work in ways that surely augur a similar solicitude for English, alongside the promise of its own 'perpetuity'. The *Dictionary*, the 'Fair Copy' confirms, has thereby become 'a work prosecuted under your Lordship's influence' (*Yale* XVIII.431). As Johnson notes with due submission: 'I here lay before your Lordship the Plan of my Design'.

As we will see, the 'Fair Copy' also presents an interesting doubleness in this respect. It is based on an earlier (but now lost) draft but reveals a later stage of Johnson's thinking. It looks back to the antecedent 'Scheme' but also clearly anticipates the *Plan* as finally published. A number of the suggestions from the earlier readers have been assimilated, yet a further layer of annotations— some by Johnson, others by Chesterfield himself (as well as by a second unknown reader)—signal further levels of negotiation and change. Paradoxically, Johnson's projections of linguistic stasis in the *Dictionary* come to exist against what can seem a striking textual fluidity. Johnson drafts and redrafts, deletes and emends. The 'Fair Copy' is marked by a pattern of on-going revision in which significant changes continue to appear.

As Reddick notes, for example, 'The principal changes Johnson made in transforming the "Scheme" into the published *Plan* appear to be intended to address aspects of a larger concern: the nature and imposition of the lexicographer's authority for linguistic decisions.'[49] Boileau—who had played a formative role in the early years of the Académie Française—is, for example, now referenced explicitly. As a new section in the 'Fair Copy' indicates, the *Dictionary*, and the normative potential it contains, is to be carefully aligned with Boileau's 'proposal to the academicians, that they should review all their impolite Authors, and correct all the Impurities which they found in them' (*Yale* XVIII.481, 483). Language academies, in another important change, now symbolize 'the highest degree of excellence' (*Yale* XVIII.488). Johnson, assuming a pose of authorial humility, fears his own work may inevitably fall short.

Authority—and the power in which this resides, as well as the means by which it might be implemented—emerges as a prominent theme. Johnson amplifies and revises his engagement with dictionary-making as prescriptive process. Chesterfield's authority is, for example, given as unquestioned. As Johnson states, Chesterfield is 'one whose authority in Language is so generally acknowledged' (*Yale* XVIII.482). Johnson is suitably deferential. His agency in the world of words is, at least rhetorically, to be secured only by dint of the power which Chesterfield has vested in him. Johnson will, he states, as Chesterfield's 'delegate', wield merely 'vicarious Jurisdiction' over the words and meanings that are encountered (*Yale* XVIII.483). The deferential diction—and rhetorical patterning of antonomasia[50]—reify a sense of hierarchy and subordination. Johnson's iterated use of 'My Lord' punctuates the revised text ('on this Province, My Lord, I entered'; 'Thus my Lord will our Language be laid down' (*Yale* XVIII.429 and 461)).[51]

Placed against the earlier 'Scheme', this is clearly a far more complex text. A new set of social relations moreover inform the metaphorical journeys—and identities—which are, in various ways, to be performed. 'Ausonius thought that modesty forbad him to plead inability for a task to which Caesar had judged him equal', Johnson notes, for example (*Yale* XVIII.482). Drawing on Ausonius's address to Emperor Theodosius, Johnson allies himself with Ausonius's submissive response ('I have no skill to write, but Caesar has bidden me.... Why should I deny that I can do what he thinks I can do?'). Chesterfield, in contrast, is allied with Caesar himself and the commands which he had issued—and in which he expected to be obeyed. As Ausonius understood all too well, 'power is masked under a courteous command'.[52] Johnson in similar ways proclaims his obedience, and a willingness to follow where Chesterfield might direct.

Other acts of submission are in evidence, too, informing the changing direction of both plan and *Dictionary*. An earlier (and markedly descriptive) inclination by which, 'with regard to Questions of purity, or propriety', Johnson had not thought to 'extend beyond the proposition of the Question, and the display of the Authorities on each side', has been displaced. Instead, as Johnson acknowledges, 'I have been since determined by your Lordship's opinion to interpose my own Judgement, and shall therefore endeavour to support what seems to me most consonant to Grammar and Reason' (*Yale* XVIII.482). Johnson's decision to introduce images of conquest and invasion clearly invokes other discourses of power, and its implementation, in the journeys he might take. New, too, is the military diction, and historical referencing, which also appears.

In other images absent from the earlier 'Scheme', Johnson is, for instance, now rendered foot soldier to Chesterfield's 'Caesar'. Johnson's immediate reference point in such figurations is the emperor Claudius who, in AD 43, sent an imperial force to Britain in a further exercise of Roman rule. Like 'the soldiers of Caesar', to whom he is now compared (*Yale* XVIII.488), Johnson must, once the sea is crossed, invade and take control. The 'new world' of words— referenced, as we have seen, by earlier lexicographers such as Blount and Phillips—is likewise repositioned. Johnson's 'new world', which, as he makes plain, is to be reached under Chesterfield's direction, offers fertile terrain for the exercise of power rather than merely disinterested or scientific exploration. The 'natives', Johnson suggests, may now be 'civilized' and unwarranted rebellion subdued.

As we have seen, Johnson's inserted metaphors readily evoke the agency (and intended rule) with which the dictionary-maker was popularly credited in prescriptive discourse. Importantly, Johnson's compliance with such ideals is now also made far more explicit.

43

Deference—and other aspects of possible subjugation—is evident in other ways too. Chesterfield's annotations, for example, often challenge the legitimacy of the constructions which Johnson had deployed in ways that give renewed prominence to the matter of correctness, and its rightful judgement. 'Is it not plough?', Chesterfield asks, for example, emending the still retained spelling of 'plow' (*Yale* XVIII.448). 'Can one properly say the *Dialect* of a profession?', he likewise demands (*Yale* XVIII.438). In Johnson's revisions to the 'Fair Copy', 'Dialect' is crossed through and the text meekly corrected in response: 'It seems necessary to the completion of a Dictionary designed not merely for Critics but for popular use, that it should comprise in some degree the *Peculiar words* of every Profession', as Johnson now writes [my emphases] (*Yale* XVIII.439). 'Is it not surer to spell *reflection, inflection* . . . from *flectare*, than *reflexion, inflexion*, &c.', Chesterfield likewise observes (*Yale* XVIII.457), contesting other forms which had appeared in the manuscript text. Etymology is, for Chesterfield, placed above custom as a model. 'Should it not be *inflections?*', he adds. Johnson's statement that '*porter a bout*' underpins phrasal structures in English such as 'to bring about' (*Yale* XXVIII.454–5) is, in similar ways, firmly disputed. 'This is no French expression', Chesterfield asserts, recommending *venir a bout d'une affaire* in its stead: '*Porter a bout* is never us'd.' Johnson submits, and revises accordingly.

Across the 'Fair Copy', the rightful exercise of power by both dictionary-maker and *Dictionary* is gradually extended. Further acts of stigmatization are encouraged, and other 'barbarities' identified (*Yale* XVIII.460). Annotations by a second (unknown) reader also enforce a heightened sense of linguistic correctness. 'Are generous, reverend, Chancelor . . . ever pronounced accurately as only of two syllables?', the reader contends (*Yale* XVIII.448). Johnson's observation that 'it may be likewise proper to remark' the ways by which, in speech, polysyllabic words such as *generous, reverend*, and *region* are contracted to disyllables (*Yale* XVIII.449) meets clear resistance. It is, on this basis, not 'proper to remark' these at all, unless in condemnation. Johnson is again seen as too liberal in inclination and intent. 'If the author quotes in his dictionary, these and simialar [*sic*] forms of expression, should he not brand them with some mark of reprobation?', the reader suggests alongside Johnson's discussion of loanwords and naturalization (*Yale* XVIII.436). Legitimacy is intentionally denied to words such as *cynosure* and *zenith* as used in English.[53]

The various drafts of both *Plan* and 'Scheme' can thereby enact a clear narrative of change. If Johnson has, we have seen, been commissioned to write a dictionary of a certain kind, the real obligations of this remit are both tightened and reinforced as we move towards the published *Plan*. Johnson's inserted metaphors set out new roles, and a clearer destination. Yet new anxieties and uncertainties can also emerge, alongside an undercurrent of resistance. As Johnson makes plain, the fact that invasions, and the kind of journeys in which power and suppression are paramount, involve a form of 'madness' cannot be denied (*Yale* XVIII.488). Conquest of the world of words is by no means a foregone conclusion. Johnson both introduces, and undercuts, the victories that popular opinion assumed. Military campaigns can be undertaken and usage attacked. Nevertheless, as 'adventurer' (here in another identity which Johnson assumes at this stage of the *Plan*), the dictionary-maker must, as we have seen in Chapter 1, also, of necessity, venture into domains where both chance and casualty intervene, and in which journeys rarely go as planned.

That journeys into words run the risk of disorientation—as well as dislocation in terms of what the dictionary-maker might be expected to perform—was, in these terms, also made apparent. As Johnson warns in a now cancelled passage, while his attention is fixed on 'distant refinements' and how these might be imposed (*Yale* XVIII.488), the real dangers might nevertheless lie in being over-whelmed by the 'mists of obscurity' which language must, in reality, present. Outside the grandiloquent ambitions which conquest and fixity alike suggest, control is by no means easy and the destinations desired all too elusive. Johnson's diction once again presages that of 'The Vanity of Human Wishes' in ways that, with hindsight, do not suggest unqualified confidence in what he sets out to do.

Dictionary-making, as Johnson already indicates, might instead have to follow an inevitably conflicted course in which desire and pragmatism point in very different directions. As he admits, the wish 'that these fundamental atoms of our speech, might obtain the firmness and immutability of constituent particles' is undeniable (*Yale* XVIII.461). Yet, as in Johnson's poetry of the dictionary years, to what extent wishes can—or should be—realized is a matter which generates issues and problems of a different kind. Whether language can be remodelled to suit human inclinations raises typically Johnsonian qualms. If lexicography is commended as an 'art', it is, as Johnson already makes plain, one which cannot, with reason, secure that which its prescriptive manifestations most desire. 'Art', Johnson stresses, cannot 'prevent' the 'mortality' of words. Instead, as he points out, 'their changes will be always informing us that Language is the work of man, of a being from whom unchangeable stability cannot be derived' (*Yale* XVIII.462).

Disconcertingly, as Johnson admits, the stasis that the dictionary-maker seeks is perhaps better seen as a 'Phantom'—an entity which, to the rational mind, must exist only in illusion and which is located far more easily in the realms of fancy and 'imagination' (*Yale* XVIII.461). As in the 'Vanity', such phantoms can delude and lead astray. As the 'Fair Copy' suggests, to pursue journeys of this kind will, for instance, require the 'Shackles' to be shed that otherwise bind the dictionary-maker, as 'slave of science', to evidence and factual enquiry. Yet, if such freedom can tempt, what it promises is thereby also rendered both insubstantial and unreal. Johnson's metaphors again problematize the nature of expectation—and its realization—in what he must perform. To follow 'imagination' is, after all, at odds which what we might expect of a work of reference—blurring generic boundaries in ways that present other conflicts of both intent and approach.[54]

The 'Fair Copy' can, in such ways, expose with particular clarity Johnson's sense of the conflicts which he faced as he set about his task. A quest to control language and impose stability can be undercut by disturbingly pragmatic reminders of the limitations of human power, while the dissonances of reason and expectation attract careful consideration. Movement and stasis are repeatedly placed in opposition. 'I know that expectation when her wings are once expanded, flies without Labour or incumbrance to heights to which Performance cannot attain', as Johnson warns in another passage that he later revised for the finished *Plan* (*Yale* XVIII.431). It is, as he indicates, 'with the cruelty of an artful Tyrant' that expectation 'offers a glimpse of 'Perfection' which nevertheless cannot be achieved. Perfection and imperfect 'Performance' exist in symbiosis.[55] Fixity is rendered a complex ideal.

As Johnson observes in due deference to his new patron, it is, of course, 'natural ... to hope that your Lordships patronage may not be wholly lost, [and] that it may contribute to the preservation of the ancient, and the improvement of modern Writers' (*Yale* XVIII.486). Johnson's modals and indicatives are, however, made carefully distinct. It is indeed 'natural to hope', and 'unavoidable to wish', Johnson affirms. This is unequivocal—these are constitutive parts of the human condition. But, by the same token, he also suggests that patronage and the dictionary 'may' contribute to the stasis which Chesterfield desired. Or, then again, they may not. Across the 'Fair Copy', as Johnson warns, what we desire and what might instead come to pass will, in language as in all else, often prove irreconcilable.

Departure and destinations: from *Plan* to 'Preface'

The finished *Plan* of the *Dictionary* would change once more. Johnson's evocative comments on the imaginative territories in which the 'Phantom' of immutability might be pursued are deleted, as are his comments on the tyrannies which unrealizable expectation will impose. As the 'Fair Copy' confirms, these sections are crossed through. If the 'Shackles of lexicography' are enforced, these now work, in essence, to a different end. They reinforce the quest for authority in language—even if Johnson's sense of doubt and equivocation is not entirely concealed. The hazards of expectation remain, if in a slightly different guise. Perhaps rightly, the *Plan* is often seen as difficult and challenging text, prescriptive and descriptive by turns, and balancing—at times precariously—between narratives of human power, deferential platitude, and a keen awareness of the kind of problems that lexicography pursued on this basis will inevitably encounter.

A further eight years of lexicographical endeavour would, of course, follow publication of the finished *Plan* in 1747. As Johnson specifies in the 1755 'Preface', to *set out*, is merely 'to begin a course or journey' (*Yale* XVIII.87). Where it ends can be very different. 'There are two things which I am confident I can do very well', as Johnson later admitted to Sir Joshua Reynolds. 'One is an introduction to any literary work, stating what it is to contain, and how it should be executed in the most perfect manner.' Johnson's other area of expertise is, he confirms, 'a conclusion, shewing from various causes why the execution has not been equal to what the author promised to himself and the publick' (*Life* I.292).[56] Plans inevitably exist, for Johnson, in a realm of hypothesis, offering confident projections of what ought to be—but which might not be accomplished. 'Such is design, while it is yet at a distance from execution', as the 1755 'Preface' would likewise confirm (*Yale* XVIII.93–4).

Johnson's 'design' had, of course, been firmly kept in public view. Alluding to the nature of Johnson's projected task, the writer David Mallet had, for example, compared Chesterfield to Richelieu and the *Dictionary*, by implication, to an academy which Johnson's endeavours might serve to realize. Richelieu's 'academy for the *French* tongue...still flourishes to the advantage of his country, as well as to the peculiar honor of his own name', Mallet noted, deftly suggesting that Chesterfield, like Richelieu, might indeed secure a language—and a reputation—which might transcend the mutability of time.[57] 'May we not flatter our hopes that some such scheme, or one yet more extensively useful, will take place, so as to be rendered effectual under your Lordship's influence?', he adjured, 'and that, ages hence, those, who are best fitted by their talents, to instruct or entertain the public, will have cause to remember, with gratitude as well as reverence, the ministry of the *Earl* of CHESTERFIELD?'[58] Swift's proposal to the Earl of Oxford (along with the linguistic stability which he too had desired) had failed. Mallet, however, looks forward with confidence to Chesterfield's role in a new campaign for linguistic reform in which such aims may indeed come to pass.

William Strahan, Dodsley's printer, had sent a missive of similar intent to *The Gentleman's Magazine* in 1749, heralding the publication of a work, now 'in great forwardness', by which 'it is hoped, that our language will be more fixed, and better established'.[59] Chesterfield, too, perhaps also prompted by Dodsley,[60] would send two commendatory letters on the subject of the *Dictionary* to Dodsley's journal *The World* in late 1754. Chesterfield's diction maintained intact the tropes of correctness and control, power and conquest from the 1747 *Plan*—even if, in a deft reversal, it is Johnson who is now figured as 'Caesar' while Chesterfield himself, in a pose of mock-humility, promises exemplary servitude and the obeisance necessary to one who controls the state of words: 'I hereby declare that I make a total surrender of all my rights and privileges in the English language, as a free-born British subject, to the said Mr. Johnson, during the terms of his dictatorship.'[61] Swift, in his earlier hopes for stasis and control, is still commended as 'ingenious', while Johnson's inauguration of a 'standard' for English is eagerly anticipated. 'Nothing can be more rationally imagined', Chesterfield declares.[62]

Johnson's corrective reading in the 1755 'Preface' of what we may 'rationally imagine' dictionaries, and language, to do is nevertheless plain.[63] Johnson publishes, as Lipking observes, a work which is, by this point, emphatically '*my* Dictionary'.[64] 'The *English Dictionary* was written … without any patronage of the great', Johnson avers

(*Yale* XVIII.111). Johnson's own famous letter to Chesterfield, written on 7 February (some two months before the *Dictionary* was published), decisively severs the formal obligations of patronage—and the link to Chesterfield. 'Is not a Patron, My Lord, one who looks with unconcern on a Man struggling for life in the water and when he has reached ground, encumbers him with help', as Johnson had demanded (*Letters* I.96). Chesterfield had, Johnson contends, in effect left him to drown in the sea of words as he strove to complete his task. Here, too, expectations of both power and safety proved awry. If, as professional writer, Johnson has a 'patron', it was, as he later declared, Robert Dodsley, the bookseller and publisher with whom the dictionary project began. 'Ithaca', as we have seen, is, in the *Dictionary*, located in *Grubstreet* rather than Chesterfield's 'outward rooms' (*Letters* I.95). As Johnson's Odyssean metaphors confirm, it is here to which he envisages his return.

As Chapter 4 will further explore, the tenor of Chesterfield's missives, and not least in their reading of language and political power, merely served to reinforce the distance which had by this point come to exist between Chesterfield and *Dictionary*, as well as Chesterfield and Johnson.[65] 'Those who have been persuaded to think well of my design, will require that it should fix our language, and put a stop to those alterations which time and chance have hitherto been suffered to make in it without opposition', as Johnson acknowledges in the 'Preface'. Yet, as he adds, he has, in this this, 'indulged expectation which neither reason nor experience can justify' (*Yale* XVIII.104). Johnson's metaphors of the dictionary-maker's journey would again recur to good effect in this respect. Chesterfield's two letters to the *World*, and the expectations on which these continue to depend, inform a further set of contrastive figurations. Power and obligation are again reversed. 'After making a hazardous and fatiguing journey round the literary world...my Lord Chesterfield sends out two little cock-boats to tow me in', Johnson stated, dismissively, to Moore. 'Does [Chesterfield] now send out two cock-boats to tow me into harbour?', he demanded of

Garrick with similar rhetorical disdain.[66] *Cock-boat*: 'A small boat belonging to a ship', the *Dictionary* confirms. The *Dictionary*, figured in Johnson's letter to Warton of March 1755 as the ship of knowledge (*Letters* I.101), proud in its great bulk, is seen as dwarfing the vessels which Chesterfield has unnecessarily despatched. There could, on a number of levels, be no greater cutting-down to size. Johnson, as he stresses, will make his own way back to shore.

Devoid of the obligations that formal patronage can bring, the 1755 'Preface' would, as a result, offer a far more trenchant vision of what dictionary-makers might do, and the routes they should follow. 'In patronage, [an author] must say what pleases his patron', as Johnson would later declare; it is 'an equal chance whether that be truth or falsehood' (*Life* 5.59). 'One who countenances, supports or protects. Commonly a wretch who supports with insolence, and is paid with flattery', as the *Dictionary* likewise explains under *patron*.[67] Payment, in these terms, is, however, conspicuously withheld. In the 'Preface', Johnson is no longer Ausonius. The hierarchical metaphors, introduced in the 'Fair Copy' and the *Plan*, do not reappear. Nor does the obeisance they had implied, or the journeys they required. Johnson is, we might note, no longer 'determined' by Chesterfield's 'opinion' (*Yale* XVIII.54), but can exercise determination of his own.

Other illusions generated by expectation rather than experience are also cast aside. In the 'Preface' Swift becomes the writer of a 'petty treatise' in which the premises of linguistic enquiry are by no means seen as secure (*Yale* XVIII.107). Indeed, as Johnson later comments, Swift's *Proposal* was 'written without much knowledge of the general nature of language'—and not least in terms of the 'certainty and stability which, contrary to all experience, he thinks attainable' (*Yale* XXII.984). References to 'Caesar' and the projected invasion—and control—of the state of language are, for Johnson, likewise confined to the past. 'Conquests', as we are told with eminently pragmatic intent, 'are now very rare' (*Yale* XVIII.105). Chesterfield's letters can here, too, receive a firm rebuff. As Johnson observes, the dictionary-maker cannot change the natural ordering of the world. It is powerlessness, rather than human power, which comes to the fore. Linguistic change, Johnson now states, is 'as much superiour to human resistance, as the revolutions of the sky, or intumescence of the tide' (*Yale* XVIII.105–6). The diction of 'The Vanity of Human Wishes' is, as have seen, redeployed to equally good effect. Ambitions to 'enchain syllables' and to 'lash the wind' encounter marked derision. Words, as Johnson makes plain, are not slaves, and lexicographers who pursue such a course are firmly condemned.[68] The doubts and pragmatism which had earlier surfaced in both 'Scheme' and 'Fair Copy' are likewise given their due. Johnson's metaphors of 'circumnavigation' as used in his letter to Warton can seem particularly apt. He can return, as we will see, in more ways than one.

3

'Excursions into books': Documenting the new world of words

An 'excursion' in modern English exhibits little of the unpredictability that marked its counterparts in the eighteenth century. Today we can, for example, book an excursion; whether to Lichfield or London, our destination will be clear. A departure from the ordinary routines by which one might travel to work or school, the excursion is a journey imbued with the expectation of pleasure.[1] Characterized by its relative brevity, excursions are usually short—a day or two at most. With similar certainty, an excursion will swiftly return us to the point where we began.

Johnson's definition is very different. In eighteenth-century English, excursions—whether literal or metaphorical—were united by a sense of potentially unregulated exploration. In line with its etymology (Latin *excursiōn-em* <*excurrĕre* 'to run out'), its essence lay in digression—and departure from the routes that might otherwise be followed. If there is a 'stated or settled path', it is the nature of the excursion to move beyond it as Johnson states under *excursion*, sense 1. As in Johnson's *Rambler* 177, excursions could, in consequence, be remote as well as wide-ranging. 'I...resolved to devote the rest of my life wholly to curiosity, and

Samuel Johnson and the Journey into Words. Lynda Mugglestone
© Lynda Mugglestone 2015. First published 2015 by Oxford University Press.

without any confinement of my excursions or termination of my views, to wander over the boundless regions of general knowledge', as Vivaculus declares (*Yale* V.168). Johnson's diction neatly aligns exploration and education, reading and discovery, here within the individual venture into words. As the *Dictionary* confirms, an *excursion* is 'An expedition into some distant part'.[2] A swift return is not expected.

Writing the *Dictionary*, as Johnson reflected in 1755, had also come to depend upon expeditions of this kind. Johnson's overarching image of circumnavigation—his 'voyage round the literary world'—rested, as he explained, on a series of discrete 'excursions into books' (*Yale* XVIII.84). Like the exploratory ventures undertaken by other more literal 'adventurers' (in which travel and the enterprise of knowledge were also firmly linked),[3] Johnson's 'excursions'—and the digressive potential they contained—were made in the interests of collecting up evidence on words and meaning, embedded together in the quotations which appear beneath the majority of entries in the finished text. As Johnson noted in December 1751 (here in writing *Rambler* 180), it was, as the *Dictionary* proved, 'only from the various essays of experimental industry, and the vague excursions of minds sent out upon discovery, that any advancement of knowledge can be expected' (*Yale* V.183). Here, too, his metaphors are revealing. Johnson's 'experimental industry' would, as we will see, be of critical import in the *Dictionary*'s formation and the knowledge it would convey. By 1755, over 2,000 'essays' of this kind would have been made, while over 116,000 citations appear across the *Dictionary*'s first edition. These, as Clifford notes, moreover represent a fraction of those that Johnson originally assembled.[4]

The dictionary as collection

Dictionaries are 'supposed, in great measure, Assemblages of other peoples', Ephraim Chambers had explained in his entry for *dictionary-writer*: 'if they rob, they don't do it any other wise, than as the Bee does, for the publick service. Their object is not pillaging, but in collecting Contributions.' Robert James's *Medicinal Dictionary* of 1742–45, on which Johnson had also worked, provided clear illustration of methods of this kind.[5] The *Medicinal Dictionary* consists 'largely of translations, abridgements, and extracts from the best-known medical texts of the day', Kaminski confirms.[6] Under James's entry for *Aer*, we find a lengthy extract from the Dutch scientist, Herman Boerhaave. In the entry for Boerhaave, we find Johnson's own biographical narrative, largely reproduced from *The Gentleman's Magazine* in 1739.

Johnson's entries in the 1755 *Dictionary* for words such as *county* (a lengthy account taken from John Cowell's *The Interpreter*) or *pea*—a thirteen-line description abstracted from the *Gardeners Dictionary* of Philip Miller[7]—reveal, for example, a process of collection which closely resembles James's own importing of authority.[8] Similar are the fourteen lines defining *elk* which derive from John Hill's *Materia Medica* of 1751.[9] All are imbricated in the text, informing what Jack Lynch identifies as the undeniably encyclopaedic tendencies which the *Dictionary* can exhibit.[10]

Nevertheless, if the *Medicinal Dictionary* provided Johnson with at least some insights into practical lexicography, it also offered the potential for critical departure. Johnson can also peruse material from earlier lexicographers with what can seem a markedly sceptical gaze. Earlier authority is, for example, often contested. 'This word is said by *Bailey*, I know not on what authority, to be derived from a custom, by which the tenants of the archbishop of York were obliged . . . to bring a lamb to the alter', he states under *lammas*. *Baldrick* is similar. If 'by some *Dictionaries* it is explained a *bracelet*', Johnson remains unconvinced: 'I have not found it in that sense.' He gives the meaning 'A girdle' instead. Johnson's independence can be marked. '*Skinner* imagines that this whole family of words may be deduced from the Latin *veho*', he declares under *ferry* (v.). Johnson's targeted use of 'imagines' does not lend credence to this view. Nor do the comments which follow: 'I do not love Latin originals; but if such must be sought, may not these words be more naturally derived from *ferri*, to be carried?'[11]

While, as Johnson admits, 'many words yet stand supported only by the name of *Bailey, Ainsworth, Philips*, or the contracted *Dict.* for *Dictionaries*', such evidence is by no means endorsed. 'Of these I am not always certain that they are seen in any book but the works of lexicographers', he writes (*Yale* XVIII.87). Entries such as those for *fatiferous* ('Deadly; mortal; destructive') or *ademption* ('Taking away; privation'), which are supported by the otherwise anonymous '*Dict.*', serve less to demonstrate the authority of earlier lexicographers than to expose the gaps in authentication which such entries suggest. As Johnson affirms, 'Many I have inserted, because they may perhaps exist, though they have escaped my notice: they are, however, to be yet considered as resting only upon the credit of former dictionaries' (*Yale* XVIII.88).[12]

It was instead by means of direct engagement, and active perusal, that Johnson endeavoured to locate evidence of words and meaning in use: 'I applied myself to the perusal of our writers; and noting whatever might be of use to ascertain or illustrate any word or phrase, accumulated in time the materials of a dictionary' (*Yale* XVIII.74). While *perusal* in modern English tends to suggest superficial browsing or rapid scanning, its eighteenth-century sense, as Johnson illustrates, was very different. It relied on close and critical engagement; it is, the *Dictionary* explains, 'to observe' and 'to examine', as well as 'to read'.[13]

Ample precedent for methods of this kind was provided by the classical dictionaries with which Johnson was familiar,[14] as well as by continental dictionaries such as the *Vocabulario* of the Accademia della Crusca. Use in earlier English works had been limited. Henry Cockeram had, for instance, read Thomas Nashe in search of evidence for his *Dictionarie* of 1623;[15] as under *argoil* and *asterlagour*, Phillips had referred to use in Chaucer's works. 'Notes or Observations upon Words, Phrases, and Passages of authentick Authors' had, in contradistinction, featured in the dictionary that

Thomas Brereton planned in 1718;[16] Addison likewise promised the use of 'Authorities...throughout' in the dictionary he outlined. Both works, however, remained unpublished. 'Our Words...lie scattered in dark Corners of our Authors', Thomas Wilson instead lamented in 1724, placing particular emphasis on the remedial endeavours that English lexicography might yet make in this respect.[17] 'For this End...it will be necessary to collect the best Words which have been introduced by our eminent Writers', he advised, 'for while good Words lie scattered in a few uncommon Books, tho' they are part of our Language, they are little known or understood'.[18]

Johnson's emphasis on collection as an integral part of his methodology was therefore particularly welcome. 'I have studiously endeavoured to collect examples and authorities', he affirmed (*Yale* XVIII.95). Since 'the deficiency of dictionaries was immediately apparent', this merely meant that 'to COLLECT the WORDS of our language was a task of greater difficulty' than he had at first supposed, he likewise acknowledged in 1755 (*Yale* XVIII.84).[19] Collection, and what was to be collected, nevertheless offered a range of other opportunities for departure and choice. Wilson's emphasis on 'best words' in 'eminent Writers' as the rightful territory for lexicographical enquiry reflected, for example, other aspects of popular language attitudes in this context. Acts of collection—and the reading this might require—were located in a privileged and hierarchical space. Deliberating in 1744 on the 'design' of an 'authoritative' dictionary, Alexander Pope revealed a similar alignment of collection and canonicity. Bacon, Richard Hooker, John Tillotson, and Dryden are among the eighteen writers he sanctions as prospective sources. Sir Walter Raleigh is, however, rejected (twice) as 'too affected' to be used as evidence. Vanbrugh, Congreve, William L'Estrange, the playwright John Fletcher, and Ben Jonson meanwhile gain a form of qualified approval as 'authorities for familiar dialogue' alone.[20] In qualitative deliberations similar in kind, Donne is given as 'superior to Randolph' and Sir William Davenant declared 'a better poet than Donne', while 'Herbert is lower than Crashaw, Sir John Beaumont higher, and Donne a good deal also'. William Cartwright and Bishop Corbett are consigned to the 'mediocre'.[21]

The idea of dictionary-making as a quantitative process by which (as in modern lexicography), frequency must determine the inclusion of a particular word or sense, remained remote. Collection for the dictionary-maker, Pope recommends, should operate within clearly normative boundaries. 'In most doubts whether a word is English or not, or whether such a particular use of it is proper, one has nothing but authority for it. Is it in Sir William Temple, or Locke, or Tillotson?', Pope stressed, 'if it be, you may conclude that it is right, or at least won't be looked upon as wrong'.[22]

Dodsley, writes DeMaria, 'clearly expected Johnson to produce a work that would resemble what Pope might have produced'.[23] Johnson, too—at least in 1747—could seem equally content to draw on Pope's transferred authority. 'Many of the writers whose testimonies will be alleged, were selected by Mr. Pope', he pointed out: 'I may be justified in affirming, that were he still alive, solicitous as he was for the success of this work, he would not be displeased that I have undertaken it' (*Yale* XVIII.55–6). In terms of collection, it is, as the *Plan* therefore confirms, an 'obvious rule' to prefer 'writers of the first reputation to those of inferior rank' (*Yale* XVIII.55). The 'best writers', 'polite writers', and 'the correctest writers' all appear as reference points, while Pope himself, as well as Addison, Milton, Dryden, and Shakespeare provide illustrative quotations where necessary. Discussing the 'familiar' sense of *toast*, Johnson turns to a citation from Pope's *The Rape of the Lock* ('The wise man's passion, and the vain man's *toast*').[24] Milton in *Paradise Lost* meanwhile demonstrates the contrastive stress patterning in words such as *dolorous* and *sonorous*: 'He pass'd o'er many a region *dolorous*' / '*Sonorous* metal blowing martial sounds' (*Yale* XVIII.38). The *Dictionary*, as an advertisement from the *London Evening Post* in April 1747 affirms (see Figure 3), was to contain 'the Words of the

To the PUBLICK,

There is now preparing for the Press, and in good Forwardness, in Two Volumes, Folio,

An ENGLISH DICTIONARY;

ETYMOLOGICAL, | EXPLANATORY;
ANALOGICAL, | And
SYNTACTICAL, | CRITICAL.

In which the Words of the English Language are traced up to their Origin, deduced through their various Fluxions and Formations, regulated in their Construction, explain'd in all the Varieties of their Meaning, and exemplified in the whole Extent of their Use, according to the Authority of our purest Writers.

To which is prefix'd,
A Critical English Grammar, and a History of the English Language, from the Age of its earliest Monuments to the Time of Queen Elizabeth.

By SAMUEL JOHNSON.

Printed for J. and P. Knapton, T. Longman and T. Shewell, C. Hitch, A. Millar, and R. Dodsley.

Figure 3. Advertisement for Samuel Johnson's *Dictionary of the English Language*, which appeared in the *London Evening Post* in April 1747.

English Language . . . exemplified in the whole Extent of their Use, according to the Authority of the purest Writers'.

To *exemplify*, as the relevant entry explains, is, of course, 'to illustrate by example'. The sense that examples in the *Dictionary* should also be exemplary ('Such as may deserve to be proposed to imitation, whether persons or things')[25] nevertheless repeatedly intervenes. Whether various writers are of 'sufficient authority' for lexicographic purposes would, for instance, early emerge as a matter of concern. If Nicholas Rowe was allowed to be a 'good poet', Johnson had used a 'bad' example which 'should not be quoted as an authority', as Chesterfield had contended in further annotations on Johnson's drafted plan (*Yale* XVIII.450). Whether 'Davis' [Sir John Davies] possessed 'sufficient authority' to be quoted at all had prompted further critical comment (*Yale* XVIII.464).[26] Here, too, Johnson is subject to intentional redirection. His projected excursions into books can, in this light, resemble the lexical equivalent of the Grand Tour, setting out the cultural highlights of English in use

59

and following the recommended routes. 'Virtually every word is propped up by a tiny history of usage by worthies', writes Lipking; it is 'a golden treasury of national wisdom', giving 'ablution from "*the wells of English undefiled*"'.[27] The *Dictionary* 'functioned as an abbreviated Great Books course', Deidre Lynch agrees.[28]

Acts of reading

Johnson, Willian Shaw notes, was an 'indefatigable reader'.[29] Nevertheless, in other problems of expectation and design, the 'feasts of literature' and attendant pleasures that Johnson envisaged as part of the process of dictionary-making did not, in fact, materialize quite as planned (*Yale* XVIII.100). A *feast*, as the *Dictionary* confirms, is characterized by its potential for abundant consumption. It is 'a sumptuous treat of great numbers', Johnson writes; it offers 'something delicious to the palate'.[30] Reading as lexicographical process proved rather different. If 'great numbers' were demanded, reading of this kind, as Johnson came to realize, could smack less of pleasure than of the need for dogged persistence, and the accretive processes by which the resources of a language might be documented. As Hawkins affirms, Johnson's work for the *Dictionary* was both arduous and 'laborious', requiring 'severe application'.[31] The 'Shackles' of the dictionary-maker which Johnson contemplates in the drafted 'Scheme' (*Yale* XVIII.461) are conspicuous. 'Being thus compelled to spend every day like the past, [Johnson] looked on himself as in a state of mental bondage', Hawkins notes.[32]

Johnson's *Rambler* essays during the dictionary years repeatedly return to the image of slow and cumulative creation, exploring the difficulty of long works which must, of necessity, rest on knowledge rather than 'fancy', and systematic enquiry rather than the 'careless glance'. As in *Rambler* 184, which Johnson wrote in December 1751, the ease and freedom of the 'writer of essays' contrasts sharply with the sustained endeavour demanded of those who, for whatever reason, are committed to projects far more expansive in time and scale. Johnson could, of course, speak from experience in both contexts. Yet it is clear, at least from this account, that the essay-writer might be said to have the easier life. He 'seldom harasses his reason with long trains of consequence', Johnson comments. Nor, he adds, do such writers need to dim their 'eyes with the perusal of antiquated volumes' or burden the 'memory with great accumulations of preparatory knowledge' (*Yale* V.201). Instead, 'a careless glance upon a favourite author, or transient survey of the varieties of life' will often suffice, supplying the 'seminal idea' which the 'warmth of fancy' can subsequently expand.

Longer works can nevertheless bring their own quiet satisfactions—and undoubted reward. As in Johnson's 'Life of Dr. Boerhaave', the consonance of knowledge with observation—and the 'slow Methods' and 'frequent Experiments' from which 'true Notions' derive—remained a subject of careful consideration. Here, too, 'the toilsome Drudgery of making Observations' had acted as a ready corrective to 'Imagination' and 'the charming Amusement of forming Hypotheses'.[33] 'All that is great was at first little, and rose to its present bulk by gradual accessions, and accumulated labours', as Johnson writes on the theme of collection in *Rambler* 83 (*Yale* IV.72). Johnson emphasizes the importance—and value—of that knowledge which is slowly but surely acquired. It is, as he observes in *Rambler* 137, only by determined industry of this kind that 'the most lofty fabricks of science' can emerge, 'formed by the continued accumulation of single propositions' (*Yale* IV.361). Here, too, excursions acquire clear value. 'The widest excursions of the mind are made by short flights frequently repeated', Johnson states; as in the *Plan*, it is 'drops added to drops' that 'constitute the ocean' (*Yale* XVIII.52).

Evidence of Johnson's reading for the *Dictionary* is particularly illuminating in this respect, emblematizing in material form the pattern of 'gradual accession' and the continued—and cumulative— value of 'single propositions'. Reading is, of course, a process which commonly leaves few traces; in ordinary circumstances, a folded corner of a page, a scribbled annotation, or a word or passage underlined in trying might indicate a reader's progress over a printed text. The books Johnson read for the *Dictionary* were, however, irrevocably changed by the experience. As Hawkins confirms, those 'he used for this purpose were what he had in his own collection, a copious but miserably ragged one, and all such as he could borrow; which latter, if they ever came back to those that lent them, were so defaced as to be scarce worth owning'.[34]

Hawkins's account of Johnson's opportunistic methods of text selection can already suggest other qualities of excursion and departure, not least when set against the deliberate (and deliberative) canon-building with which he is commonly associated. Hawkins's view that such texts, after Johnson's lexical scrutiny, were rendered 'scarce worth owning' prompts perhaps still greater dissent. Johnson's working texts, of which fourteen remain,[35] instead provide an invaluable record of some of the individual 'excursions' he made in the interests of lexicography. If in Hawkins's terms, Johnson defaced ('To destroy; to raze; to ruin; to disfigure', as the *Dictionary* explains under *deface*), he did so in ways which, importantly, still remain visible, revealing the extraordinary range of words and senses that were identified as useful evidence in the process.

Figure 4 is taken from Matthew Hale's *The Primitive Origination of Mankind Considered and Examined According to the Light of Nature*, first published in 1677.[36] A judge and lawyer, Hale was, in fact, far from being included in Pope's list of recommended authorities. In his religious writings, of which *The Primitive Origination* is one, Hale's 'extreme prolixity' is a common characteristic.[37] Few would place him, either then or now, among the 'best writers' of his era. Yet as we can see from Johnson's annotations, Hale, like the indubitably canonical Dryden or Bacon, Milton or Pope, was perused with care and diligent attention. He proved a highly productive source. Used for over three hundred citations in the *Dictionary*'s first edition, hundreds more were marked out in Johnson's progress through the text.[38]

Johnson's process of reading is rendered strikingly transparent. Underlined words pick out potential headwords while a series of

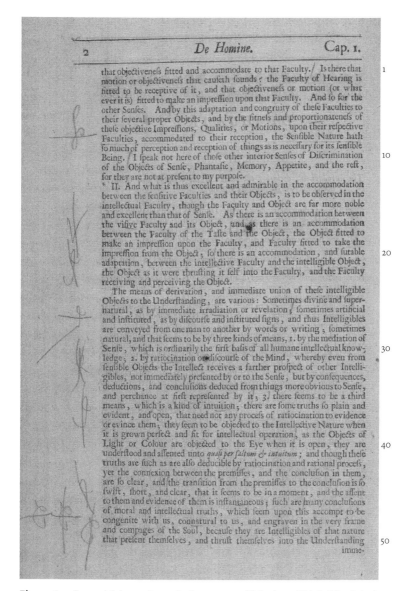

Figure 4. Samuel Johnson's marked-up copy of Matthew Hale's *The Primitive Origination of Mankind* (1677) p. 2. The Bodleian Libraries, The University of Oxford (Dep. C.25/2).

vertical lines indicate the onset and end-point of chosen quotations. These, Johnson notes, are his 'authorities'—witnesses to words in use (*Yale* XVIII.97). Further annotations fill the adjacent margin of Hale's text. Here, Johnson inscribes the initial letter of the underlined form, alerting his amanuenses—the six assistants who variously worked on the dictionary[39]—to the headword under which material was to be placed. While Johnson reads and annotates, the amanuenses copy out, creating the 'transcripts' to which Johnson also refers (*Yale* XVIII.94).[40] The dictionary hence becomes a collective process in more ways than one. Johnson's pencil marks engage with the language of the text per se but also act as a set of instructions. The assorted diagonal and vertical lines with which the capital letters in the margin are crossed through confirm a further stage of composition. Added by the amanuenses, these indicate that the citation has been duly copied and placed in dictionary order, ready for what Johnson described as the 'great labour' of interpretation (*Yale* XVIII.46).[41]

The annotated text is thereby embedded in the processes—and decision-making—which dictionary-making involves. In Figure 4, Johnson picks out words such as *visive* and *proportionateness*, *intellective, irradiation, ratiocination, intuition*, and *instantaneous*. *Connatural, congenite*, and *compage* cluster in two lines at the bottom of the page where Hale's alliterative patterning has perhaps drawn Johnson's eye. Marking is discontinuous and non-sequential, further illuminating Johnson's image of excursions in which the 'settled path' is left behind. The 'empirical impurity' which DeMaria isolates is also conspicuous.[42] If Johnson's methods are evidence-based, it is equally clear that he does not make a concordance to Hale, nor to the other texts he reads. As he acknowledges in the 1755 'Preface', his course, as in other aspects of adventure, is 'fortuitous'—guided by chance (*Yale* XVIII.84).

Johnson was, in this, by no means unaware of the difficulties of reading systematically—nor of the gaps which would inevitably appear in the *Dictionary*.[43] 'I cannot flatter myself that the collection is complete', he acknowledges in 1755 (*Yale* XVIII.87). 'He that is catching opportunities which seldom occur, will suffer those to pass by unregarded, which he expects hourly to return', he admitted; by the same token, 'he that is searching for rare and remote things, will neglect those that are obvious and familiar' (*Yale* XVIII.103). The consequence could be that 'many of the most common and cursory words have been inserted with little illustration, because in gathering the authorities, I forbore to copy those which I thought likely to occur whenever they were wanted' (*Yale* XVIII.103).

As Wimsatt confirms, Johnson's marked-up texts hence vividly emblematize the potential for both choice and divergence, as well as the difficulties this could bring. 'Imagine yourself half-way through Johnson's program of reading for the Dictionary, arriving at [a] page of Bacon's *Natural History*', Wimsatt posits: 'Which of the words and passages on the page would you mark in black lead pencil for your amanuenses to copy? Which would you pass over? By what norms would you make your selection?'[44] As in Figure 4, if *intellective* and *intuition* are chosen, it is evident that, say, *suitable* and *thrust* are not. Nor are *means* or *union* on the first line of the third paragraph, or *fit* and *perfect* on l. 39. Reading p. 4 of Hale, Johnson marks out *nobleness* and *misemployment*; reading p. 5, *quadrature* and *duplication*, *contentation*, *acceleration*, *coacervate*, *ordinable*, and *benficialness* are picked out in the first paragraph alone. Reading p. 7, a further eight words are isolated: *meridian*, *melioration*, *connaturality*, *disparity*, *eligible* (three times), *inevident*, *conjectural*, and *plurality*. Johnson picks out two words on p. 198 (*traduction*, *supposable*), while nine appear on p. 200 (*anomalous*, *mastiff*, *inermigration*, *flat-nosed*, *crisp-haired*, *fair-complexioned*, *sinewy*, *marsh-land*, and *sharp-visaged*). Other pages, for example 223–4 and 240–1, remain entirely unmarked.

Similar patterns are evident in other books. 'They are the subject of whole Volumes, and shall (some of them) be more opportunely dilated elsewhere', Robert Burton's *Anatomy of Melancholy* had stated on p. 67. If *dilated* draws Johnson's eye, the other sixteen words in this citation remain unmarked. Johnson likewise underlines *concupis-cible* ('Eager; desirous') but not adjacent words such as *appetite* and *rope*. *Twists* is underlined but not, say, *wring*, nor indeed *horse-mill*, a word that does not appear in the *Dictionary* at all. Reading Isaac Watts's *Logick*, Johnson underlines words such as *grocer* and *silk-weaver*, *credulity*, and *prismatick*.[45] Watts's maxim (on p. 355) that 'when you are called to *explain* a Subject, don't pass by, nor skip over any Thing in it which is very difficult or obscure' is framed by vertical lines, indicating the passage to be extracted. Underlining *skip over*, Johnson, however, skips over the other remaining words.[46] 'It was not easy', he writes, 'to determine by what rule of distinction the words of this dictionary were to be chosen' (*Yale* XVIII.29).

Isaac Watts's discussion of language attracted Johnson's close attention, generating citations for both *genus* and *definition* ('when we speak of the Genus and Difference as composing a Definition, it must always be understood that the nearest genus and the specifick Difference are required'; 'A Definition must be Universal'). Particu-larly interesting in this context is Johnson's reading of Watts's advice on reading itself: 'If the Books which you read are your own, mark with a Pen, or Pencil, the most considerable Things in them which you desire to remember.' Johnson underlines *pencil* in a fitting endorsement of Watts's words (even if, as we have seen, he failed to heed Watts's advice to restrict marking to books in his own possession).[47] As Watts continued (thereby providing, for Johnson's purposes, a useful citation for *bookseller*), 'It is a very weak objection against this Practice to say, *I shall spoil my book*; for I persuade my self, that you did not buy it as a *Bookseller*, to sell it again for *Gain*, but as a *scholar*, to improve your mind by it.' That one's executors might lose by such marking was, Watts stresses, to be disregarded.

Gain, even if unforeseen by Watts, remains incontestable when such marking is seen from the point of view of language historians. As in Figure 4, we can, for instance, see Johnson's attention turning to the kind of 'hard' words which might hamper fluent engagement

66

with earlier texts. Acts of reading are, in this light, not merely a means by which the raw material of the *Dictionary* is generated. Instead, as in the *Plan*, reading is repeatedly seen as an end-point for the *Dictionary* as reference work. 'It will be required by common readers', Johnson notes (*Yale* XVIII.47); 'The Reason why the authours which are yet read of the sixteenth Century are so little understood is that they are read alone, and no help is borrowed from those who lived with them or before them. Some part of this ignorance I hope to remove by my book which now draws towards its end', he explained to Warton in 1754 (*Letters* I.81). Concern for the common reader—Johnson's 'most famous critical construct', as DeMaria contends[48]—can, as here, assume prominence, rather than the strictly normative remit we might perhaps expect. What readers might need is made a matter of overt concern.

The good dictionary was, in this respect, to mediate between language and reader, facilitating understanding and furthering individual knowledge. Latinate loans are, for instance, regularly underlined in Johnson's 'excursions'. Here we might include *instantaneous*, underlined on p. 2 of Hale. Used in English from the mid-seventeenth century, this is dated to 1651 in the *OED* (twenty-six years before Hale's first edition). Similar is *congenite* ('Of the same birth; born with another') which Johnson underlines at l. 47 of Figure 4. Deriving from Latin *congenitus* ('born together'), the *OED* gives its first use in Donne in 1610. *Connatural* (in the same line) derives from Medieval Latin *connātūrālis* and was slightly earlier, first used in English in 1599 as *OED* records. *Macerate* (<the past participle stem of Latin *mācerāt*), underlined on p. 69 in Burton ('what greater folly can there by, or madness, than to macerate himself when he need not') provides a similar example, as does *exornation* (which Johnson defines as 'Ornament; decoration; embellishment'). 'Hyperbolical exornations, elegancies &c. which so many much affect', Burton stated, describing the patterns of lexical excess which characterized so many writers during the Renaissance.

Johnson's *Dictionary* is, of course, often prototypically seen as a domain of 'hard' words. Nevertheless, like opinions on the 'best writers', notions of 'ease' and 'difficulty' clearly share a certain subjectivity. 'Easiness and difficulty are merely relative', Johnson warns in 1755 (*Yale* XVIII.93). If *visive* ('Formed in the act of seeing') prompts assumptions of lexical 'hardness' for modern readers, it is, as the *OED* confirms, a word which flourished across a wide range of texts in the seventeenth and eighteenth centuries. Another Renaissance loan (< medieval Latin *visīvus*, 'seeing, sight'), its use quickly gained momentum; seven senses were in existence by the late seventeenth century.[49] The same is true of *intellective* (Figure 4, 1. 21). Now rare, having largely been displaced by *intellectual*, it had in fact been used since Middle English. *Basis*, which Johnson underlines on p. 186 of Hale, is, conversely, now an element of core vocabulary. Yet this, too, was a Latinate loan even if, like *visive*, its use had rapidly consolidated in English, gaining some nine senses by the late seventeenth century. The fact that Johnson gives five of these—against one for *visive*—is, however, some indication of their relative prominence in the English he recorded and the texts he read.

A variety of other words are underlined as well. *Unfathomable*, marked by Johnson on p. 187 of Hale, has a heritage that reaches back to Old English (revealing, too, the potential for word-formation offered by French-derived –*able* in post-Conquest English). Similar is *store-house*, underlined on the same page, which goes back to Middle English. The non-native etymon of *store* had long been forgotten by the average speaker of English (and indeed by Johnson, too, who credits it to Scandinavian rather than Provençal French).[50] *Shipping*, which Johnson underlines on p. 194, is strikingly 'easy'— a word of high frequency from Old English onwards, forming a core and unremarkable item which Johnson nevertheless remarks. *Forgetfulness*, underlined on p. 197, provides another example of Johnson's interest in ordinary rather than extraordinary use. Undeniably polysyllabic, it is composed of a set of native formatives which, without exception, go back to the earliest forms of the native tongue.

Burton, in similar ways, is the source of words such as *colly* ('a smut of coal') and *costermonger*, of *damp*, *drum*, and *dote*, *cut up*, and *culminating*, *muck-hill*, *giddy-headed*, and *fellow-feeling*. He is the source, too, of *cock-boat*, a word with which, as we have seen in Chapter 2, Johnson memorably depicts Chesterfield's 1754 missives to the *World*: 'He that erst marched likes *Xerxes*, with innumerable armies, as rich as *Croesus*, now shifts for himself in a poor cock-boat', as Burton stated in what was, for Johnson, an eminently telling conjunction.[51]

Equally clear is Johnson's habit of returning to the same word as he probes shades of meaning in use. *Plastick* is, for example, underlined several times in Hale (while *adequate*, *defection*, and *disjunctive* are, among many others, underlined on a number of occasions in Watts's *Logick*). In the *Dictionary*, conversely, it is the natural historian John Woodward (the source of some 600 citations) and the poet Matthew Prior (1664–1721) who provide the relevant evidence for *plastick*. *Adequate*, *disjunctive*, and *defection* are, respectively, supported by Watts, South, Locke, as well as the Elizabethan physician Gideon Harvey (under *adequate*); by Watts and Grew (under *disjunctive*); and by Arbuthnot, Addison, and Locke (but not Watts) under *defective*.[52] *Forgetfulness*, recorded in Hale, was supplemented in the *Dictionary* by a similar process of attention to its use by Shakespeare, Pope, and the sixteenth-century theologian Richard Hooker (who provides well over two thousand citations in the published text of 1755).[53] Hale's evidence, transcribed by the relevant amanuensis, is omitted. The same is true of, say, *store-house* for which an abundance of citations (from Hooker, Shakespeare, Holder, the Bible, Davies, South's Sermons, but not Hale) was used in the *Dictionary*. *Mastiff* ('A dog of the largest size; a bandog; dogs kept to watch the house') was another 'ordinary' word which Johnson underlines in Hale, but for which evidence in the *Dictionary* derives from Pope, Thomas More, Shakespeare, and Swift.

At other times, neither citations nor the words they supported in Johnson's reading appear in the finished text. *Marsh-land*, underlined on p. 200 of Hale ('the Up-lands in *England* yield strong, sinewy, hardy Men; the Marsh-lands...Men of large and high Stature') remains absent, just as it was from Bailey. The same is true of *flat-nosed* (underlined on the same page), as well as *compages*, used to mean 'a complex structure', which appears in the penultimate line of Figure 4. *Interlucency*, carefully underlined on p. 193 of Hale ('those parts of *Asia* and *America* which are now disjoyned by the interlucency of the Sea') represents another omission. Not all, as this makes clear, could be included—even if the evidence of Johnson's marked-up texts continues to testify to the acuity of his observation, and his engagement with a variety of words on all levels. *Interlucency*, we might note, still remains unrecorded in the *OED*. Likewise, *OED* records *complicatedness* only from 1730 where, lacking primary evidence, it relies on a secondary citation from Bailey's *Dictionarium Britannicum*.[54] Johnson, however, had already noted Hale's use in 1677.[55]

Against Boswell's later sense of lexicography as a process of assembling headwords, and then simply locating appropriate evidence (*Life* I.188), surviving evidence of Johnson's excursions into books offers therefore a very different history of the *Dictionary* and its making. Indeed, across the *Dictionary*, the diction of discovery—of what has, and has not been found—still reminds us of the realities of its formation, and of other aspects of the literary journeys Johnson made. So, too, do Johnson's first-person pronouns. 'This word I have met with only in *Spenser*, nor can I discover whence it is derived', Johnson writes, for example, under *awhape* (v.): 'To strike; to confound'. Similar are his entries for *beemol*, *geason*, and *meeken*. 'This word I have found only in the example, and know nothing of the etymology', Johnson states under *beemol*, providing evidence from Bacon's *Natural History*: 'There be intervenient in the rise of eight, in tones, two *beemols*, or half notes; so as, if you divide the tones equally, the eight is but seven whole and equal notes.'[56]

Geason ('Wonderful') is given as 'a word which I find only in *Spenser*'; 'This word I have found nowhere else', the entry for *meeken* ('To make meek; to soften') likewise attests. *Conduce* and *cote* offer parallel examples. 'In this sense I have found it only in the following passage', Johnson notes of the former, adducing Wotton as sole witness to its use: 'He was sent to *conduce* hither the princess Henrietta-Maria.'[57] 'This word, which I have found only in Chapman, seems to signify the same as *To leave behind, To over pass*', Johnson states for *cote*, affirming the limits of discovery that evidence will, at times, reveal.[58]

Collections and canonicity

Collection was, of necessity, a subject with which Johnson was intensely preoccupied during the dictionary years. What, after all, made a 'good' collection? Johnson repeatedly returns to problems of this kind, examining the nature—and value—of the selections that might be made. Was the best collection really monolithic in its contents, Johnson queries in *Rambler* 177, contemplating Hirsutus's collection of 'all the English books that were printed in the black character' or Ferratus's 'set of half-pence' in his 'collection of English copper' (*Yale* V.170). Such narrowness did not inspire. It is made to seem remote from the real concerns of life as well as from the 'useful knowledge' which Johnson instead commends. 'Nothing is valuable merely because it is either rare or common, but because it is adapted to some useful purpose, and enables us to supply some deficiency of our nature', *Rambler* 78 declares (*Yale* IV.46–7). 'All useless science [i.e. "knowledge"] is an empty boast', the epigram to *Rambler* 83 affirms (*Yale* IV.70). In the latter, collectors of shells, stones, insects, of art and mechanical science are themselves gathered up. So, too, are those who collect artefacts of the past. Yet, in a dangerous precedent for lexicography (and the principles on which this, too, operates), collections of this kind are depicted as potentially losing all meaning when abstracted from the contexts in which they once were placed. In collection, breadth—and usefulness—emerge as recurrent concerns.

Literary value, and its own assumed salience for collection, can seem equally problematic at times. As Johnson explores in *Adventurer* 138 (written in 1754) this is often contingent rather than essential: 'If a new performance happens not to fall into the hands of some, who have courage to tell, and authority to propagate their opinion, it often remains long in obscurity, and perhaps perishes unknown and unexamined' (*Yale* II.496). 'If we consider the distribution of literary fame in our own time, we shall find it a possession of very uncertain tenure', Johnson likewise warned in *Rambler* 21, written in May 1750 (*Yale* III.118). The 'pinnacles of fame' are 'slippery' (*Yale* III.114); qualitative regard is arbitrary, being 'sometimes bestowed by a sudden caprice of the publick, and again transferred to a new favourite, for no other reason than that he is new' (*Yale* III.118). Conversely, the ordinary can be devalued in popular perception merely by dint of its unremarkability. 'That familiarity produces neglect, has long been observed', Johnson writes in June 1753 (*Yale* II.383).

While the 'best writers' were, as we have seen, prominent in both expectation and advertising for the *Dictionary*, Johnson can, in such ways, also explore the problems on which such value judgements might rest. Whether Pope, as Johnson had deferentially remarked in 1747, would have no reason to be 'displeased' by the kind of collections which were in fact made for the *Dictionary* (*Yale* XVIII.56) can, in this respect, pose a number of interesting questions. If 'great writers' dominate in the finished text, there are nevertheless some marked departures. Here, too, excursion as a means of moving outside what might otherwise be expected can be apparent.

Johnson's 'excursions into books', for instance, firmly exclude Hobbes. If recommended by Pope, Hobbes's 'principles' were nevertheless disliked by Johnson.[59] Temple, whose diction was a guarantee of good English for Pope, was likewise often censured in the

Dictionary for his contraventions of common use.[60] Conversely, Johnson's reading includes Raleigh—whose work Pope deemed wholly unacceptable for the purposes of lexicography. In the *Dictionary*, evidence from Raleigh and Pope is, in fact, often placed in marked equivalence. 'If it should appear fit to bestow shipping in those harbours, it shall be very needful that there be a *magazine* of all necessary provisions and munitions', Raleigh states under sense 1 of *magazine*, defined as 'A storehouse, commonly an arsenal or armoury, or repository of provisions'. Citations from Pope, Milton, and Dryden follow. 'Useful arms in *magazines* we place, / All rang'd in order, and disposed with grace', accompanying evidence from Pope's 'Essay on Criticism' (1711) affirms. *Sad* is similar. Raleigh and Pope alike illustrate Johnson's sense 2, defined as 'Habitually melancholy; heavy; gloomy; not gay; not cheerful'. A similar parity of evidence occurs in, say, *destroyer, dispersion, organ, monument, never*, and *graft* (among others).

Elsewhere, citations from Raleigh appear alongside Shakespeare (under e.g. *carouse, champaign, dispense, dissembler, dealing*), alongside Spenser and Milton (under e.g. *deity, diet, gluttonous*), Locke (see e.g. *disability, facility, harpy*), and Dryden (see e.g. *gummy, harmful, lightsome, motion, one, pass*), as well as in hundreds of other entries. Rather than being rejected, Raleigh had, it seems, been attentively perused in the processes of assembling evidence. Indeed, by 1755, Raleigh is specified as a prime resource by which certain aspects of English might be documented: 'If the language of theology were extracted from *Hooker* and the translation of the Bible; the terms of natural knowledge from *Bacon*; the phrases of policy, war, and navigation from *Raleigh*; the dialect of poetry and fiction from *Spenser* and *Sidney*; and the diction of common life from *Shakespeare*, few ideas would be lost to mankind, for want of *English* words, in which they might be expressed' (*Yale* XVIII.96–7).[61]

Writers such as Dryden, Milton, Pope, and Shakespeare retain, of course, clear statistical prominence; as Osselton notes, around a third of Johnson's citations in the printed text derive from

Shakespeare, Milton, Addison, and Dryden.[62] Johnson's wide-ranging use of canonical writers has long been a staple of comment on the *Dictionary*, and is illuminatingly discussed in works by DeMaria, Lipking, and Lynch.[63] Documenting *crescent* (n.), Johnson's text refers to Shakespeare, Milton, Dryden, and Pope; under *quart*, Spenser, Shakespeare, and Swift alone appear; *unfirm* is similar, verified only by Shakespeare and Dryden, as is *involuntary*, documented by Locke and Pope. *Velvet* is supported by three citations, all from Shakespeare's plays. Frequency does not, of course, guarantee unconditional approval; Dryden, as we will see in Chapters 5 and 6, can often be exemplary for the wrong reasons; Shakespeare's linguistic creativity (like that of Temple) can encounter a similar critical gaze.[64] It is important, too, to remember that the citations which remain in the printed text do not, as we have seen, reflect the range of those originally assembled—nor the underlying processes by which Johnson used the whole body of citations in deriving the meanings and sense-divisions which the *Dictionary* represents.

Alongside the kind of 'eminent writers' that Wilson commends, Johnson's 'authorities, on which the credit of every part of this work must depend' (*Yale* XVIII.55) can, in practice, also include writers such as Hale, as well as, say, the physician John Arbuthnot whose works on diet and *The Effects of Air on Human Bodies* frequently appear across the *Dictionary*, or William Holder (*c.*1615–98), the author of a slim treatise on articulatory phonetics entitled *The Elements of Speech* (cited for words such as *investigate, tension, language,* and *jar*). Similar was John Mortimer (1656?–1736) whose *Whole Art of Husbandry, in the way of Managing and Improving of Land* (1707) was a canonical text in terms of agriculture if not literary culture. Perusal could, in reality, acquire a variety of objects. Other non-canonical sources include, for example, the Royalist surgeon Richard Wiseman, the printer Joseph Moxon (1627–91), or Charles Jervas whose translation of Cervantes's *Don Quixote* was published five years before Johnson's *Plan* in 1742. Scientists such as Boyle form a frequent source, though Johnson's gaze can turn equally to medical dispensatories,[65] private letters, journalism, as well as a range of recent novels. 'Mr. Gay died of a mortification of the bowels; it was the most precipitate case I ever knew, having cut him off in three days', we are, for example, informed under *precipitate*, sense 3, which Johnson explains as 'Hasty; violent'. Johnson's source was the correspondence of Pope and Swift which, as the *Dictionary* often illustrates, presents canonical writers in a rather different setting.[66]

Johnson's discussion of lexicographical 'need' in the 'Preface' serves, of course, to pre-empt criticism of at least some uses of this kind (*Yale* XVIII.94). 'Some of the examples have been taken from writers who were never mentioned as masters of elegance or models of stile', he states (*Yale* XVIII.94). Ideals of 'purity', even if vaunted in the advertising campaigns of 1747, would not necessarily be enough. 'In what pages, eminent for purity, can terms of manufacture or agriculture be found?', the 1755 'Preface' counters. 'Words must be sought where they are used', Johnson explains in yet another image of exploratory endeavour and the lexical quest. As in Johnson's entries for *probe-scissors* ('Scissors used to open wounds, of which the blade thrust into the orifice has a button at the end') or *fasciation* ('Bandage; the act or manner of binding diseased parts'), a functional dependence on certain writers in certain registers is inevitable. Wiseman's *Surgery* documents both, appearing, too, under *ossifick* ('Having the power of making bones, or changing carneous or membranous to bony substance') and, say, *oxycryate*: 'A mixture of water and vinegar' or the medical sense of *to dress*: 'To cover a wound in medicaments'. The same principles apply the entries for *picker* (One who picks or culls') and *ciderist* ('A maker of cider'), both of which are illustrated by Mortimer's *Husbandry,* or the terminology of a range of trades and crafts for which Moxon's *Mechanick Exercises* proved an invaluable resource.[67]

Nevertheless, evidence from these and similar sources was also routinely used in documenting markedly non-technical elements of the vocabulary. If Raleigh is used for terms of war and navigation as under *deck, barge,* and *keelson* ('The wood next the keel'), he also appears in Johnson's entries for *mellifluous* and *metropolitan, impassable, clarity, fashion,* and *fiction.* He appears, too, under *worldly* and *manhood* (alongside Milton), under *deathful* (alongside Sidney, Milton, and Pope), under *facility* (alongside Sidney and Bacon), and *far* (alongside Milton, the Bible, and Addison), among hundreds of similar examples. Wiseman likewise appears as witness to core lexis such as *go* and *milk,* as well as under words such as *lace* (alongside Dryden and Congreve), *rhubarb* (alongside Shakespeare), of *hard* meaning 'Difficult of accomplishment' (alongside Milton, Dryden, and the Bible), or *jack* (alongside Pope and Wilkins). Mortimer's *Husbandry* attests to parallel acts of reading, documenting the register-specific (as under *fallow* in the sense 'Ground plowed in order to be plowed again'), as well as a range of indubitably 'ordinary' words such as under *heart, inward,* and *glass.* Drafting *pale* ('Narrow piece of wood joined above and below to a rail, to inclose grounds') Johnson turns to Shakespeare, Prior, and, again, to Mortimer. Drafting *thick* ('Not easily pervious; set with things close to each other'), three citations from Dryden are accompanied by one from Mortimer. Mortimer's *Husbandry* accompanies a quotation from Dryden under *bag* (v.), and evidence from the Bible and Broome's *Notes on the Odyssey* under *beat* (sense 4).

The contiguities which result can destabilize popular expectations of a neat and formalized hierarchy by which 'great writers' alone act as authority for the use of words. That this could have been the case is often clear. In terms of need, Arbuthnot's evidence, as under *dryness* sense 1 ('Want of moisture') could easily have been omitted. Yet, instead, Brown, Denham, Bentley's *Sermons,* John Ray's *the Wisdom of God manifested in the Works of Creation* (1691), and Arbuthnot are all made to serve—collectively—as authorities for use. Likewise, Johnson places Arbuthnot alongside Shakespeare and Dryden under *talent,* or with South, Locke, and Swift under *healthy,* or with Bacon, Clarendon, Dryden, and Swift under *facilitate.*

He appears under *tepid* (alongside Milton and Dryden), *drowsiness* (alongside Shakespeare, Locke, and Crashaw), *valuation* (alongside Bacon and Shakespeare), or *intrust* (alongside Dryden and Addison). What is found, and where Johnson looks, can in such ways often depart from prototypical images of his work. As in Johnson's image of his circumnavigation of the 'literary world', texts—and citations— from a variety of sources can be brought together in the aim of documenting English in use.

The temporal restrictions originally placed on reading for the *Dictionary* can be equally subject to change. 'My purpose was to admit no testimony of living authours', Johnson had stressed (*Yale* XVIII.96); 'I have', he added, 'fixed *Sidney*'s work for the boundary, beyond which I make few excursions'. The opposite boundary was located in the Restoration of 1660.[68] Yet here, too, 'excursions' into books can venture widely from the 'settled path'. Newton, who died in 1727, is, for instance, the source of hundreds of citations in the published text, variously attributed to 'Newt.', 'Newton', or his individual works. Mortimer and Arbuthnot, Richardson and Charlotte Lennox were all still writing as Johnson composed the *Dictionary*. So, too, was Watts who was by no means among the *'wells of English undefiled'* of pre-restoration writing (*Yale* XVIII.95). A dissenting minister and educational writer, he was scarcely invested with the kind of canonical value which Shakespeare and Dryden, or Milton and Pope assume. Watts's religious non-conformity had already excluded him from attending university in Oxford. Spence, discussing lexicographical authority with Pope in 1744, had ventured to include Hooke and Middleton. 'Aye, and I think there's scarce any more of the living that you need name', Pope had replied.[69] Yet in the *Dictionary*, over five hundred citations from Watts's works appear, documenting words such as *fatalist* and *chairman*, *languor*, and *mechanicks*, as well as *dictionary* itself.

Johnson's 'fixed . . . boundary' can therefore often prove relative rather than absolute. As Read and others have stressed,[70] Johnson's documentary ventures can turn to contemporary novels and current writing in ways which necessarily challenge other popular expectations of what he should accomplish. Johnson's reading of *Robinson Crusoe* (1719) informs, for instance, the evidence used under *awning, ironwood, locker,* and *wound* (v.). Swift's *Gulliver's Travels* (1726) likewise appears under, for example, *unship* ('To take out of a ship'), *bandage, gird, jerken* ('A jacket; a short coat'), *indifferently, seem, sidle, stamp,* and *ledge.* Johnson's use of Richardson's *Clarissa,* published in the same year as the *Plan,* is both well known and pervasive (see e.g. the entries for *alive* (adj.), *deviation* (n.), *devious* (adj.), and *rakish* (adj.)). Richardson's linguistic creativity was, as Tieken Boon confirms, a marked feature of his work, though, as Keast notes, a pre-existing collection of moral sentiments from *Clarissa* also aided Johnson's use.[71] 'Full dress creates dignity, augments consciousness, and keeps at distance an encroacher', we are told under *dress*; 'women ought not to think gentleness of heart despicable in a man', the entry for *gentleness* states.[72]

That Johnson had 'cited authorities . . . beneath the dignity of such a work' was, as Garrick informed Johnson, therefore also to be among the 'animadversions' of the *Dictionary.* 'I have done worse than that', Johnson is reputed to have replied, in response to Garrick's example of Richardson as one such undignified source: 'I have quoted *thee*' (*Life* 4.4). Garrick—one of Johnson's pupils in the ill-fated educational establishment Johnson had set up in Edial, near Lichfield, and with whom Johnson first travelled to London in 1737—unknowingly provided testimony for words such as *fabulist* ('A writer of fables'), *nowadays,* and *prudish.* In other acts of markedly modern appropriation, Chesterfield, with what is perhaps barely concealed intent, would become the source of *ridiculer,* a new entry which appears in 1773: 'The *ridiculer* shall make only himself ridiculous', the accompanying citation states.

Those who in the *Dictionary* 'validate their native language as well as the book that contains it'—here in what perhaps remains Johnson's most striking act of 'excursion'—would moreover include a range of modern women writers such as Charlotte Lennox, Elizabeth Carter, Anne Moreton, Jane Collier, and Hester Mulso.[73] Carter and Mulso were, of course, also involved in the *Rambler* essays, being responsible for parts of *Rambler* 10, and *Rambler* 44 and 100 respectively.[74] Johnson was closely linked with Charlotte Lennox during the dictionary years, and has often been credited with writing Chapter 11 in the final book of Lennox's *The Female Quixote: or The Adventures of Arabella* which was published in March 1752 (Johnson reviewed it in the *Gentleman's Magazine* in the same month).[75] Nevertheless, in terms of lexicography, women—as for earlier dictionary-markers such as Robert Cawdrey, Cockeram, and Blount—were traditionally seen as the proper recipients of lexicographical instruction rather than sources of possible authority and exemplification. The *Table Alphabeticall*, as Cawdrey explained in 1604, was 'gathered for the benefit and help of ladies, gentlewomen, or any other vnskilfull persons'.[76] Blount, in a similar way, directed his *Glossographia* to the 'more-knowing Women' (and 'less-knowing Men').

Popular folk-linguistics across English history had maintained an enduring emphasis on female linguistic deficit. As Chesterfield declared in the *World* in December 1754, women, whose 'natural turn is more to . . . copiousness' than 'correctness of diction', surely offered further opportunities for the corrective enterprise of the dictionary in Johnson's hands.[77] Richard Owen Cambridge, writing later that year, made a similar point,[78] as did Johnson's close friend Hill Boothby in 1753. 'Female vanity has, I believe, no small share in the increase of the difficulties you have found', she wrote to Johnson. Referring to the need to explain 'the *general and popular language*' in the *Dictionary*, Johnson should, she advised, 'treat this vanity as an enemy, and be very far from throwing any temptation in its way'.[79]

Johnson's attitudes, and practice, proved rather different. While examples in both 'Scheme' and *Plan* are indeed resolutely male, citations from women writers are assimilated with conspicuous neutrality in the *Dictionary* proper. They exemplify rather than being made a site for control or emendation, offering the potential for instruction in ways which, here at least, reverse the gendered models of the past. Citations from Lennox's *Female Quixote* (1752) appear under *pique* and *simplicity, singular,* and *suppose, visionist,* and *volubility*; her *Shakespear Illustrated,* published in 1753, is likewise cited under *virtue, uncle,* and *unravel* (among others).[80] Mulso appears alongside Dryden under *quatrain.* A range of other citations—Jane Collier's (1753) *Essay on the Art of Ingeniously Tormenting* under *marital, pert,* and *prink,* Elizabeth Carter under *proportions*—provide other instances of female testimony, and the perusal of female-authored texts for the purposes of lexicography.[81] Patterns of contiguity and equivalence are again significant, placing Lennox alongside Pope, Locke, and Prior under *pique,* and Swift, Denham, and Bacon under *sally.*

Such testimonies by no means provide a dominant pattern in Johnson's evidence. Nevertheless, the fact of these first uses of female authority within English lexicography should not be forgotten. As under *quatrain,* if Dryden illustrates the word, it is Mulso who exemplifies the form and shares the authority of the definition. As Johnson's entry states, a *quatrain* is 'A stanza of four lines rhyming alternately: as, "Say, Stella, what is love, whose fatal pow'r / Robs virtue of content, and youth of joy? / What nymph or goddess in a luckless hour / Disclos'd to light the mischief-making boy".' If the first eight words are Johnson's, the rest belong to Mulso.[82] As in Johnson's accompanying 'Grammar', his validation of female endeavour—and changing public identity—can be conspicuous. A substantial addition in the fourth edition of the *Dictionary,* for example, draws attention to the gendered inflexion of English nouns as in *actor, actress.* Yet, observing those listed in previous grammars, Johnson adds more examples of his own: 'To these mentioned by Dr. Lowth may be added *arbitress, poetess, chauntress, duchess, tigress, governess, tutress, peeress*', and, indeed, *authoress.*[83] English, he argues, is strikingly deficient in this respect: 'We have only a sufficient number to make us feel our want.' The breadth of

Johnson's subsequent examples can perhaps surprise, alongside the equality of consideration it reveals: 'when we say of a woman that she is a *philosopher*, an *astronomer*, a *builder*, a *weaver*, a *dancer*, we perceive an impropriety in the termination which we cannot avoid'. Conversely, 'we can say that she is an *architect*, a *botanist*, a *student*, because these terminations have not annexed to them the notion of sex' (*Yale* XVIII.306–7). Comments of this kind shed, of course, an interesting light on his selection of women alongside men as authorities in the *Dictionary*, as well as on the broader communities of knowledge that this affirms.

4

The ordered state: Power, authority, and the written word

By 1767, the collocation *dictionary order* had entered the language: 'the order in which items are arranged in a conventional dictionary' as the *OED* records.[1] Nevertheless, as the history of lexicography confirms, the ordered state which language assumes once it enters a dictionary had, in reality, long been clear. Even in 1604, Robert Cawdrey—heralding the beginning of monolingual English lexicography—had carefully delineated the principles by which material was ordered in his own work. 'If the word, which thou art desirous to finde, begin with (a) then look in the beginning of this Table, but if with (v) looke towards the end', he explained, detailing how a reference work of this kind might be used. Knowing the order of the alphabet 'perfectly without booke' was, Cawdrey added, vital for readers who desire to 'profit' from the information a dictionary contains.[2]

By Johnson's time, such guidance was, of course, unnecessary, while the range of information ordered by contemporary lexicography had substantially increased. Entries in Johnson's *Dictionary*, for example, typically contain information on spelling, part of speech, etymology, as well an extensive range of senses, sub-senses, phrasal combinations, and supporting evidence. Information on

Samuel Johnson and the Journey into Words. Lynda Mugglestone pronunciation is given too, even if this is usually restricted to indicating which syllable takes the main stress. A very different state of language, as Johnson also emphasizes, had, however, long continued to exist outside the dictionary. This was 'copious without order' and characterized by 'perplexity' and 'confusion', as well as by a striking 'exuberance' of signification (*Yale* XVIII.74). As Johnson indicates in his 1755 'Preface', it is, in this light, the dictionary-maker's task to disentangle and regulate, to ascertain and receive. Order is both a process and a state to be reached.[3]

Isaac Watts's proposition ('a *dictionary*... is a collection of the words of a language') which Johnson used in illustrating the entry for *dictionary*, was, in this respect, not quite true. As Johnson wrote in 1751 in *Rambler* 83, the collection is, in effect, like the 'heaps of stone' or the 'piles of timber' for the architect (*Yale* IV.75). It is a beginning but not an end. If, for the architect, the projected building cannot exist without the basic materials which the 'heaps' provide, the same is, by extension, true of the lexicographer and language. Collection, and what is collected, can, as in Chapter 3, provide the primary substance of Johnson's *Dictionary*. Yet, in the process of composition, the underlying collection must be ordered and arranged as well as shaped to fit its new role. In so doing, the 'heaps of stone' might not all be used; some might be cast aside, others judged too small or large.

Order—and disorder—pattern in intricate ways across the history of lexicography. Chambers, Johnson, and Chesterfield would, for example, all reveal an interest in the iterated imaging of language as a 'heap' versus the wider sense of order that the good dictionary or reference book might, in various ways, provide. Encompassing language in the pages of a single book is difficult, Chambers had, for instance, affirmed in his *Cyclopaedia*; the lexicographer, he explained, must 'dispose such a Variety of Materials in such a manner, as not to make a confused Heap of incongruous Parts, but one consistent Whole'.[4] Almost twenty years later, Johnson used the same image in his *Plan* to contest the nature of what earlier lexicographers had achieved. Order remained unrealized; 'Our language...now stands in our dictionaries a confused heap of words without dependence, and without relation', he pointed out, adroitly signalling the advances which his own work would bring (*Yale* XVIII.40). The *heap*, as the *Dictionary* explained, was 'Many single things thrown together; a pile; an accumulation'. Its corresponding verb exemplified the processes that Johnson saw at stake. *Heap* was carefully ordered into three senses, each precisely differentiated and supported by appropriate evidence. The dictionary-maker was not, as in Johnson's first sense, simply 'To throw on heaps; to pile; to throw together', even if, in the processes of gathering evidence for his task, he might indeed, as in sense 2, 'accumulate' and 'lay up'. Sense 3, Johnson elaborated, was 'to add to something else'—a process which offered both continuity and advance.

Chesterfield's use of this image was perhaps predictable. Returning to Johnson's confident statements on order and reform, Chesterfield, too, condemned the disorder which characterized earlier works. 'All words, good and bad, are there jumbled indiscriminately together', he stated, dismissively, of the dictionaries of the past. Opportunities to impose a regulative 'good order' on the wider use of words had self-evidently been missed. Such authority as had hitherto existed is rendered specious: 'the injudicious reader may speak and write as inelegantly, improperly and vulgarly as he pleases, by and with the authority of one or other of our WORD-BOOKS', as Chesterfield contends.[5] Issues of gender and language are moreover made to intervene to good effect, offering additional scope for the prescriptive power that Johnson, as lexicographer, should rightfully wield. Chesterfield's image of the 'promiscuous heap' of words hence characterizes female discourse which, unregulated and out of control, presents a level of chaos which, as he warns, also threatens wider patterns of use: 'The torrents of their eloquence, especially in the vituperative way, stun all opposition, and bear away in one promiscuous heap, nouns, pronouns, verbs, moods and tenses.'[6]

Against the fixity he desires, such fluidity is made to seem trans-gressive and anomalous; here, too, the order Johnson brings is anxiously awaited. Unbeknown to Chesterfield, Johnson's patterns of 'excursion' in this respect were, of course, already clear. Women writers in the *Dictionary*, like their male counterparts, could aid in resolving rather than exemplifying the disordered 'heap' of words. Chesterfield's 'torrent', like the 'intumescence of the tide' to which Johnson in 1755 compares change in language (*Yale* XVIII.106), would remain unstilled. The expectations which Chesterfield indulged were, here as elsewhere, to receive short shrift once the *Dictionary* was published.

Order and the making of the *Dictionary*

Order, as Johnson's *Dictionary* makes plain, is, in fact, densely polysemous. On one hand, it inclines, as under *order* as verb, to the process by which things might be 'methodised' and 'fitly dis-posed', and on the other, to the diction of command and rule. The first was clearly salient to the *Dictionary* as text. Johnson, for example, repeatedly returned to the pragmatics of dictionary order in this respect, discussing the need to 'methodise my ideas' in the *Plan* and, by 1755, describing the various ways in which his own 'variety of materials' had been 'reduced to method' (*Yale* XVIII.29 and 74). Collection, as the *Rambler* essays explore, was, of necessity, a two-stage process. Collectors 'ought to amass no more than they can digest', Johnson stated, for instance, in November 1750 in *Rambler* 71 (*Yale* IV.10). 'To spend life in poring upon books' is to 'obstruct and embarrass the powers of nature' as well as 'to bury reason under a chaos of indigested learning', he likewise warned in August 1753 (*Yale* II.412). Like other collectors, the dictionary-maker must bring the process of collection to an end so that *digestion*—which Johnson defines, under sense 3, as 'the act of methodising; the maturation of a scheme'—can take place. 'He that has once accumulated learning, is next to consider, how he

86

shall most widely diffuse and most agreeably impart it', as Johnson emphasizes in 1753 (*Yale* II.413).

Nevertheless, reading some 2,000 texts had, as we have seen in Chapter 3, created a daunting mass of material for which 'digestion' was by no means easy. As both Reddick and McDermott confirm, for example, Johnson's methods of preliminary ordering foundered within a few years of beginning his work.[7] Strahan's commendations in 1749 of the 'great forwardness' of the *Dictionary*, together with the linguistic order it would bring, possess, in this light, a certain irony.[8] Behind the scenes, Johnson had been forced to abandon the organizational model on which he had hitherto relied. Two years after the finished *Plan*, order had collapsed into disorder; preliminary 'digestion' had proved all too fallible. Such tensions repeatedly informed the making of the *Dictionary*, and the struggle to encompass English in a single text.

Johnson's initial plan, as Reddick explains, had been to create what might be seen as a kind of a 'skeleton dictionary'.[9] What Johnson referred to as his 'transcripts' (*Yale* XVIII.94)—i.e. the citations which, as we have seen in Chapter 3, his amanuenses abstracted from the marked-up books—had been copied into eighty hand-made notebooks, and placed under the various headwords which Johnson also indicated as he read through the primary texts. In a further aspect of design, Johnson had also planned to flesh out the various alphabetical and semantic categories as the relevant evidence materialized. Yet, by 1749, the finite nature of the notebook page and the diversity of words, meanings, and citations which had already accumulated as a result of Johnson's assiduous annotation proved irreconcilable. Neither language nor quotations could be confined within the limits originally imposed. If material had to be ordered, Johnson's wide-ranging evidence—and the protean nature of English—clearly demanded a more fluid and flexible system. Henceforth the amanuenses recorded Johnson's marked citations on loose slips of paper. These could be arranged, and re-arranged, at will, responsive alike to Johnson's 'slow methods' and the realities of 'gradual accumulation'. Theory—and the early attempt to impose fixed categories—was, in this respect as in others, forced to yield to practical experience.

Further problems lay ahead. 'Memory' or invention, as Johnson acknowledged, would be forced to act as remedy for a number of absences which became apparent only as ordering for the *Dictionary* advanced.[10] 'This word I remember only in *Shakespeare*', he notes, for instance, under *scroyle* ('A mean fellow; a rascal; a wretch'). To *cream*, in the sense 'To take the flower and quintessence of any thing', was 'used somewhere by *Swift*', as Johnson adds with a conspicuous lack of specificity. Memory and minute accuracy in quotation did not necessarily coincide. The 'same' citation from *Hamlet* supports both *distilment* and *instilment* ('Upon my secure hour thy uncle stole, / With juice of cursed hebenon in a viol, / And in the porches of mine ears did pour / The leperous *distilment*'/ '*instilment*'). Invention, too, as the *Dictionary* confirms, might also have to supply 'an example that was wanting' (*Yale* XVIII.95). 'Reflection; prudent consideration; as he always acts with good *advice*', Johnson notes, for instance, under *advice*, sense 2. 'The act of declaring one's self bankrupt; as he silenced the clamours of his creditors by a sudden *bankruptcy*', the entry for *bankruptcy*, sense 2 confirms. Another common resource of dictionary-makers, invented examples would often be used to demonstrate meaning in unambiguous—if unempirical—ways.

The limits of the printed page, and the two folio volumes to which Johnson was contracted, led to further acts of selection. Paradoxically, dictionary order could require processes of reduction alongside expansion. 'When the time called upon me to range this accumulation of elegance and wisdom into an alphabetical series, I soon discovered that the bulk of my volumes would fright away the student', Johnson acknowledged in 1755 (*Yale* XVIII.94). Alongside 'the weariness of copying', lexicography came to comprise 'the vexation of expunging' both headwords and citations for the purposes of the printed text (*Yale* XVIII.94). This explains, of course, the gaps which, as Chapter 3 has noted, often intervene between collection—and what was collected—and the finished work. Johnson's lexical explorations in Hale, Burton, or Watts are only partly reflected in the *Dictionary* as published. By no means could all be included. By the same token, even those citations which were retained were often subject to reduction in size and scale. 'I have desired the passages to be clipped close', as Johnson reassures Strahan in 1753 (*Letters* I.73); orders to this effect had been issued to his amanuenses. To *clip*, as the *OED* confirms, was to 'cut or snip...off'—a process of physical reduction which applied not to the paper on which the quotations were inscribed, but to the length of the quotations per se.[11] It is, in terms of editing and citational evidence, a common practice in historical lexicography, as evidence from the making of the *OED*'s first edition likewise attests.[12] Yet this, too, could prove a difficult part of the *Dictionary* to bring to order. As Johnson admitted to Strahan, if instructions to 'clip close' were observed 'for two or three leaves', they were also repeatedly forgotten: 'Since poor Stuart's time I could never get that part of the work into regularity, and perhaps never shall. I will try to take some more care but can promise nothing.'[13] As Johnson indicates, only when in charge of making up the sheets for the press himself could he be sure to 'clip...close' enough.

The consequences of this particular aspect of 'digestion' were clear. As Johnson laments in the 1755 'Preface', he had, in making the *Dictionary*, been 'forced to...reduce my transcripts very often to clusters of words, in which scarcely any meaning is retained' (*Yale* XVIII.94). 'Bolingbroke argues most *sophistically*' is, as Wimsatt notes, all that remains of a once extensive citation deriving from a letter from Swift to Pope (though Johnson's meaning—if not Swift's— is arguably sharpened rather than lost in this instance).[14] Watts's once extensive citation for *pencil* ('If the Books which you read are your own, mark with a Pen, or <u>Pencil</u>, the most considerable Things in them which you desire to remember') is likewise reduced (and rearranged): 'Mark with a pen or *pencil* the most considerable things in the books you desire to remember.'[15] Across the *Dictionary*, Johnson's fondness for longer passages which reveal the full resonances of a given word in context could nonetheless often remain in evidence. A lengthy citation from Watts still illustrates *specific* while eight lines from Bacon's *Natural History* document the semantic potential of sense 3 of *weight*, defined as 'Ponderous mass'. Another eight lines from Bacon carefully illustrate *rabbit*, allowing Johnson to retell in full the anecdote which Bacon's *Apothegms* had supplied.[16]

Johnson's contemporaneous essays in the *Rambler* can, in this light, provide some interestingly double-edged comments which confirm the need for progress alongside the difficulties with which the traveller, whether literal or metaphorical, was faced: 'The traveller that resolutely follows a rough and winding path, will sooner reach the end of his journey, than he that is always changing his direction, and wastes the hour of daylight in looking for smoother ground, and shorter passages', as Johnson pointedly declared in 1750 (*Yale* III.339). 'I thought the passages too short', Johnson later stated of Addison's 'collection of examples selected from Tillotson's works'. These had, Johnson confirms, been sent to him 'too late to be of use' (*Yale* XXII.634). Here, too, the *Dictionary* remained distinctively his own.

Order, power, and the problems of prescription

Matters of this kind repeatedly confirmed the difficulty of securing dictionary order (on a variety of levels) as Johnson moved between collection and finished text. Discourses of power can seem remote; Johnson can be caught between the apparent intransigence of publishers, and the overwhelming amount of material which a dictionary of English had to include. Nevertheless, dictionary order as realized by Johnson was, as we have seen, also expected to extend to methods—and ideals—which were, by definition, more interventionist in nature. As the *Dictionary* confirmed, *order* easily inclines towards command and rule; as in Johnson's sense 5, an *order* is a 'mandate; precept; command'. It is a 'rule' and 'regulation', sense 6 adds. As in the accompanying citations, order can demand deference and subjugation, subservience and submission.

For Chesterfield, a political modelling of lexicographical control (and the subsequent submission of language and its users) clearly informs this aspect of dictionary order. As we have seen, annotations on Johnson's drafted plan in 1747 evoke the idea of a ruled language which the dictionary-maker should impose, bringing new governance to a state of language which is seen as lawless and unruled. As Chesterfield concludes in 1754, if language is to be ordered, 'we must have recourse to the old Roman expedient in times of confusion, and chuse a dictator'. Chesterfield's images both draw on and extend Johnson's earlier figurations of power, detailing the ways in which linguistic reform might be secured by Johnson's aid. As we have seen in Chapter 2, Johnson, as 'delegate' and 'soldier' to Chesterfield's 'Caesar', is, in 1747, on course to a 'new world' of words. Conquest, as a metaphor of over-arching power, informs Johnson's examination of the expectations with which lexicography was framed.[17] 'The power which might have been denied to my own claim, will be readily allowed me as the delegate of your Lordship', as Johnson had advanced of the cross-currents which authority might reveal (*Yale* XVIII.55).

Eight years later, and some five months before the *Dictionary* was published, Chesterfield—already envisaging the conquest as complete—hence depicts Johnson as triumphant ruler in a realm in which, as he writes, a new and 'lawful standard of our language' has been imposed.[18] 'A *ruler*', as the *Dictionary* explains, 'has supreme command'. Chesterfield's linguistic liberty is freely renounced in favour of the authority—and autocratic rule—which the dictionary-maker should provide. 'I will not only obey him, like an old Roman, as my dictator, but, like a modern Roman, I will implicitly believe in him as my pope, and hold him to be infallible', he avers: 'I hereby declare that I make a total surrender of all my rights and privileges in the English language, as a free-born

British subject, to the said Mr. Johnson, during the term of his dictatorship.'[19]

As both Johnson and Chesterfield explore, prescriptivism—and the linguistic ideologies on which it was based—can effectively be realised in political models of rule and conquest, of suppression and images of beneficial change. As in the prescriptive rhetoric of Snell and Swift, English was easily depicted as a realm ripe for new-found regulation in ways that might pay little attention to the rights of the 'natives' and the patterns of usage hitherto in evidence. In the 1747 *Plan*, Johnson's colonial metaphors, as Beach and Barrell observe, form part of this remit, changing the state of language which has so far existed.[20] Dictatorship—and models of absolute rule—will, as Chesterfield suggests, hence secure the obedience, and deference, by which such reform is to be implemented. For language to change, precept must be matched by practice; prescriptivism operates on two levels, encompassing both edict (and those who issue such edicts), and those who must, by compulsion, obey. Chesterfield in 1754 hence reveals an easy rhetoric in which absolute power is welcomed, and democracy willingly shed. Johnson is commended as dictator with evident approbation.

Johnson's exploration of these tropes is, as we might expect, markedly more complex. Where power is, or might be, located—and how it is be deployed—emerges as a wide-ranging issue to be resolved. Johnson's writing across the dictionary years (as well as afterwards) can, for example, probe the problem of rule—and obedience—with increasing scepticism. As Greene affirms, Johnson 'had a deep-seated aversion to an excess of the power of one rational human being over another'.[21] Autocracy in this light is problematic from the beginning.

Even in the *Plan*, as we have seen, narratives of conquest can be set against a very different appraisal of what human power might secure. 'It may be reasonably imagined, that what is so much in the power of men as language, will very often be capriciously conducted', as Johnson early makes plain (*Yale* XVIII.40–1).

Contracted to bring about a new state of words, he can, as a result, tread a fine line between discovery—in which the course may, as he states, be made easier for those who follow what he has established—and images of oppression in which language might perhaps become the dictionary-maker's subject in more ways than one. Retreat, too, remains an option. 'Sovereignty' ('Supremacy; highest place; supreme power') can, in far more categorical ways, lie with custom, as Johnson also indicates, in a force which is not easily redressed (*Yale* XVIII.50). Apparent deference to Caesar, as in the journey of conquest on which Johnson has been dispatched, can therefore co-exist with a sense of the democratic identity of language in which, as for Locke, the 'common Tye' of words and meaning governs usage and its own 'rights' within the state of language.[22]

Johnson's repeated exploration of absolute power, and the consequences of its imposition, as he wrote the *Dictionary* can nevertheless make his stated submission to Chesterfield as Caesar in 1747 seem increasingly anomalous. As in his play *Irene*, which Johnson began in 1737 but substantially revised after 1746 (it was performed in February 1749),[23] autocratic power is made the subject of highly critical review. 'Such are the woes when arbitrary pow'r, / And lawless passion, hold the sword of Justice', he declares in Act I. In *Irene*, the unhappy state which results is placed in firm contrast to 'the land . . . / Where common laws restrain the prince and subject, / A happy land, where circulating pow'r, / Flows through each member of th'embodied state' (*Yale* IV.121). Dictatorship and democracy are placed in opposition. 'Common laws' importantly act on all alike, in an equality of process which must extend to ruler as well as ruled. Johnson's entry for *common law* in the *Dictionary* derives from this same period, being written, as we know, before 1750. Here, too, 'custom' (in a very different model of prescription) takes precedence over what individual edict might seek to impose. *Common law* 'contains those customs and usages which have, by long prescription, obtained in this nation the force of laws', as the *Dictionary* explains.[24] While dictators, as the *Dictionary* indicates, are, indeed, 'invested with absolute authority', their negative connotations are, for Johnson, equally made plain. *Dictatorship* connotes 'insolent confidence', he expounds. It is not commended. As in *Irene*, autocratic power can reveal its own predispositions to lawlessness. Three years into the *Dictionary*, Johnson's examination of the effects of arbitrary decree by no means suggests either endorsement or emulation.

Johnson's readings, and re-readings, of Caesar prove equally interesting, especially when set against Chesterfield's assumptions in this respect. Chesterfield's attitudes to Caesar remain unequivocally positive. Just as Johnson is constructed as dictator in intended praise, so, too, is Caesar recommended in 1752 as a role model to Chesterfield's own son: 'How delightful is [Voltaire's] History of the Northern Brute, the King of Sweden! For I cannot call him a Man; and I should be very sorry to have him pass for a Hero, out of regard to those true heroes; such as Julius Caesar; Titus; Trajan, and the present King of Prussia [Frederick the Great].' Chesterfield advocated careful observance.[25] For Johnson, matters prove rather different. His deference to Caesar in 1747, and his endorsement of classical precedent in this respect, is not sustained. Caesar as configured in the essays of the *Rambler*, and *Adventurer* instead prompts a range of sharply critical re-assessments of power and its abuse. 'Caesar...let his ambition break out to the ruin of his country', Johnson stresses in September 1750 (*Yale* III.267). His resistance to such discourses of power and oppression is marked. 'I would wish Caesar and Cataline, Xerxes and Alexander... huddled together in obscurity or detestation', he states in 1753: 'I cannot conceive, why he that has burnt cites, and wasted nations, and filled the world with horror and desolation, should be more kindly regarded by mankind than he that died in the rudiments of wickedness; why he that accomplished mischief should be glorious, and he that only endeavoured it should be criminal' (*Yale* II.433). Writing *Rambler* 156, 'despotick antiquity' is soundly condemned

(*Yale* V.67); writing *Rambler* 158, the 'arbitrary edicts of legislators, authorised only by themselves' meet the same fate (*Yale* V.76). Johnson had little patience with the kind of patriotic cant that invoked Rome as a model, Vance firmly concludes.[26] As in Johnson's review of Thomas Blackwell's *Memoirs of the Court of Augustus* in 1756, Chesterfield's 'old Roman expedient' was to be given markedly short shrift. 'I know not why any one but a schoolboy in his declamation should whine over the common-wealth of *Rome*, which grew great only by the misery of the rest of mankind', he declared. In such processes, liberty and freedom were alike abused: 'The *Romans*, like others, as soon as they grew rich, grew corrupt, and in their corruption sold the lives and freedoms of themselves, and of one another', Johnson expounds.[27] To be commended as dictator is, Johnson suggests, by no means complimentary.

Power, and the responsibility it brings, can therefore be a complex matter in Johnson's wider thinking. Anarchy—and the absence of order—is not presented as a viable option.[28] Yet 'authority', as Johnson also makes plain, should never 'swell into tyranny' nor 'subjection...degenerate into slavery' (*Yale* XIV.251). Just rule, as Greene affirms, is, across Johnson's writing, firmly removed from dictatorship and oppression.[29] As for Locke (who is frequently cited in this regard across the *Dictionary*), Johnson's images of both society and good government habitually move in very different directions. 'If the ideas of liberty and volition were *carried* along with us in our minds, a great part of the difficulties that perplex men's thoughts would be easier resolved', as a citation from Locke states under *carry*. 'All men ought to maintain peace, and the common offices of *humanity* and friendship in diversity of opinions', a citation under *humanity* likewise confirms.

For the state of language, similar considerations can intervene, influencing the patterns of authority—and forms of power—that Johnson comes to deploy across the *Dictionary*. Johnson's processes of collection, as we have seen, already place emphasis on what 'custom' might have established—a truly autocratic dictionary would, after all, have no need of evidence to support, or contest, its claims. 'On dit', as the *Dictionnaire* of the Académie Française famously declared; what is stated as right should be information enough. Supporting examples in the *Dictionnaire* are invented in order to demonstrate the proprieties at stake.[30] Yet, even in 1748 (and in the early stages of his own work in lexicography), Johnson's sense of the problems which such autocratic regulation of language can involve is plain. Writing his 'Life of the Earl of Roscommon', Johnson mentions Roscommon's 'design of instituting a society for the refinement of the *English* language' only to adduce its failure. Rather than the endorsement of such ideals such as we might perhaps have expected—not least given the 'refinement' of language to which Johnson, too, was committed—he includes not only the salient biographical facts but Elijah Fenton's sceptical evaluation of such reformist enterprises per se.[31] Language academies, as Fenton had stressed, represent 'a design, of which it is much easier to conceive an agreeable idea, than any rational hope ever to see it brought to perfection'.

Significantly, neither Johnson nor Fenton express regret—or, indeed, realistic hope for the future—in this respect. In Johnson's 'Life' of Roscommon, theory and practice already divide; reason and the 'rational' counter what imagination might 'conceive' in ways which clearly resonate with Johnson's earlier concerns in the 'Scheme' and 'Fair Copy'. Revising the 'Life' for the later *Lives of the Poets*—long after the *Dictionary* was complete—Johnson's own scepticism would, of course, be plain: while 'the edicts of an English academy would probably be read by many', this is, he states, 'only that they might be sure to disobey them'. As in the 1755 'Preface', it is liberty rather than oppression, and suffrage rather than submission, that is affirmed (*Yale* XXI.245).[32]

Models of authority: Johnson, spelling, and the *Dictionary*

Johnson's treatment of spelling offers, in this light, a useful way of examining models of order, authority, and control as they came to be instituted across the *Dictionary*. As we have seen, Johnson's initial convictions, as expressed in the first draft of the 1746 'Scheme', and verified by his already wide reading in earlier texts, was that spelling was now relatively 'settled', even if it could not be said to be fixed (*Yale* XVIII.385).[33] Here, too, 'anarchy' was not recommended—idiosyncratic modes of spelling, as *Rambler* 51 explores, can lead to incomprehension and the failure of language in itself.[34] Nevertheless, Johnson's tolerance of some level of on-going variation was plain. Chesterfield's position was very different. Johnson's revisions to the 1746 'Scheme' accordingly defer to Chesterfield's dislike of the 'great uncertainty' which English spelling revealed. Spelling is 'in itself inaccurate, and tolerated rather than chosen', Johnson's emended text instead points out (*Yale* XVIII.37). A process of reform is embedded in what the *Dictionary* must do.

The popular mythography of Johnson's *Dictionary* suggests, of course, a domain of striking fixity and stability in this respect. 'Without a demand for linguistic authority, Johnson would not have been hired, and he knew what his readers wanted. For instance, they urgently wanted standardized spelling', Lipking notes.[35] David Crystal makes a similar point; Johnson's work is used to epitomize orthographical regulation in ways which are deemed to impact on the subsequent history of English: 'Johnson did "fix" spelling, to an appreciable extent. And people were prepared to use him as a model and follow his decisions', he writes.[36] Nevertheless, here, too, as the making of the *Dictionary* confirms, Johnson's task was by no means easy. The 'testimony' supplied by the 'equiponderant authorities of writers alike eminent for judgment and accuracy' could differ, exposing other problems of lexicographical 'choice' (*Yale* XVIII.35). If, as Johnson states, he had 'been determined by your Lordship's opinion . . . to support what appears to me most consonant to grammar and reason' (*Yale* XVIII.54), what precisely is 'reasonable' ('Just; rational; agreeable to reason', as the *Dictionary* explains) can, at times, be difficult to discern.[37]

As in Johnson's wider imaging of conquest and the world of words, tropes of conflict can swiftly come to the fore. 'The great orthographical contest has long subsisted between etymology and pronunciation', as Johnson observes in 1747 (*Yale* XVIII.35). Language, as in the entry for *contest* in the *Dictionary*, readily acts as a locus of dispute and dissent, with opponents ranged on both sides. 'Leave all noisy *contests*, all immodest clamours, and brawling language', a citation from Watts advises. Yet, to bring resolution in any 'contest' in which language is involved is, as Johnson explores, often problematic. 'It is not more easy to perswade men to agree exactly in speaking than in writing' (*Yale* XVIII.35), as he confesses in the 1747 *Plan* in words which already resonate with the problems of control.

Even in 1747, Johnson's maxims on orthography are, for instance, often explicitly aligned not with expected reform (and the kind of forcible 'perswasion' that Chesterfield might prefer) but with 'the general custom of our language' and 'the present usage of spelling' (*Yale* XVIII.36, 37). Statements made in this context—that, for example, 'All change is of itself an evil, which ought not to be hazarded but for evident advantage', and that 'as inconstancy is in every case a mark of weakness, it will add nothing to the reputation of our tongue' (*Yale* XVIII.36)—have often been taken as reflective of Johnson's adherence to fixity, and the rightful imposition of norms. Yet, as a careful reading of this section of the text confirms, Johnson's resistance is not so much indicative of his insistence on a new-found normativity—based in autocratic decree about what must henceforth be used—but, instead, of his reluctance to introduce changes which have no basis in actual usage. As his immediately preceding comments in the *Plan* make clear, 'The chief rule which I propose to follow, is to make no innovation, without a reason sufficient to balance the inconvenience of change.' Order in this light derives from common law, inclining to the *status quo* wherever possible. 'Such reasons', he adds, 'I do not expect often to find' (*Yale* XVIII.36). If reason is again prominent, it is set against the vagaries of wilful—and arbitrary—change. Johnson's caution is marked. His subsequent comments offer a careful critique of spelling reform and those who, in various ways, 'take pleasure in departing from custom' in their attempts to impose individual preferences on the language as a whole (*Yale* XVIII.36).[38]

In terms of information on spelling within the *Dictionary*, the primary focus is, of course, Johnson's specification of the headword. Set apart from the body of the entry, this is rendered visibly distinct through capitalization, hence DA'CTYLE, DA'LLIANCE (Johnson's inserted accent mark indicates the expected position of stress). As such, it provides a reference model by which Chesterfield's 'uncertainty' might indeed be resolved; while other variants might therefore exist in 'general custom', the choice of headword will, of necessity, prioritize and select. It sets out, in effect, a preferred spelling, authorized by the lexicographer and made part of the dictionary's intended role as reference book. As eighteenth-century lexicography confirms, different dictionary-makers can, of course, draw on different patterns of 'preference' in this respect. If Johnson's headwords institute forms such as *publick*, *classick*, *logick*, and *musick* as part of the reference model he provides, Benjamin Martin's *Linguæ Britannicæ Reformata*, published in 1749, conversely discards what he termed the 'redundant final *k*'. This reflected the 'old Way' of spelling, Martin argued, rather than that used by 'later Writers'.[39] 'Preference' in his *Dictionary* is given to headwords such as *music* and *logic*. '*K* is a very useless and superfluous letter ...and should not be wrote at the end of words exceeding one syllable', Buchanan's *Linguæ Britannicæ vera Pronunciatio* (1757) likewise averred.[40] Typical of the first half of the eighteenth century, Johnson's preferred *–ick* would, at least in public printed texts, largely have disappeared by its end. His cautions on reason, custom, and obedience prove, in this instance, well justified. Even if spellings with *-ick* are 'settled' within the pages of his text, this does not, as the history of English confirms, prevent the eventual dominance of other co-existing forms.[41]

As Johnson indicates, 'preference' and 'doubt' will, in fact, often work together in this respect within the *Dictionary*. As in the *Plan*, consideration of Chesterfield's concerns about 'uncertainty' inform Johnson's comments on his decision, in instances where 'orthography is dubious' (i.e. 'doubtful; not settled'; 'uncertain')[42] to give spelling 'a claim to preference' when 'the greatest number of radical letters' is preserved, or, tellingly, when the spelling in question 'seems most to comply with the general custom of our language' (*Yale* XVIII.36). As a result, if readers whose own preferred form is, say, *batchelor* consult the *Dictionary*, a corresponding entry is provided—but they also find themselves redirected to the variant *bachelor* (under which Johnson places full information on meaning and patterns of sense-division). Similar are the entries for *fosset* and *faucet* (in which readers are redirected to *faucet*, defined as 'The pipe inserted into a vessel to give vent to the liquor'), or *calif* and *caliph*, or *intire/entire*. As under *kaw* and *caw* ('To cry as the rook, raven, or crow'), Johnson can provide information on both forms, as well as appropriate evidence. Yet as befits the 'faithful lexicographer' (*Yale* XVIII.99), he also takes care to indicate which variant—in this instance, *caw*—might be preferred, at least for the purposes of the *Dictionary* and the advice it must provide. *Entire* is 'better', he likewise notes under *intire*. Yet here, too, parallel entries exist, while Hooker provides important evidence for the way in which *intire* is in fact also used in English.[43]

We can in such ways see the careful interplay of the roles which Johnson, as lexicographer, must perform. Seeking to 'register but not form', he pays due attention to the evidence of his 'authorities', and the order this suggests. Nevertheless, this does not mean that what he terms 'absurdities' and 'improprieties' are to be registered without comment, nor that guidance is withheld where necessary (*Yale* XVIII.75). Here, too, Johnson can tread a careful line. As in his entry for *plum*, certain variants—writing *plum* as *plumb*—are therefore proscribed, while the conventional spelling *plum* is instituted as norm. Spelling here is 'dubious' indeed; custom provides competing norms. 'A custom has prevailed of writing *plumb*, but improperly', Johnson explains; this represented, in essence, an analogical extension on the model of *lamb*, *comb*. 'Contest' between etymology and certain forms of usage is equally apparent. Johnson, however, unequivocally accords victory to the form that had, as in his chosen headword, long been established without the epenthetic <*b*>. As the *Dictionary* confirms, the spelling *plum* has both etymology and history on its side—as well as majority usage. *Plumb* is 'improper', Johnson concludes. In this instance, analogy had been carried too far, potentially eliding the visual distinctiveness of *plum* ('A fruit') and *plumb* ('A plummet; a leaden weight let down at the end of a line').

A similar process is at work in his entry for *conversable*. This, Johnson notes, is 'sometimes written *conversible*, but improperly'. Analogy with the cognate forms of *conversant*, *conversation* is provided as justification. Johnson's recommendation, as befits a reference book, are in line with what that which 'seems most to comply with the general custom of our language' rather than with what 'sometimes' happens. *Intrinsecal* offers a further useful example in this context. Here, Johnson's chosen spelling accords with etymology (the word, he confirms, derives from Latin *intrinsecus*, French *intrinseque*). Yet, as he notes within the entry itself, current practice does not agree: 'This word is now generally written *intrinsical*, contrarily to analogy.' As a result, while contest is resolved in one direction by the choice of *intrinsecal* as headword, other supporting information can already suggest that victory, at least quantitatively, might lie in another direction entirely. Januslike, the entry remains conflicted; authority points in two directions, divided between etymology and current practice. If the headword reveals 'preference' (*Yale* XVIII.77), it does not, as Johnson is careful to explain, therefore necessitate autocratic rule. Spellings with *intrinsical* instead appear across the *Dictionary*, as in a citation from Hale under *discongruity* ('There is want of capacity in the thing, to sustain such a duration from the intrinsical *discongruity* of the one to the other'), or that from Locke under *extrinsical* ('Outward objects, that are *extrinsical* to the mind; and its own operations, proceeding from powers intrinsical...when reflected on by itself, become also objects of its contemplation, are the original of all knowledge'). Johnson's entries for *jelly/gelly* offer a similar tension. The 'proper orthography' is *gelly*, he notes, commending a form in which etymology (< Latin *gelatinum*) receives its due. Nevertheless, *jelly* also gains an entry of its own, supported by evidence and appropriate citations from Shakespeare, King, and Pope.

The spelling which appears within citations was, moreover, as Johnson indicates, by no means to be seen as insignificant. 'I have left, in the examples, to every authour his own practice unmolested, that the reader may balance suffrages, and judge between us', Johnson states in 1755 (*Yale* XVIII.77).[44] As the *Dictionary* confirms, the practice of *suffrage* is that in which the individual is given a 'vote' or a 'voice in a controverted point'. In terms of Chesterfield's political metaphors, dictatorship can, as such, seem particularly remote. Instead, in Johnson's account of the methods he has deployed, while the headword acts as guide, this does not necessarily either fix or settle. Here, power transparently moves from dictionary-maker to dictionary-user who must 'balance' the evidence as they see fit.[45] Variants, Johnson stresses, remain 'unmolested'—undisturbed by unnecessary intervention.[46] Spellings with, say, *intire* as well as *entire* hence appear across the text; as under *medly*, citations from Addison and Walsh deploy *medley*, whereas a quotation from Hayward uses *medly*. Under *vitious*, Dryden's *vicious* and Ben Jonson's *vitious* co-exist. *Inferrible* and *inferible* offer other alternative spellings; Johnson's headword attests the latter, a citation from Brown the former. *Jerken* (which Johnson defines as 'a jacket; a short coat; a close waistcoat') provides a similar example. *Jerkin* appears by virtue of South's *Sermons*, as well as Swift's *Gulliver's Travels*. Johnson's *jerken*, to which he gives 'preference', seems heavily outnumbered.

Johnson's *Dictionary* can, in these and other ways, provide a surprising amount of information on the co-existing variants of eighteenth-century spelling. If, in the entry for *gaol*, the spelling *goal* is not recommended (this, Johnson makes clear, is best seen as an incidental error, presumably prompted by the unfamiliar sequencing of <ao> in English words),[47] he offers strikingly neutral evidence on the co-existence of *gaol* and *jail*. Johnson gives preference to *gaol* (presumably on the basis of the etymology (< French *geol*)), though a detailed entry for *jail*—with supporting evidence from Shakespeare, Clarendon, and Dryden—is also provided. As Johnson observes, in reality, the word 'is written either way' and 'commonly by later writers *jail*'. His diction is descriptive; both *jail* and *gaol* are recorded with marked objectivity while the direction of on-going change is also pointed out.

Comment within individual entries is, in this light, often highly illuminating. *Tricker*, for instance, 'is often written *trigger*', Johnson states in the relevant entry. Here, too, observation—and the salience of 'equiponderant authorities' (*Yale* XXVIII.35)—can self-evidently come to the fore. In the accompanying citations, Newton and Butler use *tricker*, Locke uses *trigger* (as Johnson's entry for the latter also confirms). 'I know not which is right', Johnson adds. Uncertainty is embedded in the forms the *Dictionary* records. The entry for *embassy* affirms a similar potential for choice: 'It may be observed, that though our authors write almost indiscriminately *embassador* or *ambassador*, *embassage* or *ambassage*; yet there is scarcely any example of *ambassy*, all concurring to write *embassy*.' Usage, in this respect, attests an 'indiscriminate' variation which Johnson again describes. As under *dependency*, the selection of one form (in the headword) can be followed by a categorical—and neutral—affirmation of flux: 'This word, with many others of the same termination, are indifferently written with *ance* or *ence*, *ancy* or *ency*, as the authors intended to derive them from the Latin or French.' For these words at least, victory in any 'orthographical contest' can, it seems, go either way. Authority is shared—and verified—between equivalent norms of practice.

Given prototypical expectations of Johnson's work, this diction of 'indifference' and uncertainty is particularly worthy of note.[48] *Indifferent*: 'Neutral; not determined to either side', the *Dictionary* explains. 'Many words are written uncertainly with *en* or *in*', Johnson states, for example, under *en*. *Bond*, he likewise records, 'is written indifferently, in many of its senses, *bond*, or *band*'. *Imbrue* is similar: 'To steep; to soak; to wet much or long. This seems indifferently written with *im* or *em*.' 'I have sustained both modes of writing', he affirms.[49] Variation seems embedded in English usage in ways which Johnson is not inclined to change. *Dependent/ dependant* provide parallel examples. 'This, as many other words of like termination, are written with *ent* or *ant*, as they are supposed to flow from the Latin or French', Johnson writes under *dependent*.[50]

Johnson's metalanguage—and a pervasive habit of hedging ('perhaps', 'sometimes') in the comments that he makes—can, as a result, often sit at odds with the narratives of reform and imposed power that Chesterfield, and others, awaited. 'This is sometimes, perhaps not improperly, written *discursive*', he states under *discoursive*. Similar is *jerk* which, Johnson notes, 'is sometimes written *yerk*'. 'Believe' and 'think' likewise often appear in favour of the autocratic imperatives on which prescriptive rhetoric conventionally relies. As under *oddly*, Johnson can posit a form which he might have preferred yet which is, as he indicates, nevertheless rejected against that validated by 'custom' and 'present usage': 'This word and *oddness*, should, I think, be written with one *d*; but the writers almost all combine against it.' In Johnson's explanation, 'suffrage' again triumphs over dictatorship and reform as decreed by the individual will. As in the accompanying headword, Johnson's reference model is aligned with 'the writers' (and provided with <dd>). It is, by the same token, moved away from what Johnson 'thinks', and his personal predilection for a single <d>.

Griffon and *hale* confirm processes similar in kind. If we are told for the former that this 'should rather be written *gryfon*, or *gryphon*', nevertheless, as Johnson adds, 'it is generally written *griffon*'. Johnson's headword agrees with the latter. 'This should rather be written *hail*', the entry for *hale* ('Healthy; sound') likewise confirms, but the headword again conforms to practice rather than such theoretical precepts and reform. Even when Johnson's modals ('should be', 'should rather be') suggest the conventional markers of prescriptive, and proscriptive, discourse,[51] they are, as here, often be accompanied by statements which return us to the rather different realities of language in use. 'This word should...be spelled *sprite*, and its derivatives *spritely*, *spriteful*', Johnson avers, for instance, under *spright*. But, as he adds, 'custom has determined otherwise'. *Spright*, the headword duly affirms. A corresponding headword *sprite* is also given, though this gains a single citation in support. *Spright* is instead provided with four senses, and seven citations. This 'should, I think, be written *outrageous*', Johnson writes in a similar mode under *outragious*. But here, too, 'custom seems otherwise', and it is this to that Johnson's headword accordingly defers. 'I have followed custom', he states with similar intent against the various possible variants of *shew* and *strew*. 'Perhaps', he conjectures, the form *strow* 'is best', on the grounds that it 'reconciles etymology with pronunciation'. Yet, as he makes plain, 'the orthography of this word is doubtful'. In the *Dictionary* he follows, instead, what 'is generally written'.

As such examples suggest, if Johnson 'settles', his practice inclines not to what he defines, under *settle* sense 6, as 'To fix; to make certain or unchangeable' but rather to that given in the preceding sense: 'To determine; to affirm; to free from ambiguity'. Johnson clarifies and explains in ways which, as we will also see in Chapter 5, can give close attention to the range of variants which eighteenth-century usage continued to reveal. Widely evident across the citational evidence that Johnson provides, such variation can moreover appear with striking frequency in Johnson's definitional structures too. If *surgeon* is, for instance, selected as headword, the currency of *chirurgeon* as competing form is by no means obscured.[52] Johnson's corresponding entry for *chirurgeon* makes plain the pattern of change, and the prevalence of co-existing forms. 'It is now generally pronounced, and by many written, *surgeon*', he writes. Entries across the *Dictionary* will, in turn, often combine the two, such that a *sea-surgeon* is 'A chirurgeon employed on shipboard' while a *barber-chirurgeon* is, in contrast, 'A man who joins the practice of surgery to the barber's trade'.

Contemporary variation in the use of double consonants is equally apparent. While for Lass, 'by the eighteenth century, the previously rather capricious use of double consonant graphs (either to indicate short vowels or simply as typographic variations) has been stabilised', this is not a conclusion which Johnson's *Dictionary* necessarily supports.[53] Instead, a range of variant forms coexist such that, say, an *ale-knight* is 'A pot-companion; a tippler' while an *ale-house* is 'A house where ale is publickly sold; a tipling-house'. Likewise, *balance* appears as headword, and *ballance* in a range of definitions (see e.g. *distemper*, sense 5: 'Want of due ballance between contraries'; *to turn*, sense 4: 'To change the state of the ballance'). *Penny* and *peny* (see e.g. *grain*, sense 5: 'The smallest weight, of which in physick twenty make a scruple, and in Troy weight twenty-four make a peny weight') provide other examples. *Penny* and *halfpenny* appear as headwords while the etymology for the latter records that it derives from *half* and *peny*. It is defined as 'A copper coin, of which two make a peny'.[54]

Both Osselton (1984) and Tieken Boon van Ostade have drawn attention to the flux of forms which appear in Johnson's private writing, using this to affirm a divide between 'epistolary spelling' and print, and between 'private' and 'public' standards of use.[55] It is, nevertheless, clear that in the entirely public form of the *Dictionary* similar aspects of variability are, in reality, widely in use. *Chappell*, *chapell*, and *chapel*, for instance, appear in Johnson's correspondence (sometimes even in the same letter),[56] while relevant headwords in the *Dictionary* record both *chapel* and *freechappel* (the latter deriving from *free* and *chappel*, as Johnson explains). *Hil* and *hill* are similar; *muckhill* is defined as 'a dunghil', while *uphill* and *downhil* appear as headwords. Other images of contemporary variation appear in the conflicting testimony of *wain* and *wane* (*decrease*, sense 2. 'The wain; the time when the visible face of the moon grows less'), or *opake* and *opaque* (see e.g. *darkness*, sense 2: 'Opakeness'; *pellucid*: 'not opake'; *shadowy*: 'opake'; *lightsome*: 'not opake'). Meanwhile, *opaque* appears as headword and in the glosses Johnson provides for *dillucid* and *transparent* (both are 'not opaque'). Other variations can be located in *skreen* and *screen* (*umbrella*: 'a skreen used in hot countries to keep off the sun, and in others to bear off the rain'; *umbrage*: 'Shade; skreen of trees'; *cover* 'a screen'; *fight* 'something to screen the combatants in ships'), or *croud* and *crowd*. For the latter, the headword in the *Dictionary* (for both noun and verb) follows *crowd*, Johnson's private practice the former. Practice within the body of the *Dictionary* is diverse, though *croud* is strikingly prominent. *Accloy* is hence defined as 'To fill up, in an ill sense; to croud, to stuff full' and *accoil* as 'To croud, to keep a coil about, to bustle, to be in a hurry'. *Aggroup* is 'To bring together into one figure; to croud together: a term of painting', while *cloud* (sense 4) is 'Any thing that spreads wide; as a croud, a multitude'.

Similarly prominent are *risk* and *risque*. If *risk* appears as headword, it is by means of *risque* that a range of words, including *danger*, *dangerless*, and *depone* are defined. 'Risque; hazard; peril', 'Without hazard; without risque; exempt from danger', and 'To risque upon the success of an adventure', Johnson's definitions respectively aver. Such forms unite private spellings, as in Hester Thrale's 'he...would rather run the Risque of spending the Night on board',[57] and the public text of the *Dictionary*. While we cannot, of course, be sure that the spelling which appears in the definitions accords with Johnson's underlying manuscript text (though the forms he used in his private letters certainty provide appropriate precedent), the lack of attention—and normative intent—directed to these variations is undeniable. They remain moreover across the different editions of the *Dictionary*.[58] Seen from this position,

Johnson's text does not suggest a writer who was unduly preoccupied either with control or conquest. In terms of orthographic variation, testimony extends from headword to citations (and the diversities that these record), to aspects of definition.[59]

Johnson's attitudes towards spelling reform are, in this light, especially telling. To what extent he would seek to include himself amongst those desirous of the 'reformation and settlement of our orthography' is doubtful. 'There are, indeed, some', he writes, 'who despise the inconveniencies of confusion' and 'seem to take pleasure in departing from custom, and to think alteration desirable for its own sake' (*Yale* XVIII.36–7). Yet, as Johnson indicates, there are clear limits to reform in this respect. While the history of English was littered with idiosyncratic schemes by which spelling might be rectified and changed,[60] Johnson reveals a sharply satirical distancing in his accounts of their achievements and approach: 'I suppose', he writes, 'they hold singularity its own reward, or may dread the fascination of lavish praise' (*Yale* XVIII.37).

The *Grammar* which appears as part of the prefatory matter for the *Dictionary* confirms a similar stance. In ways which already presage Johnson's revisions to his 'Life' of Roscommon (and the scepticism about reform which this reveals), images of national conquest—and the legitimacy of individual rule—are firmly cast aside. 'Who can hope to prevail on nations to change their practice, and make all their old books useless?', Johnson demands. Moreover, 'what advantage would a new orthography procure equivalent to the confusion and perplexity of such an alteration?' (*Yale* XVIII.295). Johnson's rhetorical questions affirm his own position of dissent. Describing the orthographic endeavours of would-be reformers such as Alexander Gil or Charles Butler, it is clear that, for Johnson, as for Locke, communication—and what both regard as the true ends of language—can be impeded by injudicious change or wilful reformation in which 'each man had his own scheme' (*Yale* XVIII.299–300). Johnson, as he stresses, will write in order to provide 'a guide to reformers, or terrour to innovators' (*Yale*

XVIII.295).[61] Guided by reason, 'I have', as Johnson confirms in the 'Preface', 'attempt[ed]...few alterations'. Neither 'narrow views' of correctness nor 'minute propriety' are, in reality, deemed sufficient cause to 'disturb...the orthography of [our] fathers' (*Yale* XVIII.78).

5

Meaning, governance, and the 'colours of words'

The 'great labour' of the *Dictionary* lay, of course, in ordering of a different kind. As in Johnson's definition of *lexicographer*, the dictionary-maker must 'detail the signification of words'—offering, as Johnson indicates in the *Plan*, a mode of definition in which 'brevity, fulness, and perspicuity' (*Yale* XVIII.46) must all come to the fore. As the *Dictionary* explains, *perspicuity* lay in the qualities of 'Clearness to the mind; easiness to be understood; freedom from obscurity or ambiguity'. It was for the dictionary to 'take away our doubts about words', as William Warburton had earlier affirmed to Joseph Spence in 1744.[1] Against a dominant—and highly negative—rhetoric of uncertainty, the good dictionary offered the prospect of resolution for words and the meanings they should possess.

As in Warburton's image of the dictionary as a 'compass' ('The instrument composed of a needle and card, whereby mariners steer', as Johnson explained under *steer*, sense 9),[2] lexicography was seen as a means of guiding users in the right direction amidst the perplexity of the 'sea of words'. Sophia, in Fielding's *History of Tom Jones* (1749), is, for instance, directed to the dictionary as a reference book to remedy her erroneous conflation of *hate* and *dislike*. 'Will you never learn a proper Use of Words?', Mrs Western

Samuel Johnson and the Journey into Words. Lynda Mugglestone
© Lynda Mugglestone 2015. First published 2015 by Oxford University Press.

admonishes: 'By Hatred . . . you mean no more than Dislike'.[3] Hester Thrale's acquaintance, Mrs Wallace—who described 'how She had been admitted when abroad to the *Refractory* of some Friars in France or Italy'—was, as Thrale's comments reveal, in need of similar redress.[4] *Refractory* meant 'Obstinate; perverse; contumacious', as Johnson's *Dictionary* carefully explained. A *refectory* was, in contradistinction, a 'room of refreshment; eating room'. Supporting evidence neatly confirms this contrastive use. '*Refractory* mortal! if thou will not trust thy friends, take what follows; know assuredly, before next full moon, that thou wilt be hung up in chains', Arbuthnot states in his *History of John Bull*. 'He cells and *refectories* did prepare, / And large provisions laid of winter fare', Dryden had written, to very different ends, in 'The Hind and the Panther' (1687).

Johnson's elaboration of *hate* and *dislike* was particularly detailed, even if it appeared too late for Sophia in *Tom Jones* (who had been advised to 'consult *Bailey's Dictionary*' instead). *Hate* as a verb is illustrated by four citations; six exemplify its corresponding noun. *Dislike*, Johnson explains, is 'To disapprove; to regard without affection; to regard with ill-will or disgust'. To *hate* is qualitatively distinct; it is, Johnson adduces: 'To detest; to abhor; to abominate; to regard with the passion contrary to love'. Bailey's *Universal Etymological Dictionary* simply defined *hate* as 'to bear ill will to'. *Dislike* had not been defined at all. Other entries in Johnson's *Dictionary* confirm a similar process of advance; Johnson's extensive sense-divisions engage with meaning in ways which widely reveal the play of connotation and denotation by which the same word is used across a range of contexts.

Nevertheless, as Joseph Spence indicates, the extent to which doubt might, in matters of meaning, really be resolved by the aid of lexicography could prompt doubts of its own. Warburton's idealized conceptions of the dictionary's role elicited a certain scepticism in this respect. Discussing the trio of *parsimony, covetousness,* and *avarice,* Warburton had, for example, proclaimed that the first was 'saving what is one's own', the second 'the desiring what is another's', and the third 'the doing both to excess'. As Spence added, however, 'I always thought that frugality was saving what was one's own, in a good sense, and parsimony in a bad; that avarice was the same, only to a greater excess, and that covetousness was a vicious desiring of what was another's.' This, he concluded, 'may help to show the difficulty of fixing the definitions'. Doubt, for Spence, is made to qualify the lexicographical enterprise per se. 'How should we get the public to agree in these and like definitions, when almost any two men you talk with would be found to differ about them?', he demanded.[5]

Spence isolated what would long remain a problematic issue in lexicography. On one hand, being definitive was often seen in terms of the imposition of fixed and immutable meanings—and the kind of rule which Johnson was, ideally, to impose. 'Everie man, by the *Lexicon* may trulie know and boldly warrant the meaning and sense of the words, which hee useth', as Snell had declared in 1649: 'the signification...will bee alwaies undoubted and certain, without variation and change, and held to an immutabilitie'.[6] As for Swift or, indeed, Strahan,[7] certainty of this kind is depicted as highly desirable. Conversely, as Spence postulates, if meaning is to be imposed merely at the will of the dictionary-maker, the senses which other speakers prefer—and use—might well be ignored. Whether such high-handed methods would really remove doubt was debatable. Yet, as Spence's own examples proved, an unsettled range of significations seemed possible when such prescriptive (and proscriptive) models were absent.

Johnson's entries for Spence's disputed words provide, in this light, a useful test case for both method and approach. *Avarice*, for instance, is defined as 'Covetousness; insatiable desire'. Accompanying citations from L'Estrange and Shakespeare neatly demonstrate the sense of excess which both Warburton and Spence identify. '*Avarice* is insatiable; and so he went still pushing on for more', writes L'Estrange; 'There grows / In my most ill compos'd affection, such / A stanchless *avarice*, that were I king, / I should cut off the nobles for their lands', Malcolm confesses in *Macbeth*. *Parsimony*, in contrast, is explained as 'Frugality; covetousness; niggardliness; saving temper'. While Spence had restricted *parsimony* to negative meaning alone, for Johnson, it was clear—as his evidence confirmed—that the possession of a 'saving temper', together with the careful regard for individual economy which this comports, cannot be regarded as faults per se. Yet *parsimony* also has the potential to become negative, veering towards stinginess and the 'niggardly' (Johnson's definition of the latter as 'avaricious' or 'sordidly parcimonious' [*sic*] is telling). 'The ways to enrich, are many: *parsimony* is one of the best, and yet is not innocent; for it withholdeth men from works of liberality', as a supporting quotation from Bacon affirms.

Covetousness, Johnson specifies, is meanwhile implicated in avarice and parsimony alike; it is defined as 'Avarice; inordinate desire of money; eagerness of gain'. His evidence likewise supports the 'good sense' of *frugality* on which Spence comments; citations from Bacon, Waller, and Dryden all provide appropriate illustration. Meaning is nevertheless calibrated in ways which again move well beyond Spence's sense of the word. If *frugality* is glossed as 'thrift' and 'good husbandry', it can, Johnson reveals, also be aligned with *parsimony* and the negative resonances this acquires. As an illustrative citation from Arbuthnot indicates: 'The boundaries of virtues are indivisible lines: it is impossible to march up close to the frontiers of *frugality*, without entering the territories of parsimony.' Or, as Johnson stresses in a similar mode in the 1755 'Preface', 'the shades of meaning sometimes pass imperceptibly into each other'; if 'on one side they apparently differ', they can move ever closer on the other. 'It is impossible to mark the point of contact', he concludes (*Yale* XVIII.91).

Arbuthnot's words resonate in ways which, for Johnson, clearly engage with the wider problems of meaning and its determination. As Spence acknowledges, both he and Warburton had based their judgements on what they 'thought' about words. Meaning here depended on opinion or, as the *Dictionary* explains, on what is otherwise seen as 'Perswasion of the mind, without proof or certain knowledge'. Doubt, in these terms, is inevitable. Opinion, as Johnson's wider thinking confirms, is often depicted as problematic.[8] 'The opinions of others whom we know and *think* well of are no ground of assent', as Locke states, here in a citation deployed under *think*.[9] As the entries for *frugality, parsimony, covetousness,* and *avarice* instead confirm, it was only by scrutinizing a range of 'testimonies' that meaning can emerge. 'The solution of all difficulties, and the supply of all defects, must be sought in the examples, subjoined to the various senses of each word', Johnson writes in 1755 (*Yale* XVIII.93). 'He...back'd his opinion with quotations', as a quotation (under *quotation*) from Prior affirms, illustrating meaning and process alike.

In these entries at least, Johnson's careful differentiation of sense rests on certain foundations. Opinion is transcended by observation; collection—and interpretative engagement with what has been collected—enable and create the entries that we see. Doubt is allayed not by the assumed certainties of prescriptive (and proscriptive) discourse, but by the careful probing of language and Johnson's assembled evidence of its use. Knowledge, above all, is made *demonstrable*: 'That which may be proved beyond doubt or contradiction; that which may be made not only probable, but evident', as Johnson's entry for this word confirms.

Criticism and correctness: The dictionary-maker as judge

If Johnson's handling of evidence in his entries for *frugality* and related words suggests a strongly descriptive approach within his 'world of words' then it is salutary to recall, as Chris Pearce stresses, 'the standard assessment' of Johnson's work as lexicographer—one in which his definitions are 'brilliant', his etymologies 'wretched', and his comments on usage 'prescriptive and capricious'.[10] Johnson is 'by reputation', Siebert notes, 'the most prescriptive of English lexicographers'.[11] As for Romaine, Johnson is circumscribed by a set of prescriptive and proscriptive commonplaces.[12] As Sledd and Kolb conclude, Johnson had, it seemed, indeed given the age the kind of dictionary it wanted—regulative, prescriptive, and firmly engaged with the remit of standardization and stability.[13] In Lynch and McDermott's set of *Anniversary Essays* on Johnson's *Dictionary* in 2005, adjacent chapters on description and prescription articulate opposing positions. Appropriating Johnson's own legal diction, McDermott argues for the defence and Barnbrook for the prosecution.[14] Johnson's testimony, and the evidence of the *Dictionary*, is appropriated on both sides. Doubt and certainty can be equally prominent in this respect, offering conflicting interpretative trajectories of what Johnson does or does not do.

Such conflicts lie, in some ways, at the heart of lexicography. As Hartmann reminds us, dictionary-making is, even for modern descriptive dictionaries, a domain in which prescription and description inevitably have a complex relationship. Lexicography, he writes, has 'always and essentially been a kind of codification which lies somewhere between linguistic description and prescription, between the specification of actual usage and the setting of potential norms, between observation of what speakers and writers do and remediation in situations of communicative conflict'.[15] It offers a continuum of practice in which reference models must be provided and norms identified, together with the opportunity to advise—and perhaps intervene—where usage might seem awry.

That Johnson recognized a similar conjunction is likewise clear. As in the 1755 'Preface', he can, as we have seen, comment on the fundamental 'duty of the lexicographer' by which usage is to be 'registered' rather than 'formed'. Yet, he notes, too, the regulative function which the dictionary-maker must play when language is deemed to reveal 'improprieties' and 'absurdities' (*Yale* XVIII.75). Judgement is, in this light, inevitable. His task, he explains, is to 'collect the testimonies on both sides, and endeavour to discover and promulgate the decrees of custom' (*Yale* XVIII.50).

Judgement as outlined in the *Plan* can nevertheless incorporate discourses of power in which intended agency is marked. Set against the lawlessness of the 'new world' in which the dictionary-maker might venture, Johnson can depict lexicography as a process in which 'barbarous' words should be 'eradicated', as well as 'civilised', as part of the 'conquest' of English which might be made. Johnson's diction of 'branding'—by which, as he indicates, 'barbarous words' are to be 'branded' with 'some note of infamy'—offers, for example, other mechanisms by which rule might be imposed as well as change effected (*Yale* XVIII.53). As McDermott notes, Johnson's diction of legal process is conspicuous.[16] A *brand*, the *Dictionary* confirms, is 'A mark made by burning a criminal with a hot iron, to note him as infamous' (*brand* (n.), sense 4). Seen in terms of language and its use, such judgement is, by implication, both unambiguous and ineradicable. 'Publickly branded with guilt; openly censured; of bad nature', Johnson's entry for *infamous* clarifies. 'Persons *infamous*, or branded with any note of infamy in any publick court of judicature, are, *ipso jure,* forbidden to be advocates', a citation from John Ayliffe's *Parergon Juris Canonici Anglicani* (1726) states in apposite illustration.

'Just animadversion', as Johnson indicates, should operate in similar ways. In other images in which the dictionary-maker is rendered judge, *animadversion* mediates between specifically legal uses in which punishment is temporal rather than spiritual, as well as those in which 'severe censure' or 'reproof' is deemed the rightful course.[17] Such methods, as the *Plan* confirms, will provide a means of determining whether words are to be 'acquitted' or condemned (*Yale* XVIII.45), offering too, the potential for legitimate restraint. Animadversion, Johnson notes, might serve to constrain 'barbarities in our conversation' which otherwise 'may in time creep into our writings' (*Yale* XVIII.44). The *Dictionary*, as Hodgart affirms, was to be 'a legislator of standard meanings'—a means by which Johnson was rendered 'fit and ready to govern the kingdom of letters'.[18]

Johnson 'revolutionized judgmental indication', Allan contends, stressing the diversity and extent of his proscriptive practice in this respect.[19]

As we might expect, such governance as implemented in the *Dictionary* is complex, offering continuities with the 1747 *Plan* (and the imposition of power it explores) as well as other patterns of departure. In terms of lexicographical tradition, precedent already existed for the kind of branding that Johnson at first envisaged. An obelisk in Phillips's own 'new world' of words indicates words from which approval is withheld; Kersey in his *Dictionarium Anglo-Britannicum* continued the same practice.[20] Johnson nevertheless decided on a different route as he sought to bring material for the *Dictionary* into order. Rather than 'marks of infamy' which might be realized in a specific set of symbols, the *Dictionary*'s entries reveal a wide-ranging qualitative metalanguage which is typically integrated within the body of the definition, elaborating and extending both meaning and the conditions of use.[21]

Diction of this kind allows, of course, for greater nuance and detail than a single proscriptive marker might have done. Yet the negative orientation of many such comments in Johnson's *Dictionary* is undeniable. Evaluative comment is marked; a word such as *coxcomical*, defined as 'Foppish, conceited', is deemed 'Unworthy of use'. Propriety, and its calibrated presence and absence, suggests other patterns of cultural value and reform. *Aversion*, we are informed, is used 'most properly' with *from*, 'less properly' with *to*, and 'very improperly' with *towards*. Gay's use of *head* ('very improperly applied') prompts judgement in which the sense of incorrectness is plain. Testimony does not work in Gay's favour; evidence is cast aside. Adjectival uses of *extempore* and *antiquary* are similar. 'It is sometimes used as an adjective, but very improperly', Johnson concludes of the former. As under sense 3 of *prejudice*, supporting evidence can provoke expostulation—and highly critical acts of reading: 'This sense, as in the noun, is often improperly extended to meanings that have no relation to the original sense.' 'Who', Johnson demands, 'can read with patience of an ingredient that prejudices a medicine?'[22]

Johnson specifies, too, a range of 'bad' and 'vicious' words, offering the kind of public proclamation of 'bad nature' which his definition of *infamous* outlines. Here we might include *fraughtage*, defined as 'lading; cargo' and illustrated by a citation from Shakespeare's *Comedy of Errors* ('Our *fraughtage*, sir, / I have convey'd aboard'), as well as *furnace, patronage,* and *period* in their use as verbs. 'He *furnaces* / The thick sighs from him', states a citation from *Cymbeline*; 'Your letter he desires/ to those have shut him up, which falling to him, / *Periods* his comfort', the messenger in Act 1 of *Timon of Athens* avers. All are 'bad', as is *trainy*, used by Gay and defined as 'belonging to train oil' ('Oil drawn by coction from the fat of a whale'), or *youthy*, glossed as 'young; youthful' and used as a deliberate stylistic departure in *Spectator* No. 296: 'The scribler had not genius to turn my age, as indeed I am an old maid, into raillery, for affecting a *youthier* turn than is consistent with my time of day.' *Insolence* ('To insult; to treat with contempt') is perhaps still worse, being adjudged 'a very bad word'. Supporting evidence from King Charles ('The bishops, who were first faulty, insolenced and assaulted') does not secure exemption.

While *viciousness*, as Johnson explains, is to be seen as distinct from active criminality (inclining rather to 'habitual faults' than 'criminal actions'), the sense of perceived transgression is plain. '*From* WHENCE' is a 'vitious mode of speech', we are informed under *whence* (sense 7) alongside evidence from Shakespeare and Spenser. Similar is '*From hence*'—'a vitious expression, which crept into use even among good authors, as the original force of the word ... was gradually forgotten', as Johnson avers under *hence*, sense 8. Here, too, the process of 'animadversion' seems at work, applied to uses deemed 'unjust' and which have, without such justification, 'crept' into use. The prepositions which appear in constructions such as *from whence* or *from hence* are deemed redundant and otiose. Johnson's own use, as in his definition of *body* sense 3, instead illustrates the proprieties at stake: 'A person; a human being; whence somebody.' *Whence*, Johnson asserts, means, in its own right, 'From what place' or 'From which place or person'.[23] In the norms the *Dictionary* recommends, such changing patterns of use are constructed as error while remediation is attempted through both example and advice. 'A word that has crept into conversation and low writing, but ought not to be admitted into the language', Johnson states of *shabby* with similar intent.

Disannul presents a parallel case: 'This word is formed contrary to analogy by those who not knowing the meaning of the word *annul*, intended to form a negative sense by the needless use of the negative particle.' Such usage—even if by 'good writers'—proceeds from misapprehension, Johnson contends. Intentionally reasoned interpretation prompts convictions of its 'absurdity'—and rightful proscription; *annul*, he observes, already signified the negative sense intended. *Disannul* 'ought therefore to be rejected as ungrammatical and barbarous', Johnson adjures; here, corrective rule proceeds not from 'the decrees of custom'—and Johnson's stated 'promulgation' of such—but from the codification of practices by which the state of language might be improved.[24] Attributions of 'barbarity' in the *Dictionary* meanwhile take us back to the image of lexicography as colonial enterprise in which 'civilisation' (and rigid governance) might bring wide-ranging cultural change. 'Uncivilised', Johnson notes in explanation of *barbarous*. Thenceforth, *banter*, and *wabble* are (among others) all found wanting in this respect. 'A barbarous form of an unnecessary word', Johnson likewise states for *viz*. Its frequency within his assembled citations is ignored.

Johnson's critical practice

A range of critical comments across the *Dictionary* will therefore steer the user in certain directions—and away from others. In Johnson's acts of remediation, words and meanings are identified which are, for whatever reason, disfavoured and which should not, henceforth, be used. Johnson's 'talent for criticism, both preceptive and corrective', as early observed by Hawkins, is marked.[25] Johnson's diction is qualitative, evaluative—and often, it seems, transparently subjective.

Criticism—and the role and responsibilities of the critic—was nevertheless a topic which also attracted Johnson's careful consideration both during and after the dictionary years.[26] As in Johnson's highly satirical *Idler* 60 and 61 (which he wrote in 1759), Dick Minim, an erstwhile brewer's apprentice, proclaims critical opinions on 'beauties and defects' with apparent confidence after reading a 'few select authors', as well as taking part in some coffee-house conversations on 'language and sentiments' (*Yale* II.185). It is perhaps unsurprising that Minim, like Roscommon,[27] is made a ready advocate of an 'academy of criticism'—an institution that might 'receive or reject', instilling national standards of elegance and taste. 'He whom nature has made weak, and idleness keeps ignorant, may support his vanity by the name of a critick', Johnson caustically observes (*Yale* II.184–5). Criticism here receives its own critical review. Both its basis—and its rationale—are seen as important.

In Johnson's engagement with good critical practice, primary rather than secondary engagement is repeatedly commended. Rather than opinion, it is books and wide reading, Johnson states, which inform sound judgement. The critic should not succumb to temptation, issuing judgements merely because these are expected. More rigorous foundations are required, Johnson suggests, lest criticism becomes an act of wilful censure, aggrandizing the critic perhaps—but failing to inform judgement, and subsequent practice, in any real sense. When subject to unreasoned criticism from all sides, even 'Mr. Rambler' can, Johnson notes, be lost in the sea of words: 'I cannot but consider myself amidst this tumult of criticism, as a ship in a poetical tempest, impelled at the same time by opposite winds, and dashed by the waves from every quarter' (*Yale* III.130). Criticism prompts, as a result, a further set of prescriptions in Johnson's work. 'It is', he writes in *Rambler* 92, 'the task of criticism to establish principles; to improve opinion into knowledge; and to distinguish those means of pleasing which depend upon known causes and rational deduction, from the nameless and inexplicable elegancies which appeal wholly to the fancy' (*Yale* IV.122).

Rambler 93, written in 1751, reveals similar deliberations. 'The duty of criticism', Johnson stresses, 'is neither to depreciate, nor dignify by partial representations, but to hold out the light of reason, whatever it may discover; and to promulgate the determinations of truth, whatever she shall dictate' (*Yale* IV.134). Truth, reason, and knowledge are yoked together, subordinating 'fancy'—and the subjective appreciation of 'inexplicable elegancies'—in ways which should, at best, foster sound critical exegesis. Criticism, Johnson writes, should 'reduce those regions of literature under the dominion of science, which have hitherto known only the anarchy of ignorance, the caprices of fancy, and the tyranny of prescription' (*Yale* IV.122). Johnson's political metaphors are, as we have seen in Chapter 4, commonplace in his work. Yet, as *Rambler* 92 suggests, if ignorance is productive of anarchy (and a fundamental lack of governance), unwarranted prescription (and proscription) can equally be a form of tyranny which the good critic should resist, whether in the state of language or elsewhere.

To what extent Johnson's theory of a principled criticism, articulated as he wrote the *Dictionary*, also informs his critical practice on words and their use remains therefore an interesting question. Johnson's interest in language, usage, and 'the light of reason' is, for instance, undeniable in his later *Lives of the Poets*. Addison's broken metaphor in ll.161–2 of his *Letter from Italy* ('Fired with that name — / I bridle in my struggling Muse with pain, / That longs to launch into a nobler strain') attracts, for instance, firm censure. 'To "bridle" a "goddess" is no very delicate idea; but why must she be "bridled?"', Johnson demands. If it is 'because she "longs to launch"', this is, he notes, 'an act which was never hindered by a "bridle"'. As Johnson concludes, 'She is in the first line a "horse", in the second a "boat"; and the care of the poet is to keep his "horse" or his "boat" from "singing"' (*Yale* XXII.651). The lines have moved into unreason; sense has been strained too far. Johnson as critic intervenes.

Gray is likewise seen as challenging 'the utmost limits of our language' in lines 13–19 of 'On a Distant Prospect of Eton College'. His use of 'gales' as 'redolent of joy and youth' prompts Johnson's critical dissent. A *gale*, as the *Dictionary* confirms, is 'A wind not tempestuous, yet stronger than a breeze'. In Johnson's deductive processes, Gray's lines yoke incompatible spheres of meaning. The capacity of a gale to evoke joy is limited; *redolent* is moreover 'sweet of scent', as Johnson further explained.[28] Johnson's censure of 'buxom health' in the same poem rests on similar principles. 'Gray seems not to understand the word', Johnson declares (*Yale* XXIII.1464). As the *Dictionary* affirms, the sense-divisions which *buxom* supports sits uneasily with Gray's chosen collocation. 'Health' seems neither 'obedient' or 'gay', nor 'wanton' or 'jolly'. Such patterns lie, in essence, outside what Johnson defines as *acceptation*: 'The meaning of a word, as it commonly received'. Informed by common practice ('our language') rather than poetic idiosyncrasy, Johnson's censure is both unequivocal and to the point.

Similar processes, and very similar diction, appear in the *Dictionary*. Swift's use of *quaint* to mean 'Affected; foppish' is, for example, firmly condemned: 'This is not the true idea of the word, which *Swift* seems not to have understood', Johnson states. Swift—like Gray— has used words in ways which depend on the idiosyncratic and individual, rather than a shared understanding of sense. If Johnson explains Swift's usage, and provides appropriate testimony, he also distances it from the senses which dictionary-maker and critic should alike commend. *Quaint* in the *Dictionary* means 'Nice; scrupulously, minutely, superfluously exact; having petty elegance' (sense 1), or 'neat, pretty, exact' (under sense 3), as well as 'subtly excogitated' under sense 4 (in what is arguably one of Johnson's less successful definitions). Swift's misguided use hence stands as one of the 'absurdities' or 'improprieties' which the dictionary-maker must, of necessity, constrain (*Yale* XVIII.75).

Similar is Spenser's use of *quaint* to mean 'quailed; depressed'. This is used 'I believe by a very licentious irregularity', Johnson notes. Locke's influence can seem pervasive. 'The chief end of language, in *communication*, being to be understood, words serve not for that end, when any word does not excite in the hearers the same idea which it stands for in the mind of the speaker', as Locke had stressed, here in a citation which Johnson deploys under *communication*.[29] 'Language being the conduit whereby men convey their knowledge, he that makes an ill use of it, though he does not *corrupt* the fountains of knowledge, which are in things, yet he stops the pipes', as Locke likewise states, in the *Dictionary*, under *corrupt*.[30] Rather than bringing 'understanding', we can, in such uses, run the risk of misapprehension. Usage can, Locke suggests, rightly be identified as 'ill' when meaning is potentially awry. The danger of such use, he adds, is that it will 'lead himself and others into Errors'.

Johnson's entries for *bellows* and *kickshaw* offer useful illustration in this respect. We are informed both of common usage (what 'we say'), as well as the creative departures which individual writers reveal. 'It has no *singular*; for we usually say *a pair of bellows*; but *Dryden* has used bellows as a *singular*', Johnson explains for the former. Here, if the conduit of language, in Locke's sense, is not entirely blocked, the flow of understanding is nevertheless impeded. Dryden's unconventional form is observed (and explained), but it is also firmly distanced from the patterns the *Dictionary* must recommend for wider use. Prescription and description unite in the recommendations that the dictionary as reference model must provide. *Kickshaw* reveals a parallel process. 'This word is supposed, I think with truth, to be only a corruption of *quelque chose*, something', Johnson writes. Yet, as he adds, '*Milton* seems to have understood it otherwise; for he writes it *kickshoe*, and seems to think it used in contempt of dancing.' Milton's 'ill' use of *magnetick* to mean 'magnet' is similar, being carefully separated from the meanings which the *Dictionary* endorses for wider use.

If we return to Johnson's 'bad' and 'improper' words, a similar set of processes is, in fact, often in evidence, informing the 'rigour of interpretative lexicography' in Johnson's hands (*Yale* XVIII.90). *Head*, Johnson states, for example, in a highly detailed entry, habitually refers in English to the 'top' or 'fore' part of an object or concept. As such, it can denote, as in sense 22, the 'Dress of the head' or in sense 20, the 'Upper part of a bed' or, as in senses 23 and 24, the 'Principal topicks of discourse' or the 'Source of a stream'. Yet it cannot, except with difficulty (and 'very improperly' as Johnson states), be 'applied to roots'. Even if evidence exists, as Johnson concludes in sense 30, this is anomalous when placed against the norms of use attested elsewhere. Gay's usage ('How turneps hide their swelling *heads* below') requires elucidation, hence its inclusion. Yet, given the *Dictionary*'s role as reference book, *head* in this sense cannot be recommended. Judgement is given, and Gay's use proscribed. The verdict, however, proceeds from the wider consideration of evidence and the 'suffrage' of language in use.

Peal, given as 'improperly' used by Shakespeare 'for a low dull tone', presents a similarly conflicted semantic space. Peals in English habitually ring out; a *peal* is 'A succession of loud sounds: as, of bells, thunder, cannon, loud instruments', Johnson explains. Hayward, Addison, Milton, and Dryden all offer testimony in support. Shakespeare's creative departure in Act III of *Macbeth* ('The shard-borne beetle with his drowsy hums / Hath rung night's yawning *peal*') conversely fractures this shared sense of meaning. Just as Johnson had noted in the *Plan*, even the 'correctest writers' can depart from habitual patterns of use (*Yale* XVIII.50); their role as model was not guaranteed. As Johnson explained, while 'we usually *ascribe* good, but *impute* evil', neither can, as a result, be seen as fixed in 'our licentious language': 'the use of these words, nor perhaps of any other, is so established as not to be often reversed by the correctest writers'. Shakespeare served, in effect, to prove his point, reversing the connotations of *peal* to denote what is 'dull' rather than 'bright' and, as in *Henry VI, Part II*, deploying *pilgrimage* to refer to 'time irksomely spent' ('In prison thou hast spent a pilgrimage, / And, like a hermit, overpast thy days'). Its conventional meaning, Johnson indicates, was rather different: 'A long journey; travel; more usually a journey on account of devotion'. The appearance of *exorcist* to mean 'An enchanter; a conjuror' in *All's Well that Ends Well* provides a further example of such potential conflicts in both sense and understanding.

Uses of this kind are therefore ingenious and arresting—but, as the *Dictionary* makes plain, they also deliberately depart from the patterns of meaning by which 'common English' must be defined. They are, in the *Dictionary*, hence identified as 'improper'. *Skyed* (defined as 'Enveloped by the skies' and declared to be 'unusual and unauthorised'), or Dryden's use of 'resume again' under *resume*, sense 4 ('improperly, unless the resumption be repeated') offer similar illustration. In line with his ideals of perspicuity, Johnson elides the obscurities and ambiguities which might otherwise prevent understanding. In each case, evidence is documented and explanation provided. Yet, if 'the rules of stile' are, as Johnson stressed, 'like those of law', these must arise, he adds, 'from precedents often repeated'. In this important respect, the laws laid down in the *Dictionary* are made those of 'common law' by which all are, in reality, to be ruled (*Yale* XVIII.50). Johnson's metalinguistic comments hence separate such idiosyncratic forms from those which 'common readers' might usefully adopt. If Johnson judges, judgement again proceeds from the complex role that the *Dictionary* as reference book must fulfil.

There can, conversely, be miscarriages of justice. As Johnson admits in *Rambler* 93 (*Yale* IV.132), 'critics, like all the rest of mankind, are very frequently misled by interest'. 'Interest'— Johnson's 'Share; part in any thing; participation' (*interest* (n.), sense 3)—can, in this light, expose judgement to the kind of subjectivity we see under *like*, *shabby*, or *shambling* in which the interpretative salience of evidence is rejected in favour of other claims where, at least with hindsight, 'fancy' can be conspicuous and power can, in reality, be used to different ends. Johnson's antipathy to *shabby* is, as we have seen, marked; the prevalence of *like* in the sense 'Near approach; a state like to another state' does not produce the approval we might, at least empirically, expect. Evidence is weighed, and found wanting; the form is 'common, but not just', Johnson decrees. 'This use is more frequent, though less just', he likewise observes under *trivial* in the sense 'Light; trifling; unimportant; inconsiderable'. Why *shambling* is 'bad' remains unclear. Here, too, dictionary order can point in different directions. In terms of the 'light of reason' (and modern descriptive practice), Johnson's objections can seem awry, and his diction of 'animadversion' misplaced; he seems to support not the 'decrees of custom', but edicts of his own.

Johnson, as David Crystal remarks, will at times 'back the wrong horse';[31] remediation is attempted when none is, in reality, required. As even in the later *OED*,[32] it can be tempting to see innovation as error and 'barbarism' as a product of ignorance—of 'not knowing' the 'proper' forms of words. Johnson can be an all too human lexicographer, using evidence as a means of calibrating meaning and usage, but being pulled, ineluctably, at other times by the sway of language attitudes, or his own patterns of preference. *Precarious* offers similar illustration; the changing patterns of sense-division are attributed to infelicity and lack of skill. 'No word is more unskilfully used than this with its derivatives', Johnson declares; 'It is used for *uncertain* in all its senses; but it only means uncertain, as dependent on others.' In similar ways, he can intentionally resist the change of word-class by which *miniature* and *extempore* are 'improperly' used as adjectives, or soundly condemn the use of *viz*, a contracted form of Latin *videlicet*. Johnson here moves closer to his original remit, in which judgement might secure the regulative order which English, for many, seemed to lack. Johnson's stated 'endeavours' to support, and 'promulgate the decrees of custom' do not always succeed (*Yale* XVIII.50). The state of language can be governed in different ways—democratic and open to 'suffrage' in most parts, but with occasional pockets of the overtly dictatorial. As Beal stresses, prescriptivism is, of necessity, a continuum, on which writers—and, indeed, even the same writer—can be differently located at different points.[33]

Nevertheless, as under *buxom*, we should note that the *Dictionary* can also reveal processes by which Johnson—here precisely like his readers—can, in fact, find his own 'opinion' being improved into knowledge, and the 'tyranny of prescription' left behind. *Buxom* 'means only *obedient*' even if it is 'is now made, in familiar phrases, to stand for *wanton*', Johnson had, for example, categorically stated in 1747 (*Yale* XVIII.51). 'It originally signified obedient', the *Dictionary* conversely acknowledges. Johnson's evidence in 1755 is made to confirm a neutral process of change and polysemy. *Buxom* in the *Dictionary* has three senses, illustrated by seven citations.[34] None is labelled 'familiar'; by the same token, it does not 'only mean' 'obedient'. *Lesser*, as the various editions of the *Dictionary* confirm, informs, in time, a similar pattern of acceptation. 'A barbarous corruption of *less*, formed by the vulgar from the habit of terminating comparatives in *er*; afterwards adopted by poets, and then by writers of prose', Johnson notes in 1755, attesting a process of change and diffusion in which the usage of the mass of the people (the 'vulgar') gradually spreads to the educated minority. As elsewhere, reading the semantics of eighteenth-century English can be complex; 'corruption', as, indeed, in comparable uses in the *OED*, often refers to change of external form,[35] while 'barbarousness', as we have seen, is undeniably negative, confirming the unlicensed departures that usage (and its acts of 'usurpation') can bring. Yet, as in the fourth edition of the *Dictionary* in 1773, Johnson can acknowledge that *lesser* has, in reality, 'all the authority which a mode originally erroneous can derive from custom'. What might initially have seemed error has, in time, been drawn within the 'sovereignty of words' (*Yale* XVIII.50) and the 'decrees of custom' which these reveal.

As in Fussell's image of the *Rambler* essays as 'dynamic enter-prises', we can therefore at times see a similar impetus in the *Dictionary* too.[36] Authority is complex, challenging where one might originally have desired to go. As Johnson concludes—with Horace—under *latter*: '*Volet usus Quem penes arbitrium est, & vis, & norma loquendi*'.[37] Dictatorship—and the illusions of power the dictionary-maker might entertain—must, he notes, ultimately be left behind. 'Use will require it, in whose hands is the judgment, power, and standard of speech', states Horace. Here true 'judge-ment' must—irrespective of individual desires—derive from the process of 'suffrage' and the common law of words.[38]

Doubt and the art of definition

At least quantitatively, Johnson's prescriptivism remains in fact a relatively minor aspect of his work. Qualitative judgements of vari-ous kinds are, Allen notes, appended to just over 2 per cent of Johnson's entries.[39] Attributions of 'barbarous' and 'barbarity' appear, as McDermott confirms, a mere twenty-one times in the 1755 *Dictionary*.[40] 'Viciousness' is rarer still, appearing in a scant handful of instances.[41] As Siebert contends, the negative metalan-guage which appears under words such as *shabby* or *whence* 'does not mean that the work as a whole is rigorously prescriptive, any more than the presence of a few humorous definitions . . . justifies the conclusion that most of Johnson's definitions are eccentric and subjective'.[42]

Instead, Johnson's reasoned apprehension of meaning, govern-ance, and the use of words can involve close consideration of the 'rules of style' and the contextual variations which thereby emerge, as well as a diction in which variation, doubt, and uncertainty can, as for spelling, displace the expected certainties of proscriptive dis-course. 'Discovering' the 'decrees of custom' is, as Johnson often reminds us, is by no means easy. '*Shakespeare* seems to have used this word for *anchoret*, or an abstemious recluse or person', he states, for example, under *anchor* in another attempt to deduce the meaning at stake. Similar is *gad*. 'It seems to be used by *Shakespeare* for a stile or graver', sense 2 affirms. 'Active; nimble; shifting to and fro. Such seems to be the meaning here', Johnson suggests under *wimble*. His metalanguage confirms the difficulty of judgement and interpretation alike. 'An ugly face; such, I suppose, as might be hewn out of a block by a hatchet', he states under *hatchet-face*. Johnson's entry for *dere* (v.) is particularly noteworthy. 'Some think that in the example it means daring', he points out. If Johnson glosses *dere* as 'To hurt', his readers—here in other processes of 'suffrage'—are nevertheless invited to bring their own judgement to bear on the evidence he provides.

Similar are Johnson's entries for *persuade* and *angry*. Here, precept and practice are placed in careful apposition. To *persuade* (sense 2) is, Johnson notes, 'To influence by argument or expostulation'. As such, he adds, '*Persuasion* seems rather applicable to the passions, and *argument* to the reason'. Yet, as in other aspects of Johnson's examination of English in use, what might seem preferable is not that which necessarily happens: 'This is not always observed', he concludes; usage varies, and the neatly contrastive distinction Johnson postulates is not sustained in practice. *Anger* as revised in the 1773 edition prompts a parallel process; we can be presented with a rational case for how language should be used. Yet this is, in turn, countered by what in reality takes place. 'It seems properly to require, when the object of anger is mentioned, the particle *at* before a thing, and *with* before a person', Johnson states. Nevertheless, as in *Rasselas*, we can 'differ from ourselves' (*Yale* XVI.105). 'This is not always observed', Johnson notes. Observation and discovery inform the information which is provided, in place of the diction of categorical rule. Norms remain variable, within and outside the *Dictionary*.

'To observe' in entries of this kind can therefore encompass the consideration of what writers (and speakers) do, as well as Johnson's own processes of remark.[43] His diction can be strikingly tentative, variously marked by 'perhaps' or 'seems' or the subjunctive in line with the doubts that must, in language, all too reasonably remain. 'Vile; worthless. Perhaps grating by the sound', Johnson postulates for *scrannel*. 'The meaning of this compound is doubtful', he confesses under *dew-burning*: 'Perhaps it alludes to the sparkling of dew'. 'Of this meaning I am doubtful', he writes under *stadle* (sense 3), adducing its possible sense as: 'A tree suffered to grow for coarse and common uses, as posts or rails'. 'It is doubtful whether this word be adjective or adverb', the entry for *headlong* (adv.) likewise admits. Similar is *vicety*: 'Of this word I know not well the meaning', Johnson notes.

Even notions of correctness can generate the same response. Johnson makes plain the problem of subjectivity, and 'partial representation'. 'I know not whether *Milton* has used this word very properly', Johnson writes under *lackey*, defined as 'To attend servilely'. His entry for *blush* (n.) is particularly interesting. As Johnson notes under sense 3 ('Sudden appearance'), this 'seems barbarous, yet', as he continues, it is 'used by good writers'. That illustrative example is given from Locke ('All purely identical propositions, obviously and at first *blush*, appear to contain no certain instruction in them') adds further weight to testimony of this kind as well as contributing to Johnson's qualitative hesitation. Johnson's subjunctives can, in similar ways, discomfit expectations of proscriptive exhortation. 'To obtain a dispensation from; to come to agreement with', he notes, for instance, in explaining *dispense* sense 5. Yet his uncertainty is conspicuous. Both modality ('may') and subjunctive ('be') qualify what might otherwise be advanced: 'This structure is irregular, unless it be here supposed to mean, as it may, to discount; to pay an equivalent.' Johnson carefully probes the possibilities of meaning; a definitive answer is absent.

Prescription can, as under sense 2 of *prejudice*, hence move towards carefully modulated advice which engages with the variable norms of use. Discussing the on-going change by which *prejudice* was, in the eighteenth century, increasingly being used to denote 'detriment' or 'injury', Johnson turns again to the subjunctive: 'It were [i.e. "might be"] therefore better to use it less.' Caution is necessary; the change is incomplete; usage might go either way. He resorts, too, to 'perhaps': 'perhaps *prejudice* ought never to be applied to any mischief, which does not imply some partiality or prepossession'.[44] While, as he states, 'In some of the following examples its impropriety will be discovered', precisely which ones these are is not made plain. An extensive set of citations from Shakespeare, Bacon, Locke, and Addison is provided. Here, too, the reader must decide, subjecting authority, impropriety, and Johnson's 'assembled authorities' to careful scrutiny.

Johnson's *Dictionary*, as such entries confirm, will not necessarily 'take away our doubts about words' or supply the 'conquest' and dictatorship which Chesterfield and others awaited. As under *shelfy*, we can, in contradistinction, be firmly reminded of what is not known or understood, in processes in which power is abdicated and meaning remains profoundly unsettled. 'I know not well the meaning in this passage, perhaps rocky', Johnson writes; 'Of this word I know not the meaning', the entry for *stammel* likewise observes. *To grudge* (sense 5) presented similar problems. The subjunctive again comes into play: 'To give or have any uneasy remains. I know not whether the word in this sense be not rather *grugeons*, or remains; *grugeons* being the part of corn that remains after the fine meal has passed the sieve.' Just as Collier had stated, here in a citation which Johnson deploys under *dogmatick*, it is learning which 'gives us a discovery of our ignorance'. 'It keeps us', he adds, 'from being peremptory and dogmatical in our determinations.'

Reason and the 'colours of words'

Across the *Dictionary*, a play of style and sense can therefore emerge in which correctness is relational, and meaning rendered more or less appropriate depending on the context in which particular words are used. Rather than the rigid binarisms of right and wrong that we prototypically expect, Johnson's engagement with meaning and what he later termed the 'colours of

words' (*Yale* XXI.183) will, in such ways, inform a closely calibrated analysis in which considerations of style, register, and tone
illuminate the information he provides. As under *brat*, while this
signifies 'a child', Johnson also stresses the 'contempt' on which
such uses depend. Explaining sense 7 of *fellow* (n.), Johnson draws
attention to the ways in which it is 'used sometimes with fondness;
some times with esteem; but generally with some degree of contempt'. Likewise, *notable*, when signifying 'Careful; bustling',
acquires overtones of 'contempt and irony' while *die*, 'used in the
style of lovers', takes on the sense 'To languish with affection'.
Disoblige, as Johnson specifies with delicate apprehension, is 'A
term by which offence is tenderly expressed'. If *addict* (v.) acquires
a 'bad sense' in the *Dictionary*, this, too, operates in descriptive
rather than prescriptive ways, indicating not condemnation but
the play of negative connotation. 'It is commonly taken in a bad
sense; as, *he addicted himself to vice*', as Johnson's invented
example makes plain.[45]

If Johnson lacks the modern terminology of register, it is this
which is often apparent in the comments that he makes, whether in
terms of style or the lexical and semantic variations that particular
contexts of use comport. As Iamartino stresses, meaning for Johnson is therefore densely connected to the pragmatics of use, to
collocation, and the semantic prosodies that language can reveal.[46]
Johnson notes, for example, the 'commercial' sense of *accrue*, as well
as that of *advice* and *instant*. Finance informs the entry for *defalcate*
while the diction of 'workmen' appears under, for example, *batten,*
batter, camber, bedding, moulding, and *dawk* ('A cant word among
the workmen for a hollow or incision in their stuff'). Johnson
comments on the 'dialect of trade' under *handsel* and that of 'sea-
men' in sense 11 of *foul*. *Cradle* likewise gains a sense used 'with
surgeons' ('A case for a broken bone, to keep off pressure') and
another 'with shipwrights' ('A frame of timber raised along the
outside of a ship by the bulge, serving more securely and commodiously to help to launch her').[47]

Johnson's stated disregard for 'mercantile...diction' does not therefore necessarily reflect his practice in the *Dictionary* itself (*Yale* XVIII.103).[48] Professional registers can be surprisingly diverse. Specific uses 'in anatomy' characterize *canal* (sense 3) while *elect* (sense 3) is applicable 'in theology'; grammarians necessitate other attributions of sense and meaning, as under sense 3 of *analogy* ('By grammarians, it is used to signify the agreement of several words in one common mode'). Under *alert*, Johnson distinguishes 'military' and 'common' senses (under sense 1 and 2 respectively). *Abduce* is given as 'A word chiefly used in physick or science'; 'chymical cant' is discussed under *gibberish*, 'military cant' under *fascine*, and the 'cant of taylors' under *cabbage*. Such uses illuminate Johnson's sense of *cant* (sense 2) as one aspect of professional 'jargon'—'A particular form of speaking peculiar to some certain class or body of men', he explains. *Peccant* is hence 'chiefly used in medical writers', while *chit* is, Johnson notes, 'a cant term with maltsters' who use it to mean: 'The shoot of corn from the end of a grain'. That poets necessitate other divides is made clear under words such as *bounteous* or *bespeak*; 'chiefly poetical', Johnson states under sense 4 of the latter. 'Out of use, except in poetry', the entry for *welkin* ('the visible regions of the air') likewise confirms.

Other aspects of Johnson's metalanguage work, in effect, to the same end, elaborating connotation alongside denotation, and probing the tonal landscape of language in use. As for *ludicrous*, the salience of historically accurate acts of reading is clear. In modern English, this is clearly pejorative, offering an easy alliance with habits of proscriptive thinking. For Johnson, as his definition affirms, the *ludicrous* instead inclines to that which is 'burlesque; merry; sportive; exciting laughter'.[49] As in *Rambler* 168, it is contextual, embedded in the consideration of decorum—as well as the web of associations, or the sense of the ridiculous, in which linguistic humour often resides (*Yale* V.126). Johnson's use in the *Dictionary* is similar, offering a descriptive normativity in which the associative norms of style and meaning work together. As under *jaunt*, the 'ludicrous' and 'solemn' act in mutual redefinition. Exploring the ways in which *jaunt* (n.) 'is commonly used ludicrously', Johnson can draw attention to other forms of stylistic departure; it is used 'solemnly by *Milton*', he adds. Under *deadly* (adv.), senses 1 and 2 specify meaning in all too serious ways. 'In a manner resembling the dead', Johnson notes for the former; 'Mortally', sense 2 amplifies. Yet, given the polysemies of use, *deadly*, as sense 4 explains, is also 'sometimes used in a ludicrous sense, only to enforce the significa-tion of a word'. 'John had got an impression, that Lewis was so *deadly* cunning a man, that he was afraid to venture himself alone with him', as Arbuthnot had written in his *History of John Bull*. Here the 'ludicrous', and the comic exaggeration it comports, is set apart from other meanings of the word; it characterizes a particular stance, and intended tone.

Johnson's comments on *quoth* ('now only used in ludicrous language'), or *naughty* ('Now seldom used but in ludicrous censure') provide parallel examples. Shakespeare's use of 'naughty' as a syno-nym for 'evil' was no longer tenable. Used of an adult in eighteenth-century English, the connotative values were very different. The metalanguage of 'burlesque' operates in a similar way, being used in the *Dictionary* to characterize *collop* ('child'), or in commenting on the prosodies of *doughty* which, as Johnson notes, 'is now seldom used but ironically, or in burlesque'. Language, as Johnson explains, is, in reality, a prime vehicle for the *burlesque*. Defined as 'Jocular; tending to raise laughter', *burlesque* is characterized by the presence of 'unnatural or unsuitable language or images'. At issue is decorum, and its deliberate incongruity for the purposes of humour.[50]

Johnson's 'low' words offer similar illustration. Such labels are habitually orientated to particular contexts of style and use rather than acting as proscriptive markers per se. High style connotes the formal; the low, in contrast, is used to characterize the colloquial and conversational, the robustly idiomatic and informal in John-son's world of words. Like the 'familiar', the 'low' hence often denotes orality, and the kind of style which is, as the lexicographer

James Murray later observed, removed from the 'dignity' of print.[51] Yet such words, as Johnson carefully explains in October 1751, are low only by convention. 'Our opinion . . . of words, as of other things arbitrarily or capriciously established, depends wholly upon accident and custom', he states. In reality, words only become low 'by the occasions to which they are applied' or, he warns, by 'the general character of those who use them' (*Yale* V.126). As for Locke, such signification is to be understood as arbitrary rather than innate: 'No word is naturally or intrinsically meaner than another', Johnson explains (*Yale* V.126).[52] Nevertheless, as Boileau had observed (and as Johnson here acknowledges), it is undeniable that 'a mean or common thought expressed in pompous diction, generally pleases more than a new or noble sentiment delivered in low and vulgar language' (*Yale* XVIII.125). Words of this kind are, Johnson admits, often disfavoured as a result; such negative reactions 'operate uniformly and universally across all classes'. Here, too, the difficulties of the dictionary-maker are plain.

Yet Johnson's stress on the linguistic consequences of what is merely arbitrary association is revealing. Words move, in effect, up and down in the associations they reveal. *Death's door*, as the *Dictionary* confirms, 'is now a low phrase' but, as Johnson's diction indicates, it was not always such. To be at *death's door*, as Johnson explains, hence treats of death but in ways remote from the solemnity of formal discourse. Similar is his entry for *good now*; characterized as 'a gentle exclamation or entreaty', it is also 'now a low word' though its origins—and earlier pattern of use—were different. In similar ways, *to ding* is 'low'—glossed as to 'bluster' and to 'bounce' (the latter signifies 'to boast; to bully' in 'familiar speech', as the relevant entry explains).[53]

Conversation and orality will, across the *Dictionary*, bring their own stylistic norms. *Adventuresome* is a 'low word, scarcely used in writing', Johnson notes. *Mucker* ('To scramble for money; to hoard up') is restricted in similar ways. If 'used by *Chaucer*,' it is, he specifies, 'still retained in conversation'. 'A word scarcely used but in low conversation', Johnson likewise notes for *despisable*. Johnson's sense of *clever*, sense 4, is similar—this is a 'low word', he notes, 'without a settled meaning', and confined to 'burlesque' and 'conversation'.[54] *Confounded* offers a further example, its vigorous colloquialism (in the sense 'hateful' or 'detestable') illuminated by the accompanying citation from Swift: 'Sir, I have heard another story, / He was a most confounded Tory; / And grew, or he is much bely'd, / Extremely dull before he dy'd.'

Reading the metalanguage of the past nevertheless often brings challenges of its own. Johnson's 'vulgar' words sound firmly pro-scriptive but, as Wild points out, they often participate in similar patterns, frequently being allied to the common and colloquial in other aspects of register and its role in language use.[55] 'Vulgarly reputed unwholesome', Johnson notes under *dogdays*, for example, drawing on popular conceptions about 'days in which the dogstar rises and sets with the sun'; a *foliomort* is 'vulgarly [i.e. commonly, by the masses] called *philomot*', he likewise affirms. In the *Diction-ary*, *philomot* gets its own entry, the currency of this alternative form being confirmed by its use in Addison's *Spectator*. As a citation from Watts elaborates under *simple*, '*Simple* philosophically signifies sin-gle, but vulgarly foolish'; Watts differentiates, in effect, between ordinary and scientific use. If *pretty*, as we are informed, is a 'very vulgar use', the accompanying citations from Abbot, Bacon (twice), Boyle, and L'Estrange should urge caution before we impose our modern—and highly negative—patterns of signification. *Pretty*, as Johnson's definition explains, is common and colloquial, and widely used as an intensifier. Similar patterns underpin Johnson's com-ment that *perilous*, in other changes in progress, is deemed 'vulgarly *parlous*' while *verjuice* is 'vulgarly pronounced *varges*'.

Nevertheless, as in the 'vulgar eyes' which appear under *cabinet* in the illustrative citation which Johnson provides from Swift ('In vain the workman shew'd his wit, / With rings and hinges counterfeit, / To make it seem, in this disguise, / A *cabinet* to vulgar eyes'), *vulgar* can (especially in the days before the General Education Act of

1870), also, of course, encompass a sense of uneducatedness in an era in which education was by no means a common property. Such shades of meaning point towards its later social downshifting— evident perhaps in Johnson's statement that *arse* is a 'vulgar phrase, signifying to be tardy, sluggish, or dilatory', in a sense verified by evidence from Butler's *Hudibras*: 'For Hudibras wore but one spur, / As wisely knowing, could he stir / To active trot one side of 's horse, / The other would not hang an *arse*.' If usage is common, it is also robustly colloquial in ways which might not be suitable for polite company. The prosodies of use are complex. As in *Rambler* 168, it is easy to approve delicacies of diction which characterize 'elegant writing or conversation'—less easy when these same words have passed into general use, being 'debased by vulgar mouths' (*Yale* V.127).[56]

Even *cant* can benefit from considerations similar in kind. Whether, as in the stated intentions of the 1747 *Plan*, the *Dictionary* will restrain such forms and 'secure our language from being over-run with cant, from being crowded with low terms, the spawn of folly or affectation' can, in reality, prompt further doubts and other images of departure (*Yale* XVIII.42). Professional 'cant' is, as we have seen, widely recorded, while the alliances of cant with slang are confirmed in ways which often prove equally illuminating. To *canary* is 'A cant word, which seems to signify to frolick', as Johnson notes against Shakespeare's use in *Love's Labour Lost*. *Fap* 'seems to have been a cant word in the time of *Shakespeare*', he states, adducing a meaning 'fuddled; drunk'. *Bamboozle* ('to deceive; to impose upon') is, in a similar way, defined by its affinities to slang rather than its use in 'pure and grave writings' – in which, as Johnson indicates, such usage would be incorrect indeed. Johnson's entry for *scruze*, and the interest in colloquial discourse this reveals, still provides an antedating of some 150 years for comparable evidence in the *OED*: 'This word, though now disused by writers, is still preserved, at least in its corruption, *to scrouge*, in the London jargon.'[57] Johnson's dismissive definition of *cant* as 'barbarous jargon' doesn't necessarily do justice to the care with which he documented such usages, and anatomized the meanings that they bear across a wide range of texts.

Cant, as Johnson's entry confirms, is therefore densely polysemous, encompassing the 'corrupt dialect used by beggars and vagabonds'— here in a form of language which had long had its separate lexicographic tradition[58]—as well as the clichéd and formulaic maxims which, deemed 'formal and affected', reveal the 'whining pretension to goodness' that Johnson firmly condemns in sense 3. 'Clear your mind of cant', he insisted to Boswell (*Life* 4.221). Here, Johnson's disapproval can indeed be plain. 'My mother', as he later recounted to Hester Thrale, 'was always telling me that I did not behave myself properly; that I should learn *behaviour*, and such cant'.[59] Johnson's sensitivity to style, as DeMaria affirms, was acute—and widely verified across the *Dictionary* in ways which repeatedly move outside the rigid binarisms of right and wrong, or conquest and control, in order to guide users to consideration of the tonal range with which words are, in reality, deployed.[60]

6

Defending the citadel, patrolling the borders

'My citadel shall not be taken by storm while I can defend it, and
...if a blockade is intended, the country is under the command of
my batteries', Johnson wrote to Strahan in November 1751. 'I shall',
he continued, 'think of laying it under contribution to morrow
Evening' (*Letters* I.50–1).[1] As Johnson's letter indicates, the *Dictionary*, and the words it contains, could readily become a territory to be
defended. It is the 'country'—a state of language which is by this
point well equipped with batteries of Johnson's own devising. The
'citadel', as Johnson's *Dictionary* explains, is a fortress or castle, the
place where arms are kept. Johnson's metaphors set out a war in
which words—as both territory and ammunition—are paramount.

Strahan's 'blockade', on the other side of this metaphorical conflict, conversely refers to the booksellers' threat to sever vital
supplies—in this respect, the paper to be used as well as the payment
which was due for Johnson's (and the amanuenses') work. Following the dictionary crisis of 1749,[2] it was, as both Johnson and
Strahan were well aware, almost a year since new copy had been
delivered. Johnson's own blockade could, from this point of view,
already seem well established. Johnson had, in 1746, presciently
described the agreement on which he and the booksellers had

Samuel Johnson and the Journey into Words. Lynda Mugglestone
© Lynda Mugglestone 2015. First published 2015 by Oxford University Press.

entered as a 'treaty' (*Letters* I.41). Five years later, this had, it seemed, already broken down. A state of siege was possible, with the lines of conflict firmly drawn.

In the event, Johnson would, of course, find himself forced neither to attack nor defend. His 'batteries' remained unused, the citadel intact; Strahan's threatened 'storm' was averted. The book-sellers demanded a meeting with Johnson at which terms were to be discussed and resolution reached. The *Dictionary* proceeded slowly but securely to publication three and a half years later. Johnson's military metaphors—situating language, and specifically lexicography, in a threatened realm of words—nevertheless resonated with a wider set of tropes which, as in the 1747 *Plan*, easily rendered language a site of conflict and potential invasion, of attack and of necessary defence. Questions of citizenship, and the naturalization—or otherwise—of loanwords, all impact on the wider identity of 'English'. As Chesterfield stressed, the border territories of language might, for the dictionary-maker, require careful scrutiny. Johnson's ambitions to 'discover the coast' (*Yale* XVIII.58) could, in this light, present other difficulties for the lexicographer's intended course.

As we will see, disputes over the legitimate territories of language (and languages) were by no means uncommon by the eighteenth century, as were associated perceptions of lexical migration and settlement, incursion and defeat. Patrick Hanks's comment that 'We must bear in mind that foreign borrowings would not have seemed such a prominent feature of English to Johnson as they do to us' can, in this respect, demand careful examination.[3] Here, too, issues of power—as well as conquest and submission—were marked. As Sir Thomas Browne—a frequent source in the *Dictionary*—had warned, 'Nations that live promiscuously, under the Power and Laws of Conquest, do seldom escape the loss of their Language with their Liberties.'[4] John Wilkins, a prominent member of the Royal Society, made a similar point in 1668: 'the Laws of forein Conquests usually extend to Letters and Speech as well as

Territories; the Victor commonly endeavouring to propagate his own Language as farre as his Dominions.'[5] Yet, as the history of English demonstrated, conquest could also take place in other, less obvious, ways. Lexical enrichment, deriving from foreign sources, could extend the native word-hoard—but also potentially over-power it. 'If too many Foreign Words are pour'd in upon us, it looks as if they were design'd not to assist the Natives, but to Conquer them', Dryden observed in 1697.[6]

Recent history confirmed the on-going salience of these debates. Writing in the *Spectator* in the early eighteenth century, both Swift and Addison drew attention to the ambiguities of victory and defeat, conquest and conquered. Britain, Addison noted with patriotic pride, was indeed in the ascendant in the War of Spanish Succession (a conflict then in its tenth year, and in which Britain was opposed to both France and Spain). Nevertheless, the cross-currents of power and dominance in the lexicon were very different. 'Our Warriors are very Industrious in propagating the *French* Language, at the same time that they are so gloriously successful in beating down their Power', he pointed out; the soldiers 'send us over Accounts of their Performances in a Jargon of Phrases, which they learn among their Conquered Enemies'.[7] Addison raised questions of transparency as well as need. 'When we have won Battels which may be described in our own Language, why', he demands, are 'our Papers filled with so many unintelligible Exploits, and the *French* obliged to lend us a Part of their Tongue before we can know how they are Conquered?' Paradoxically, a new Norman conquest, occupying language if not land, could seem imminent. 'The present War has so Adulterated our Tongue with strange Words, that it would be impossible for one of our Great-Grandfathers to know what his Posterity have been doing', Addison averred, deploying other familiar tropes in which linguistic change and potential incomprehensibility combine.[8] Johnson read his words attentively. Addison's cautions reappear in the *Dictionary* in telling illustration of *adulterate*, defined as 'To corrupt by some foreign admixture; to contaminate'.

Chesterfield's letter to the *World* in November 1754 revealed a similar preoccupation with identity and the national tongue, as well as the role which lexicography might play in such domains. Global as well as local considerations intervene. Conquest is rendered a feat of words as well as strength in Chesterfield's account of the spread of French as global language during the reign of Louis XIV; if 'the success of [Louis's] arms first opened the way', it was, he adds, equally clear that 'a great number of most excellent authors who flourished in his time, added strength and velocity to it's progress'. Reified as a form of lexical colonialism, such 'progress' is, importantly, now seen as extending to English too. 'I have therefore a sensible pleasure in reflecting upon the rapid progress which our language has lately made, and still continues to make, all over Europe', Chesterfield remarks. Led by writers such as Newton, Swift, Pope, and Addison himself, this is given as 'A nobler sort of conquest, and a far more glorious triumph, since graced by none but willing captives!'[9]

While this alignment of language and territorial advance is commended (at least when seen in terms of the native tongue), other anxieties self-evidently remain. Greater defence at home is required, Chesterfield stresses; complacency is unwise. The danger that English might 'be overwhelmed and crushed by unnecessary foreign ornaments' is not to be forgotten. Johnson's forthcoming *Dictionary* would, Chesterfield suggests, make its own contribution to the advance of the national tongue.[10] More significantly, he also anticipates the increased stringency towards non-native words which it would bring. 'The time for discrimination seems to be now come', Chesterfield avers: 'Toleration, adoption and naturalization have run their lengths.'[11] Loanwords offered other opportunities for rule. Issues of protection and defence, and power and suppression, are firmly brought to the fore.

Defending the citadel of words

Johnson's diction, in both *Plan* and the 1755 'Preface', clearly shares some of this historical as well as ideological positioning. While the

144

Dictionary was published in a rare interval of peace, work on it began during the closing years of the War of the Austrian Succession (1740–48) in which Britain was opposed to France, as well as Spain, Prussia, and Bavaria. 1744 had also seen an attempt at a more literal invasion of Britain in which France had been thwarted only by the weather and the deterrent effect of a large British fleet despatched to the Channel.[12] Yet even the peace of 1755 was arguably notional rather than actual. Hostilities of various kinds had already broken out. Language and national anxieties easily combine.[13] By May 1756, Britain and France were once again at war. Conflict would not end until 1763.[14]

Popular concerns about identity, invasion, and subordination are echoed in Johnson's spirited rejection in 1755 of the idea that Britain might, in the future, be reduced 'to babble a dialect of *France*' (*Yale* XVIII.109). While invasion is, at this point, posited as a specific consequence of translation,[15] Johnson also sets 'dialect' against 'language', configuring subordinate against superordinate. He envisions—and resists—a state of conquest and subjugation in which not only England, but English too, has been subsumed into French. A *nation*, as the *Dictionary* confirms, is defined at least in part by its speakers and the language they use. It is 'A people distinguished from another people; generally by their language, original, or government'. As in his stated intent to seize the 'palm of philology' (*Yale* XVIII.109), Johnson's 'Preface' cuts French dominance in language—and lexicography—down to size. Linguistic proficiency and *babbling* enact their own patterns of discrimination. Denoting a 'copious stream of speech', *babbling* also evokes the meaninglessness (and irrationality) which such unwarranted fluency might bring; a *babbler* is 'An idle talker; an irrational prattler', the *Dictionary* explains, offering additional illumination for Johnson's patriotic slight towards the French.

As for Addison, the trajectories of occupation and independence can be matched by a sense of prescriptive (and proscriptive) resolve. 'Forgive my Transports on a Theme like this, / I cannot bear a

French metropolis', as Johnson had early declared in his poem 'London' (*Yale* VI.53); that the capital might become 'the common shire of Paris' was seen as no cause for celebration. To *Frenchify*, as the *Dictionary* records, evoked other forms of potential usurpation by which both language and culture might come to change. Documented with reference to Shakespeare's *As You Like It*, and William Camden's *Remaines Concerning Britaine* (1567), Johnson's entry testifies to a form of resistance which was, in fact, widely reified in linguistic as well as cultural terms.[16] 'To infect with the manner of France; to make a coxcomb', Johnson's accompanying definition states. As in James Smythe's *The Rival Modes* (1727) or Samuel Foote's *The Englishman in Paris* (1753), pointed satire could be directed at fashionable French affectation, especially as realized in an excess of imported diction from across the Channel. Johnson's targeted use of *flambeaux* in describing the activities of Melissa in *Rambler* 191 (*Yale* V.234) is similar. The 'tyranny...of fashion' (*Yale* XVIII.74) all too easily introduced other forms of oppression and potential rule. French as cultural signifier, as Hannah Grieg has recently demonstrated, offered *bon mots* for the *bon ton* and *beau monde* in ways which smacked of exclusivity and membership of a social elite.[17] By such means, as the *Dictionary* confirms, French *dernier* had—at least for certain sections of society—come to exist alongside English *last*, and French *gout* (deemed 'affected cant' by Johnson) alongside *taste*.

The fact that 'Our language, for almost a century, has, by the concurrence of many causes, been gradually departing from its original *Teutonick* character, and deviating towards a *Gallick* structure and phraseology' is, in Johnson's 'Preface', therefore recorded with regret (*Yale* XVIII.95). Still more deleterious, Johnson makes plain, are the structural changes to which such widespread borrowing might, if unimpeded, lead. While, outside the *Dictionary*, the Anti-Gallican society, founded in 1745, waged war against the importation of French goods,[18] in Johnson's patriotic rhetoric dictionary-maker and dictionary-users are to unite in a similar campaign against the 'traffick' of words. 'Our endeavour', Johnson declares, ought to be 'to recal' English from unwarranted importation and its consequences (*Yale* XVIII.95); it is 'our ancient volumes', reflective of the national heritage, which should instead be made 'the ground-work of stile'.[19]

Here at least Johnson and Chesterfield seem in accord. Patriotism and prescriptivism will, it seems, dovetail with precision. As in the *Plan*, preserving the 'purity' of the 'English idiom' was part of the 'chief intent' Johnson specifies. This 'seems to require nothing more than that our language be considered so far as it is our own', he added (*Yale* XVIII.29). As Johnson proclaims, he had 'attempted a dictionary of the *English* language' in a 'scheme of including all that was pleasing or useful in *English* literature', and which is characterized by 'examples and authorities from the writers before the restoration, whose works I regard as *the wells of English undefiled*' (*Yale* XVIII.74, 94, and 95). In making the *Dictionary*, 'a national purpose was clear from the outset', Cannon affirms.[20]

Writing French resistance

Dictionaries, like other texts, perhaps inevitably reveal a world-view in which the partisan and parochial can be all too apparent. Johnson's work is no exception. His imaging of invasion in 1755 nevertheless contrasts sharply with the dictionary-maker's potential to invade and rule the 'new world' of words which the 1747 *Plan* had advanced (*Yale* XVIII.58). Johnson has, in effect, changed sides. He writes from within the state of language in which incursion is formally to be resisted. It is the 'injury of the natives' which he now contemplates, as well as the kind of redress that the dictionary-maker might make. As he states of the practices adopted in the *Dictionary*, 'The words which our authours have introduced by their knowledge of foreign languages, or ignorance of their own, by vanity or wantonness, by compliance with fashion, or lust of innovation, I have registred as they occurred, though commonly only to censure them, and warn others against the folly of naturalizing useless foreigners to the injury of the natives' (*Yale* XVIII.85). Johnson's morally orientated metalanguage, in which the sins of 'vanity', 'lust', and 'wantonness' all appear, does not suggest encouragement. In Johnson's syntax, 'foreigners' and 'natives' are rendered antithetical. Within the *Dictionary*, associated images of language and identity can assume a range of forms. 'A mode of speech peculiar to the French language', Johnson notes, for example, under *Gallicism*. Indicating one way in which intended boundaries might be enforced, what is deemed 'peculiar' ('Appropriate; belonging to any one with exclusion of others') to one language cannot, Johnson suggests, easily pertain to another. 'In English I would have *Gallicisms* avoided, that we may keep to our own language, and not follow the French mode in our speech', an accompanying quotation from Henry Felton avers.[21] Johnson's entries for *Latinism* and *Grecism* mark out other territorial divides.[22] *Anglicisms*, in contrast, occupy a very different domain. Defined as 'A form of speech peculiar to the English language; an English idiom', these, Johnson confirms, were entirely consonant with the aims of the *Plan*. Unmarked throughout the *Dictionary*, they reflect what 'we' do, as in Johnson's comments on the distribution of *shore* and *bank*: 'We say, properly, the *shore* of the sea, and the *banks* of a river, brook, or small water'.[23] 'We now say, *to roast a man*, for *to teaze him*', he states under *grilly* (v.): 'We', as the *Dictionary* makes clear, are transparently British—not French or Greek.[24]

'Nosism' and its associative tribal 'we' can, as Paul Rastell suggests, prove a highly effective ideological tool.[25] As in Johnson's entry for *comport* ('To bear; to endure'), this underpins the contrastive—and potentially incompatible—identities which appear. *Comport* in this sense, we are informed, is 'a Gallick signification, not adopted among us'. Supporting evidence from *The Civil Wars* by the poet and historian Samuel Daniel (1585–1623) is provided but, Johnson indicates, by no means to be seen as representative. In other manifestations of prescriptive and proscriptive resolve, Johnson's stance, as under sense 6 of *manage* ('To treat with caution or decency'), can seem deliberately combative. 'Not to be imitated', Johnson instructs. It is a 'Gallicism'—an idiom which is, by definition, not 'peculiar' to English (and hence firmly distinct from the other five senses of *manage*, all of which remain unmarked). Similar concerns appear under *give*. Sense 1 ('To rush; to fall on; to give the assault') is 'A phrase merely French, and not worthy of adoption'. Senses 3 ('To move') and 5 (the idiom 'to give into') are similarly set apart. A 'French phrase', he notes for both. Use of *delices* ('Pleasures') or *renounce* when signifying 'To declare renunciation' prompts similarly restrictive judgments. 'A mere Gallicism', Johnson states of the latter.

Such boundaries are frequently in evidence; *tour* used to signify 'Turn; revolution' is 'rather French than English', while *attend* in the sense 'expect' is 'French'. 'This sense is purely Gallick', Johnson likewise specifies under *flatter* sense 3. Explained as 'to please, to sooth', testimony is provided by Dryden's translation of De Fresnoy's *De Arte Graphica* ('A consort of voices supporting themselves by their different parts make a harmony, pleasingly fills the ears and *flatters* them').[26] 'This word, like *charges* in the same sentence, is merely gallick', Johnson writes under *disinteressement*, here with reference to supporting evidence from Prior: 'He has managed some of the charges of the kingdom with known ability, and laid them down with entire *disinteressement*.' 'A French word which with many more is now happily disused', the entry for *souvenence* ('Memory; remembrance') observes. Evidence of obsolescence can prompt approbation rather than regret.

While principles of 'projected gain', as McMahon notes, often account for the processes of lexical transfer from one language into another,[27] Johnson's stance can seem markedly oppositional. As under *ruse* (explained as 'Cunning; artifice; little stratagem; trick; wile; fraud; deceit') or *transpire* in the sense 'To escape from secresy to notice', ideas of need, or necessary supplementation, are resisted. *Transpire* is 'a sense lately innovated from *France*, without necessity'; *ruse* is 'a French word neither elegant nor necessary'. Dryden's

attempted importation of French-derived *fraischeur* in his 1661
'Panegyric' on Charles II's coronation ('Hither in Summer-ev'nings
you repair, / To taste the *fraischeur* of the purer air') encounters
a particularly scathing response. 'A word foolishly innovated by
Dryden', Johnson declares.

Dryden's desired meaning could, of course, have been conveyed
with greater transparency by either of the interpretative glosses Johnson provides; 'freshness' and 'coolness' were alike well-established
in English, offering, from Johnson's point of view, further evidence
of Dryden's wilful deviation and unwarranted appropriation in this
respect.[28] *Prosternation* prompts a similar probing of the rational
case for loanwords and their importation. Even if this derives from
Latin rather than French, it is, Johnson declares with proscriptive
resolve, 'not to be adopted'. Both lexical and semantic utility seem in
doubt. Explained as 'Dejection; depression; state of being cast down;
act of casting down', *prosternation* belonged to a domain which, as
Johnson's own experience confirmed, was already replete with syn-
onyms. The *Dictionary* documents *despair, dejection, melancholy,*
and the state of being *dark*; Johnson in his letters writes of 'black fits'
and, in another metaphor, of the 'black dog' of depression.[29] As he
noted, his policy in the *Dictionary* was to admit, at least by preference, only those 'additions of later times . . . such as may supply real
deficiencies' and 'are readily adopted by the genius of our tongue'
(*Yale* XVIII.105, 95). *Prosternation* fails, for Johnson, on both
counts.

Chesterfield's diction of 'discrimination' can, in such ways,
acquire a range of correlates in Johnson's own prose. That all
words are 'not equally to be considered as parts of our language'
was, for example, plain from the beginning. As Johnson had stressed
in 1747, a lexicon is complex, containing 'different classes' (*Yale*
XVIII.31, 33); if some words are 'naturalized and incorporated',
others inevitably 'still continue aliens'. In Johnson's state of language, these are not 'subjects' but 'auxiliaries', demanding different
forms of representation (*Yale* XVIII.31). 'It will be proper to print

those which are incorporated into the language in the usual character, and those which are still to be considered as foreign, in the italick', he states of the methods the *Dictionary* would adopt (*Yale* XVIII.33). Johnson's italics offer a form of visual segregation, easily revealing the 'alien' status of, say, French-derived *fricassee, quelquechose,* or *canaille.* The latter, defined as 'The lowest people; the dregs; the lees; the offscouring of the people', is, for instance, 'a French term of reproach' (and thereby distinct from the unmarked 'a term of reproach' used in entries for words such as *barbarian* and *demi-man*). While, as Richardson's *Clarissa* confirmed, *canaille* could indeed be used in English,[30] it remained, for Johnson, resonant of the unassimilated 'other' whose identity as 'auxiliary' resides in another nation entirely.

Naturalization and the use of words

As Isabel Balteiro comments, the treatment of foreign words can be a particularly useful index when attempting to gauge prescriptive or descriptive orientation within lexicographic practice. The careful recording of words which exist on the linguistic periphery verifies the presence of the descriptive, she contends; the prescriptive, in contrast, often sets out a range of qualitative and evaluative parameters of desirability. If a targeted silence on disputed forms appears in some works, it is Johnson who, for Balteiro, exemplifies other aspects of prescriptive practice in this regard. As in Johnson's *Dictionary*, she postulates, 'mentioning the undesired word in one way or another may be more effective', not least 'since the non-appearance of a form may be interpreted by the user as simply... neglect or an omission'.[31] In terms of lexicography, Balteiro concludes, an approach characterized by a 'descriptive prescriptivism' might, in the end, prove best—one in which the patterns of actual usage are described alongside additional information on language attitudes and reception, including 'on whether a form may be accepted by some and refused by others'.[32]

The extent to which Johnson would, in reality, endeavour to defend the 'citadel' of language or, indeed, sustain a lexical 'blockade' can, in this light, present a range of interesting issues across the *Dictionary*. Johnson's rhetoric of stalwart defence is not necessarily maintained. As we will see, if reason—and a rational exploration of what English might seem to need—points in one direction, the historical mutability of the national tongue, as well as the salience of usage can direct attention to perspectives which are very different in kind. Johnson's entry for French-derived *finesse* provides a useful example. This could, as Johnson's definition proves, easily be glossed by words such as 'artifice' and 'strategem'. While also loans, these were now well established in English use, exemplifying the process by which 'aliens' could indeed be enfranchised within the native tongue. 'These words have been *enfranchised* among us', Johnson's entry for *enfranchise* records, adducing Isaac Watts in support. *Finesse*, Johnson indicates, remains outside such processes. Placed in italics, it manifests the kind of visual segregation Johnson describes in the *Plan*. It is 'an unnecessary word', he notes, drawing on the kind of reasoned resistance we have already seen at work under *fraischeur*.

Yet, as Johnson indicates, the on-going momentum of change is also clear. *Finesse* 'is creeping into the language', he adds. While the diction of need suggests resistance and 'animadversion', Johnson's present progressive nevertheless orientates the entry towards continuity and duration. The entry is balanced between desire and pragmatism, between the wish to withhold admission and the sense that English is already on the move. A careful engagement with recent practice moreover presents other forms of 'suffrage' (and authority) for readers of the text. 'A circumstance not much to be stood upon, in case it were not upon some *finess*', Hayward confirms in illustration of its use. Such patterning is by no means uncommon. Against the stasis Chesterfield (and others) desired, we are instead made to confront the realities of naturalization as a process by which, as Johnson states, 'an admission into common speech' must secure entry into English (*Yale* XVIII.31), just as 'aliens' will, in time, become 'natives' depending on the facts of use. For some words, of course, this process is yet to begin. As the *Plan* explains, 'the state of aliens' inevitably distinguishes some forms used in English. For these, the retention of non-native phonology, spelling, or morphology indicates, as Johnson carefully explains, that 'no approaches towards assimilation' have been made (*Yale* XVIII.32). As under French-derived *beau* (n.), he clearly feels it necessary to add information on how *beau* is to be pronounced ('It is sounded like *bo*'), as well as on its non-native pattern of inflection: it 'has often the French plural *beaux*'. Similar is *amour* where, as Johnson explains, 'the *ou* sounds like *oo* in *poor*' (rather than *ou* in native words such as *house*). The state of being 'fully naturalised', Johnson notes, removes such distinctive markers.[33] *Delice* and *dernier* offer further examples. Identified as 'merely French' (a fact confirmed by the Gallic enunciation they required), Johnson's metalanguage draws attention to the absence of assimilation. To be 'merely' French, as the entry for *merely* explains, is to be 'simply; only' French—unlike, say, the fully naturalized *frequent* or *loyal* which, while French in origin, receive no such additional comments. Johnson's *merely* signifies 'for this and for no other purpose',[34] foregrounding the 'alien' as well as the consciously Francophonic patterns on which importations of this kind often relied. Whether Johnson's intent is proscriptive is debatable; 'French', like 'gallick' (or, indeed, *grecism*), affirms the facts of non-naturalization and continued identity in Johnson's 'state of aliens'. 'A trifle; a thing of no importance: a word not naturalised', Johnson likewise notes for *bagatelle* in 1773.

Johnson's entries for *perdue* and *phenomenon* conversely occupy a very different point in his modelling of change. Here, if the borders of Englishness have been crossed, Johnson's absence of resistance is striking. 'This word, which among us is adverbially taken, comes from the French *perdue*, or *forlorn hope*', he explains for the former. While nosism is again conspicuous, it is orientated to a different end; the processes of assimilation, Johnson explains, underpin a change of grammatical form as *perdue* moves from Gallicism to an idiom of eighteenth-century English. *Phenomenon* depends on a similar process. Initially adopted as *phænomenon*, the ligature *æ* had, Johnson indicates, unambiguously signalled its alien status. Yet, as he expounds, the fact of 'being naturalised' has 'changed the *æ*, which is not in the English language, to *e*'. Assimilation and adoption are enacted in usage, gradually bringing *phenomenon* into line with other English words.

For Johnson, naturalization of this kind is to be encouraged; *æ*, as he points out, 'seems not properly to have any place in the English'. As a result, while *phænomenon* remains as a variant spelling, it is not endorsed. History, as Johnson makes plain, instead affirms a long-standing process of naturalization in this context. 'The *æ* of the Saxons has been long out of use', he states, 'being changed to *e* simple'. In turn, 'in words frequently occurring, the *æ* of the Romans is, in the same manner, altered'.[35] Similar comments attend the ligature *œ*, where considerations of 'our language' also intervene.[36] 'This is no English word', Johnson comments under *defoedation* ('The act of making filthy; pollution') in 1773. 'At least, to make it English, it should be written *defedation*', he adds in clarification.[37] As in the *Plan*, the process of 'making English' is confirmed by 'conformity to the laws of speech' into which new words are— and, importantly, continue to be—'adopted' (*Yale* XVIII.32).

Sublime (n.) and *verdant* ('green') confirm similar acts of on-going adoption, if at other points on Johnson's cline of naturalization. 'This word is so lately naturalized, that *Skinner* could find it only in a dictionary', Johnson writes, for instance, under the latter.[38] He provides early testimony from Milton, though the phrasing of his definition rightly indicates the word's recent and wider use.[39] If *sublime* is, in origin, also a 'Gallicism' (and hence 'peculiar to the French language'), usage has likewise served to remove such restrictions, rendering it, as Johnson specifies, 'now naturalized'. To refer to 'the grand and lofty style' by means of the *sublime* has become part of English, as recent citations from Pope and Addison duly attest. 'The sublime in writing rises either from the nobleness of the thought, the magnificence of the words, or the harmonious and lively turn of the phrases, and that the perfect sublime arises from all three together', Addison stressed in 1713.[40]

Words such as *adroitness* and *adroit* exist in the *Dictionary* at a different point of naturalization again. 'Neither this word, nor *adroit*, seem yet completely naturalized' into English, Johnson's entry for the former states. If *adroitness* remains without illustrative citation, Charles Jervas's introduction to his recent translation of Cervantes's *Don Quixote* (posthumously published in 1742) is used to verify *adroit*. As here, Johnson's temporal modifiers carefully map the currents of change. 'Now' and 'lately', as we have seen, document the processes of adoption for *sublime* and *verdant*. Johnson's use of 'yet', in contrast, signals both the level of diffusion as the *Dictionary* was composed, as well as indicating the potential for further change. *Yet*, when preceded by a negative, signifies 'at this time' or 'hitherto' as Johnson explains.[41] As a result, if naturalization—as under *adroitness*—'yet' remains incomplete, later language history, Johnson presciently suggests, may well tell a different story. Johnson's entry for *access* (sense 4) is similar. This, he writes, 'is sometimes used, after the French, to signify the returns or fits of a distemper'. However, it 'seems yet scarcely received into our language'. Here, usage remains variable; if used 'sometimes' (as in the supporting citation from Samuel Butler), *access* in this sense can still display conscious reference to its origins, being used 'after the French' rather than being fully assimilated. Nevertheless, as Johnson indicates, this, too, may come to change. What is 'now' or 'yet' is by no means reflective of the future state of English. As under *enceinte*, which has a similar temporal restriction in the *Dictionary* ('Inclosure; ground inclosed with a fortification. A military term not yet naturalised'), Johnson can simply note the patterns of restricted use in the liminal spaces of where 'English' might be said to be.

Johnson's often-assumed assiduity in taking up arms in the cause of the national tongue can, as such entries confirm, demand some reassessment. Against Chesterfield's desire for certainty, Johnson's fondness for hedges such as 'seems', alongside his patterns of temporal qualification, can again carefully focus attention on the possibilities of on-going change and variation. Norms, as under *access*, are made relative rather than absolute; comment, as under *mensal* (defined as 'Belonging to the table; transacted at table') or *trait* can turn to the limits of both frequency and use. 'Conversation either *mental* or *mensal*', Richardson stated, for instance, in *Clarissa* in 1747. Here, the source language is Latin (<*mensalis*) rather than French, but the constraints of assimilation and use remain the same.[42] 'A word yet scarcely naturalised', the *Dictionary* avers in ways which again suggest the latitude for future change. *Trait* ('A stroke; a touch') is accorded a similar liminality. 'Scarce English', Johnson writes. It remained, for Johnson, on the borders of adoption—'alien' rather than 'denizen',[43] a fact confirmed by its pronunciation /treɪ/ (rather than assimilated /treit/) across eighteenth- and nineteenth-century English. As the *OED* notes, its modern and dominant sense emerges only from the early 1750s.[44] Johnson's use of *scarce*, as the *Dictionary* confirms, refers to the quantitative. To be *scarce* is to be 'not plentiful'; 'rare; not common'.[45]

Even Johnson's use of 'Gallick', or his varied attributions of 'Gallicism', can, in this light, suggest other complexities of descriptive and prescriptive practice. If, as under *trait*, *delice*, and *dernier*, the 'Gallick' and 'French' demarcate naturalized and unnaturalized in Johnson's state of language, does this set out what must be seen as an essentially proscriptive boundary? Or, as in similar uses in the *OED*, does it instead engage with the realities of language practice— and the play of marked and unmarked forms, aliens and denizens, in a language on the move? *OED1*'s division of 'aliens' and 'denizens', for example, closely resembles the parameters which Johnson explored.[46] *Correction*, in the sense 'The condition of being corrected or correct (in style)', and *garnish* ('Furnished or fitted with accessories') are both identified as 'Gallicisms'. So, too, (among many others) are *debit* in the sense 'to put into circulation; to spread (news) etc', *approfound*, defined as 'To go deeply into, to search the depth of (a subject)', and *arrestation*, deemed 'more or less a Gallicism' in the sense 'apprehension by legal authority'. A '"Frenchy" kind of diction', the *OED*'s entry for *Gallicism* explains, indicating the presence of reference models in which non-native patterns remain dominant.[47] *Frenchy*, the *OED* explains, is 'characteristic of what is French (as opposed to English, etc.); French in nature, French-like'.[48] In the *OED*, in line with its own objectives, the aim is to describe—rather than proscribe—the patterns of use which are observed, isolating, too, the border territories in which words move.

Johnson's own definition—and use—of *Gallicism* can, in reality, suggest similar patterns. Gallicisms, he notes, can be further identified by idioms such as 'he *figured* in controversy; he *held* this conduct; he *held* the same language that another had *held* before'. While the individual lexemes in such examples are English, the tenor—and mode of expression—remains resolutely French. A similar interpretative stance informs, say, *give* in the sense 'to move' (*give*, sense 3), as well as Johnson's comments on Dryden's 'The Hind and the Panther' (1687) in which *renounce* is used to mean 'To declare renunciation'. 'On this firm principle I ever stood; / He of my sons, who fails to make it good, / By one rebellious act renounces to my blood', Dryden stated. Yet, as Johnson clarified, Dryden's idiom was entirely dependent on French *Renoncer à mon sang*, rendering it descriptively anomalous in English—even if entirely natural to French. This, too, was 'a mere Gallicism'.

Johnson raises, in effect, wider questions about the nature of loans and lexical borrowing. 'He that has long cultivated another language, will find its words and combinations croud upon his memory; and haste or negligence, refinement or affectation, will obtrude borrowed terms and exotick expressions', he observes (*Yale* XVIII.108). Such usage is positioned in the liminal territories where, depending on the competence of the individual speaker, elements from different languages can cross and intersect in complex ways. As Durkin has stated of transfers of this kind, the extent to which forms of this kind are, in reality, loans or whether they should instead be seen as code-switches facilitated by the bilingual or multi-lingual speaker, is an issue of some significance.[49] Just as Johnson reminded Baretti in June 1761, 'To use two languages familiarly, and without contaminating one by the other, is hardly to be hoped' (*Letters* I.197).

Johnson's 'Latinisms' offer similar examples. *Inoffensive* is 'A Latin mode of speech' when used to mean 'unembarrassed; without stop or obstruction', he notes under sense 4. 'These two senses are scarcely English, being borrowed from the Latin idiom', the entry for *dishonest* explains. In English, *dishonest* had come to mean 'Void of probity; void of faith; faithless, wicked; fraudulent'. It did not, as for Dryden in translating Virgil (in the illustrative example that Johnson supplies), signify either 'disgraced' or 'dishonoured'.[50] The senses are 'borrowed', Johnson points out—but not adopted or naturalized. That translation could be a 'pest', as the 1755 'Preface' states (*Yale* XVIII.108), is, in such instances, plain. Johnson's opposition is nevertheless not directed to translation per se (a domain in which he, of course, began his literary career) but rather to its perceived abuse and to what, in modern English, we might deem 'translationese'.[51] To *translate*, as the *Dictionary* confirms, is rightly 'To interpret in another language; to change into another language retaining the sense'. Using *dishonest*, a word long naturalized in English, with a sense which Latin alone sustained, was, in contrast, a clear contravention of what the good translation, and translator, should demand.[52]

Naturalization, Johnson stresses, was instead to be seen as a collective rather than individual process. As in Dryden's use of *renounce* or *falsify*, the extent to which a change can be facilitated—or restricted—merely by the individual is debatable. Dryden, as Johnson's extensive entry for *falsify* explores, could indeed propose both justification and need for the words and senses he deployed. 'His Crest is rash'd away; his ample Shield / Is Falsif'd, and round with Jav'lins fill'd', Dryden had written in Book 9 of his translation of Virgil's *Aeneis*.[53] As he admitted, the word had not met the approval of his friends (who 'quarrel'd at the word falsify'd as an Innovation in our Language'). Yet, as he demanded, 'Why am I forbidden to borrow from the *Italian*, a polish'd language, the word which is wanting in my Native Tongue?' The 'polish' of other vernaculars is set against the postulated deficit of English; at issue was Dryden's decision in translating Virgil to yoke an Italian sense to the already naturalized *falsify*. Dryden's departure was marked: 'To pierce; to run through', Johnson explains of the meaning which results.

Johnson gives Dryden's argument in full: 'I used the word *falsify*, in this place, to mean that the shield of Turnus was not of proof against the spears and javelins of the Trojans, which had pierced it through and through in many places.' Yet, as Johnson indicates, the success—or failure—of such attempted appropriation depends, in reality, not on the will of the individual but on the wider acts of use by which words and senses will, indeed, become part of 'received' English. Given 'all this effort', Dryden 'was not able to naturalise the new signification', Johnson stresses. As for Locke, language cannot be controlled by a single writer. Instead, as Johnson points out, a given meaning needed to be 'copied'—and adopted—by others. History—and the common facts of use—proved Johnson's point. *Falsify* was 'used by Dryden in avowed imitation of Italian *falsare*', the *OED* notes; supporting evidence merely echoes that which Johnson had provided over a century earlier.[54] *Fraischeur* and its own absence of naturalization, or French-derived *milice* ('standing force')—'a word innovated by *Temple*, but unworthy of reception'—confirm processes similar in kind, as does *perfectionate*, given as another 'word proposed by *Dryden*, but not received'. Nor, in Johnson's opinion, was this 'worthy of reception'. *Ignore* provides a further example. 'This word *Boyle* endeavoured to introduce; but it has not been received', Johnson states, here for a word for which reception would, ultimately, be very different. 'Words are offered to the public by every man, coined in his private mint, as he please; but it is the receiving of them...that gives them their authority and currency, and not the mint they came out of', as Locke likewise stressed.[55] Here, too, Johnson was in clear agreement.

Border crossings

Issues of purism and patriotism, as Gilmore notes, often unite in accounts of Johnson.[56] He is the 'true-born Englishman', as Boswell writes (*Life* 2.300); Johnson's often-cited gibes about the French easily foreground other aspects of conquest and defeat in this respect.[57] Yet, as Gilmore stresses, Johnson's treatment of words of non-native origin is, in reality, wide-ranging as well as balanced. Fewer than fifty entries exhibit Johnson's restrictive terminology of 'Gallicism' or 'merely French'; tens of thousands are, in contrast, entirely unmarked. Even Johnson's qualified comments on natural-ization are, as we have seen, often—as under *pace* and *access*, *dishonest*, and *renounce*—applied to a single sense or idiom, while the remainder of the entry is registered without comment. Even Johnson's intended imposition of italics as a form of visual segrega-tion is by no means consistently sustained; like the use of tramlines in the later *OED*, the border territories remain complex, and deci-sions fraught with subjectivity. *Messieurs*, which does appear in italics, is not specified as either 'Gallick' or 'merely French'; entries for *feuillage* ('A bunch or row of leaves'), *feuillemort* (the highly specific 'The colour of a faded leaf'), or *tete a tete*, are similar. Conversely, words such as *eclairissement*, *habiliment*, *habilitate*, and *habilitation* all appear without italics; *clique*, *coterie*, *manoeuvre*, or *vogue* provide parallel examples. *Manche*, 'a sleeve'—a word which might prompt certain reservations as to its 'Englishness' today—is likewise unitalicized and unmarked; *regnant* ('Reigning; predominant; prevalent; having power') provides a further example, even though—morphologically at least—it clearly inclines towards

French rather than the native tongue.[58] *Couchee* as noun ('Bedtime; the time of visiting late at night') is treated with similar equanimity. Johnson's practices of 'discrimination' can seem strikingly liberal. *Purist*, as the *Dictionary* confirms, also derives from French. Its definition is telling: 'one superstitiously nice in the use of words'.

The legacies of a range of other languages meanwhile confirm the identity of eighteenth-century English in a strikingly multilingual space. 'Our language is well known not to be primitive or self-originated, but to have adopted words of every generation, and either for the supply of its necessities, or the encrease of its copiousness, to have received additions from very distant regions', Johnson had stressed in 1747 (*Yale* XVIII.41). Rhetorical (and topical) ambitions for 'purity' already co-exist with 'distant regions' by which the real extent of importation into English is affirmed. 'In search of the progenitors of our speech, we may', Johnson reminds us, need to 'wander from the tropic to the frozen zone, and find some in the vallies of Palestine and some upon the rocks of Norway'. Purism was a problematic ideal. 'A *True-Born Englishman*'s a Contradiction, / In Speech an Irony, in Fact a Fiction', as Defoe had caustically observed, describing the 'Roman-Saxon-Danish-Norman' tongue that English had already become.[59]

Johnson's metaphors of circumnavigation do not, of course, suggest a commitment to the narrowly parochial; his model of English can, in this respect, prove both diverse and inclusive. Spanish *chocolate* and *renegade*, *peccadillo* and *matadore* ('A hand of cards so called from its efficacy against the adverse player') are recorded without comment. As under *cimeter* (which gains an etymology from Spanish and Portuguese), Johnson carefully records his research in Bluteau's *Portuguese Dictionary*.[60] *Lingo* (defined as 'Language; tongue; speech') is, Johnson notes, also Portuguese in origin—even though, in English, it seems a 'low cant word' as the accompanying (highly colloquial) citation from Congreve's *The Way of the World* (1700) confirmed. *Caftan* is derived from Persian ('Persick' in Johnson's text); *caravan* and *caravansary* ('A house built in the Eastern countries for the reception of travellers') from Arabic; and words such as *mumble, brabble,* and *nag,* from Dutch. *Maranatha* is given as 'Syriack', as is *mammon.* If the 'rocks of Norway' do not specifically appear, words attributed to Danish are common (see *blink* (v.); *call* (v.); *down,* meaning 'soft feathers'; or *flit* (v.), 'to fly away'). Turkish is given as the source of *mufti* ('The high priest of the Mohametans') and *janizary* ('One of the guards of the Turkish king'), of *divan* and *beglerberg* ('the chief governor of a province among the Turks'), and (among others) of *mosque* and *turban. Bamboo, banana, ananas,* and *pineapple* meanwhile reflect other exotic importations in which lexicon and changes in material culture are closely bound together. Words from Italian (see e.g. *piazza; portico; passado*), Latin, and Greek abound. Johnson derives *chaffer* ('To treat about a bargain; to haggle; to bargain') from German *kauffen* 'to buy', and *mum,* 'ale brewed with wheat', from German *mumme.*[61]

Johnson's own engagement with other languages presents a further corrective for the limited linguistic horizons he is often assumed to have. Johnson refers to learning Dutch, Italian, and Spanish,[62] to his reading (and writing) of Greek and Latin.[63] He asks Richardson in 1755 for copies of *Clarissa* translated into various languages (*Letters* I.93),[64] and writes to William Drummond of a 'zeal for languages' which is, in his own case, perhaps too unrestrained: 'Every mans opinions...are a little influenced by his favourite Studies. My zeal for Languages may seem perhaps rather over-heated even to those by whom I desire to be well esteemed' (*Letters* I.270). It is to more—rather than fewer—languages which Johnson resolves to apply himself in his prayer on the 'Study of Tongues'.[65]

Against other popular stereotypes, Johnson's French letters to Louise Flint and to Marie Hyppolyte, Comtesse de Boufflers-Rouverel (*Letters* I.321–2 and I.360) confirm fluency rather than infelicity, as does his ready translation of, say, Lobo's *Voyage to Abyssinia* in 1735 or Jean Pierre de Crousaz's *Commentaire sur la traduction en vers de M. Abbe Du Resnel, de l'Essai de M. Pope sur l'homme*, which he published in 1739.[66] Johnson as English lexicographer can likewise turn to French analogues in, say, defining *alive* and *sinistrous*. 'In a popular sense, it is used only to add an emphasis, like the French *du monde*; as, the *best* man *alive*; that is, the *best*, with an emphasis', he notes under *alive*. 'Absurd; perverse; wrong-headed; in French *gauche*', the entry for *sinistrous* elaborates. As writer too, Johnson can deploy forms he deemed French—rather than English, using *problematical* 'as the French say' in writing to Hester Thrale in 1777 (*Letters* III.95) or *de pis en pis* in 1773.[67] 'Toûjours strawberries and cream', as he writes in July 1771, offering an eloquent metonym for life at Streatham with the Thrales (*Letters* I.370).

The end of toleration?

Toleration, as the *Dictionary* explains, is 'Allowance given to that which is not approved'. It is itself a loanword, assimilated into English from Latin *tolero*. It serves, in a range of ways, to embody the complexities which the *Dictionary* reveals. As in the 'Preface', Johnson's treatment of loanwords can incline to the dynamics of registering rather than forming, as well as regulating 'absurdity' when necessary—as his comments on Dryden's attempted importation of *fraischeur* or the Italian-influenced use of *falsify* confirm. That Temple's use of *milice* is 'unworthy of reception' or that *ruse* is a French word without utility will also become part of the interpretative role that Johnson assumes. As in Chapter 5, metalinguistic comment of this kind is, however, also habitually accompanied by descriptive testimony—and carefully assembled evidence of use. As under *finesse*, if Johnson might prefer the state of language to be different, the currents of change—as his accompanying evidence confirms—clearly continue on their way. As under *falsify*, what the individual might desire is placed against what other users choose to do and say in using the native language.

As Johnson makes plain, precisely the same considerations apply to any recommendations which he himself might make in this context. 'This sense, though unusual, perhaps unexampled, is necessary in the English, unless the word *imbue* be adopted, which our writers seem not willing to receive', he writes, for instance, under *imbibe*. He provides a single example from Newton: 'Metals, corroded with a little acid, turn into rust, which is an earth tasteless and indissolvable in water; and this earth, *imbibed* with more acid, becomes a metallick salt.' Johnson, like Dryden, can advance the case for need. This is a 'word, which seems wanted in our language', the entry for *imbue* further explains. Nevertheless, as Johnson adds, even if 'proposed by several writers', *imbue* has 'not yet' been 'adopted' into general use. Johnson, as he recognizes, must likewise wait for 'the rest' to manifest the patterns of adoption he sees as beneficial. The *Dictionary* cannot, by itself, control the patterns of change, even if—as reference work—it might inform as well as guide in certain directions. Johnson's entry for *pictorial* ('Produced by a painter') provides a similar example. 'A word not adopted by other writers, but elegant and useful', Johnson states, providing a citation from Sir Thomas Browne in support: 'Sea horses are but grotesco delineations, which fill up empty spaces in maps, as many *pictorial* inventions. . . .' If Johnson commends *pictorial*, the wider realities of adoption must rest with the language in use.

Here, too, pragmatism frames the human desire for control and codification. As Johnson noted with pointed reference to the Académie Française in 1755, dictionary-makers cannot, in reality, repulse lexical intruders nor retain fugitives (*Yale* XVIII.105). If combat can be ventured, the extent to which naturalization can be either stopped or sanctioned by the will of the individual is placed in doubt. Ambitions to control the borders of French discourse are firmly set against the linguistic realities which have instead ensued. 'The *French* language has visibly changed under the inspection of the academy', he declares: 'their vigilance and activity have hitherto been vain' (*Yale* XVIII.105). As Johnson reminds his own readers (in a further corrective for any unwarranted assumptions they might retain in this respect about the nature of language and lexicography): 'The embodied criticks of *France*, when fifty years had been spent upon their work, were obliged to change its oeconomy, and give their second edition another form' (*Yale* XVIII.112). Successive editions of the *Dictionnaire* confirm the limits of human power; the dictionary changes in response to usage, not usage in response to dictionaries. The same applies to English, as another living and modern tongue.

Loanwords, and the play of naturalization they reveal, can in such ways prove highly resonant of the wider complexities of governance within the world of words. As Johnson would have fully understood, the fact that *gout*, meaning 'A taste', remains unnaturalized in English owes less to his own specification of dislike than to the collective resolve of English speakers for whom *taste* as lexeme has so far proved sufficient. It would likewise by no means have surprised him that the French-derived *rapport*, given in the *Dictionary* as introduced by Sir William Temple but 'not copied by others', would later move along the cline of naturalization, nor that *ruse* would, in time, prove more necessary that he had allowed.[68] Nor perhaps would the fact that, as *Rambler* 80 confirms, *flatter*—in a sense judged indisputably 'Gallick' in the *Dictionary*—is already crossing the border in Johnson's own prose.[69] 'The hill flatters with an extensive view', as Johnson wrote, unintentional illustrating this sense in December 1750 (*Yale* III.56). Johnson, in a similar way, provides the *OED*'s sole illustration of *correction* in another 'Gallicism' of the *Dictionary*: 'No poetry lasts long that is not very correct; the ballance therefore seems to incline in favour of correction.... So certain is it that correction is the touch-stone of poetry', Johnson's 'Preface' to Charlotte Lennox's 1759 translation of *Brumoy's Greek Theatre* declared.[70]

Chesterfield, by the same token, would also find himself illustrating a range of new lexical items in the *OED*, such as *brusquerie* (dated to 1752 in Chesterfield's use), *debut* (1751), *denouement*

(1752), *desoevre* (1750), *dessous des cartes* (1756), *faute de mieux* (1766), or *hors de combat* (1757). Principle and practice again divide. Chesterfield's levels of 'toleration' prove theoretical rather than actual; his multilingualism, as such entries confirm, easily produced further fluidities on the borders of discourse. Boswell, too, would exemplify further processes of change; as the 1791 *Life* confirms, *trait* had made its way into his familiar discourse while *jeu d'esprit* appears in characterizing Johnson's own zest for life.[71] Even in 1754, as Cambridge records, new forms of conflict and contact were making their way into English, bringing other 'exotics' in their wake. A vocabulary of 'West India phrases' might be needed for the coming year, he warns; words such as *palanquin*, *nabob*, *junk*, and *sepoy* already illustrate the on-going processes of contact and change by which, as Johnson was aware, no living language could remain unmoved.[72]

7

History and the flux of time

Hope, Johnson wrote in *Rambler* 67, 'begins with the first power of comparing our actual with our possible state' (*Yale* III.354). The present, in this respect, often prompts discontent of various kinds. 'No man is pleased with his present state', as Johnson declared, echoing Horace, in October 1750 (*Yale* III.334). Hope, in contrast, is able to console, offering 'supplemental satisfactions' and images of a perfected state of life (*Yale* III.221). As for Cupidus in *Rambler* 73, it is by 'recourse to futurity' that the 'perplexities and vexations' of the present are to be resolved; as in *Rambler* 41, imagination, and the 'anticipation of events to come', easily construct 'pleasing scenes' which are remote from the difficulties of everyday life. As Johnson states, 'With regard to futurity, when events are at such a distance from us ... we have generally power enough over our imagination to turn it upon pleasing scenes, and can promise ourselves riches, honours, and delights, without intermingling those vexations and anxieties, with which all human enjoyments are polluted' (*Yale* III.224). Hope, he adds, can 'solace us with rewards, and escapes, and victories', defeating those concerns by which the present is cast down.

Language and, in particular, contemplation of the mutability and flux which marked the native tongue, could, as we have seen, prompt similar trajectories. As for Swift, the linguistic present is

Samuel Johnson and the Journey into Words. Lynda Mugglestone
© Lynda Mugglestone 2015. First published 2015 by Oxford University Press.

made redolent of imperfection. 'Its daily Improvements are by no means in proportion to its daily Corruptions', he had stressed;[1] an excess of monosyllables, loanwords, alongside other recent 'Abuses and Absurdities' all rendered English other than it might be. 'Schemes of the future' for Swift (*Yale* III.224) instead present utopian images of a stable tongue which is, 'by some Method', rendered immune from the processes of decline and change. 'Supplemental satisfaction' is located in the state of linguistic timelessness which the future might secure. Instead of the 'perpetual Variations of our Speech', it would, Swift declares, be far better to 'have our Language, after it is duly correct, always to last'.[2] Defoe and Snell, Stackhouse and Thomas Sheridan had, in similar ways, situated the linguistic failings of the present against the salience of future reform, and the beneficial stasis that should, in time, result.[3] Prescriptivism—located in the perceived dissonance between language as it is and how it might instead be used—easily correlates with temporal patterning of this kind.

Johnson, too, as in the 1747 *Plan*, can present his own corrective visions of futurity. Drawing on the example (and precedent) of Boileau, lexicography was, as we have seen, easily depicted as a means by which undesirable change may be prevented, especially in terms of its perpetuation of English into 'any distant time' (*Yale* XVIII.54). Popular tropes of duration and preservation, of stasis against mutability all act as defining properties of Johnson's 'idea of an English dictionary' (*Yale* XVIII.57). 'Who upon this survey', as Johnson had demanded, 'can forbear to wish, that these fundamental atoms of our speech might obtain the firmness and immutability of the primogenial and constituent particles of matter, that they might retain their substance while they alter their appearance, and be varied and compounded, yet not destroyed?' (*Yale* XVIII.44).

Johnson's visions of futurity can, however, also articulate a highly conflicted space. While expectations of a corrective lexicography framed Johnson's work on the *Dictionary*, drawing on popular ideals of stasis and control, Johnson himself early problematizes assumptions by which the 'tyranny of time' might be resisted by the dictionary-maker, and the changefulness of words controlled (*Yale* XVIII.74). As in other aspects of language, what one might 'wish' for English can, of course, easily tempt the dictionary-maker into particular vanities about the world of words. As in 1755, that Johnson can 'wish...that [language] might be less apt to decay, and that signs might be permanent, like the things which they denote' (*Yale* XVIII.79) is plain. Nevertheless, if desires of this kind—and the hopes they encompass—take lexicography in one direction, an all too realistic engagement with language and the currents of change can, as in Johnson's drafted 'Scheme', already point in the other. The 'Desire' for a fixed and stable language is a 'Phantom' (*Yale* XVIII.461), he admits. Like other aspects of *fancy*, this reflects 'an opinion bred rather by the imagination than the reason'.[4]

As Johnson repeatedly explored, time and its effects were, for language, ineluctable. Words would, in this respect, often be rendered strikingly human subjects; even when gathered in the *Dictionary*, their visual stasis is illusory. Instead, as Johnson notes, they are 'like their author' such that 'when they are not gaining strength, they are generally losing it' (*Yale* XVIII.44). Aikon's emphasis on Johnson's 'engagement with human temporality' proves an enduring aspect of the *Dictionary* too.[5] Irrespective of what one might 'wish', as Johnson points out, the flux of words acts as an all too timely reminder that language 'is the work of man, of a being from whom permanence and stability cannot be derived' (*Yale* XVIII.44).

That change can be regretted is often clear. As Chapter 5 has explored, on-going change can cause concern. As under *precarious*, it can seem 'unskilful', a means by which the distinctions of the past are lost. As in the extension of *miniature* from noun to adjective, the dictionary as reference model can evaluate and decide in favour of the past. Yet, across the *Dictionary* and its making, change can also be depicted as closely entwined with the regenerative properties by which language, like nature, must 'bud' as well as 'fall away' (*Yale*

XVIII.110). 'Though art may sometimes prolong their duration, it will rarely give [words] perpetuity', Johnson carefully explains (*Yale* XVIII.44). Offering other conflicted journeys for the diction-ary-maker, the *Plan* can simultaneously advance and retreat from stability as the end-point of lexicographical endeavour. Hope, and its realization, can be rendered sharply distinct. What might be envisaged as ideal can, as Johnson recognizes, be widely at odds with the reality of a living speech. 'Successive alterations... are usual in living languages', Johnson explains, for example, under *dribble* (n.), negotiating the transitions by which time and change of form intersect.

Writing the past

Time and its linguistic patterning is, in a variety of ways, firmly embedded in the *Dictionary*. A complex metalanguage—of what has been attested 'anciently' or 'formerly', of what is 'obsolete' or 'mod-ern', or, indeed, of what 'should' or 'ought to be' in the future— informs a range of entries. 'It will be proper that the quotations be ranged according to the ages of their authors', as Johnson noted already in 1747, setting out another aspect of intended design: 'By this method every word will have its history, and the reader will be informed of the gradual changes of the language, and have before his eyes the rise of some words, and the fall of others' (*Yale* XVIII.56–7). While this is not consistently realized—'observations so minute and accurate' are themselves 'to be desired rather than expected', as Johnson reminds us in yet another corrective to both hope and human aspiration (*Yale* XVIII.57)—the influence of such ideas is evident at a range of points. As under *modernism*, Johnson can endeavour to locate the point of birth. 'A word invented by *Swift*', Johnson writes, undoubtedly aware of the ironies involved. Swift's supporting citation both deployed and castigated innovation: 'Scrib-blers send us over their trash in prose and verse, with abominable curtailings and quaint *modernisms*', as he had stressed in 1737.[6] *Witticism* is credited to Dryden in a similar way though, unlike his attempted importation of *fraischeur*, *witticism* had clearly been adopted into wider use.[7] Similar is *gas*. 'A word invented by the chymists', Johnson notes.

Johnson's attitudes to change and innovation are, here at least, strikingly neutral. 'In every word of extensive use', as Johnson affirms in the 1755 'Preface', 'it was requisite to mark the progress of its meaning, and show by what gradations of intermediate sense it has passed from its primitive to its remote and accidental signification' (*Yale* XVIII.91). In this respect, change succeeds change so that 'the original sense of words is often driven out of use by their metaphorical acceptations' (*Yale* XVIII.92). In principle, as Johnson states of the structure that his entries should manifest, 'Every foregoing explanation should tend to that which follows, and the series be regularly concatenated from the first notion to the last.'[8]

As in the entry for *extravagant*, we can, for example, map the trajectories of time and change across the various sub-divisions that Johnson provides. The earliest meaning, specified as 'Wandering out of his bounds', fades into obsolescence. 'This is the primogeneal sense, but not now in use', Johnson notes under sense 1. In time, newer meanings such as 'Wasteful, prodigal; vainly expensive', documented under sense 5, rise into prominence. Addison in *Spectator* No.243 (dated 8 December 1711) provides appropriate illustration in the *Dictionary*: 'An *extravagant* man, who has nothing else to recommend him but a false generosity, is often more beloved than a person of a much more finished character, who is defective in this particular.'

We can in such ways be reminded of the slow but inevitable movement of words in time. As Johnson states in his entry for *against* in the sense 'In provision for; in expectation of' (sense 8), 'This mode of speaking probably had its original from the idea of making provision *against*, or in opposition to a time of misfortune, but by degrees acquired a neutral sense.' Change, as here, moves 'by degrees'—offering a series of infinitesimal shifts which the dictionary-maker might, with sufficient evidence, perhaps be able to recover.[9] As under *quite,* 'its present signification was gradually introduced', Johnson affirms. Genesis and demise, alongside the narrative impetus of history, can in such ways shape the life of words across a range of entries. Johnson's habit of biographical thinking, as adduced by Catherine Parke, can seem equally evident in the *Dictionary.*[10]

Writing language history was, of course, part of Johnson's lexicographical project from the beginning. Dodsley carefully draws attention to Johnson's comments in this respect in the commendatory 'puff' he wrote in the *Museum* in 1747.[11] Similarly, specific reference appears in Chesterfield's letter to the *World* in November 1754.[12] Here, too, contemporary 'want'—and envisaged fulfilment—are plain: 'A history of our language through it's several stages' was 'still wanting', while 'Mr. Johnson's labours will now, and I dare say, very fully, supply that want'.[13] The 'History' which prefaces the published *Dictionary* was nevertheless one of the last elements to be composed—an 'extempore' work, as DeMaria suggests, which drew on a number of other works, notably Warton's *Observations on the Faerie Quene of Spenser* (published in March 1754), as well as James Greenwood's *Essay towards a Practical English Grammar.*[14] As realized by Johnson, it offers a vast sweep of historical time, beginning with the Saxons (and the inception of Anglo-Saxon Britain) and ending with Thomas Wilson's *The Arte of Rhetorike* in the sixteenth century.

As Christopher Vilmar contends, 'It is difficult to imagine many readers not driven by the demands of research perusing Johnson's "History of the English Language", with its dozens of quotations in Old and Middle English.'[15] Nevertheless, readers who do examine it are forced to confront Johnson's unqualified engagement with the facts of linguistic mutability. Retellings of the same text—here Boethius's *Consolation of Philosophy*—by King Alfred in Old English,[16] Chaucer in late Middle English, and George Colvile in 1556 focus the reader's attention on the flux of words and form which have, historically, characterized the native tongue. If Robert of

Gloucester (who died in 1147) had been used by Warton to exemplify what he termed the 'last dregs' of original 'British' composition,[17] Johnson, as in his entry for *dribble*, will instead explore the nature of 'transition' and the processes of gradual change. Gloucester, Johnson writes, seems 'to have used a kind of intermediate diction, neither *Saxon* nor *English*; in his work therefore we see the transition exhibited' (*Yale* XVIII.162). History, for Johnson, hence exemplifies 'the deduction of the *English* language, from the earliest times of which we have any knowledge to its present state' (*Yale* XVIII.125). As he elaborates, he had 'deduced the *English* language from the age of *Alfred* to that of *Elizabeth*; in some parts imperfectly for want of materials; but I hope, at least, in such a manner that its progress may be easily traced' (*Yale* XVIII.263). To *deduce*, the *Dictionary* explains, was 'To draw in a regular connected series, from one time or one event to another'.[18]

Writing the past nevertheless differs sharply from those imagined futurities by which, as we have seen, a range of figures in Johnson's *Rambler* essays can be preoccupied. As Johnson explains in August 1750 in *Rambler* 41, 'the future is pliant and ductile'. It can, as such, 'be easily moulded by a strong fancy into any form'. The past, in contrast, is already fixed in ways which will, of necessity, render the operations of 'fancy' and imagination problematic. 'The objects of remembrance have already existed, and left their signature behind them' in ways that, as Johnson emphasizes, 'defy all attempts of rasure or of change' (*Yale* III.224).[19] Writing historical time, for Johnson, is an act which is therefore made singularly unresponsive to fanciful reconstruction.[20] The dictionary-maker must instead engage with evidence and observation, and with processes which rely on 'deduction' and reason rather than fancy and imagination. As in his definition of *historian* ('A writer of facts and events; a writer of history'), or indeed of *history* itself (sense 1: 'A narration of events and facts delivered with dignity'; sense 3: 'The knowledge of facts and events'), this will inevitably bring different imperatives into play.

Johnson's 'excursions into books' could, in this respect, affirm their own historical utility, as well as suggesting still other patterns of departure for Johnson's intended course. As we already have seen in Chapter 3, the historical limits (from Sidney to the writers of the Restoration) which Johnson originally envisaged are regularly contravened. At one side, Johnson moves beyond his intended terminus of the Restoration to document what he terms 'modern' English and the diction of the 'present'.[21] At the other, he ventures in 'excursions' of a different kind (*Yale* XVIII.96) into a range of early writers, examining the evidence which they too offer in terms of lexicography. This aspect of Johnson has often been neglected.[22] What Johnson referred to as his 'zeal for antiquity' (*Yale* XVIII.96) can, however, be marked. Robert of Gloucester, for example, does not only appear in Johnson's 'History' but also acts as a witness to time and change in the *Dictionary* itself. 'It appears in *Robert of Gloucester*, that this word signified anciently any one perverse or obstinate of either sex', Johnson notes under *shrew*, defined as 'A peevish, malignant, clamorous, spiteful, vexatious, turbulent woman'. A citation from Robert of Gloucester opens the entry: 'There dede of hem vor hunger a thousand and mo, / And yat nolde the *screwen* to none pes go.' It then proceeds by way of Shakespeare, L'Estrange, as well as Dryden, to conclude in Addison's *Freeholder* No. 23, which had been published in March 1715. Johnson's intent that 'each word shall have its history' is, in such ways, fully supported. 'It is in the work of Robert of Gloucester written *luther*', Johnson likewise states under *lither* (adj.), a word he defines with reference to Gloucester's use as 'bad, sorry, corrupt'.

Johnson can, in similar ways, turn to Chaucer. 'To *brede*, in *Chaucer*, is to *deceive*', he explains, for instance, under *braid* (adj.). This is glossed as 'An old word, which seems to signify *deceitful*' and illustrated by a citation from Shakespeare's *All's Well that Ends Well*. Johnson's entries for words such as *con* and *mucker* likewise gain historical verification from Chaucer's use. *Con* is given as deriving from Saxon *connan* 'to know'; 'as in *Chaucer, Old wymen*

connen mochil thinge; that is, Old women have much knowledge',
Johnson notes. *Mucker* ('To scramble for money; to hoard up; to get
or save meanly') demonstrates, as we have seen, other continuities
between past and present, and the rise and fall of words: it is given as
'a word used by *Chaucer*, and still retained in conversation'.[23]
Citations from Chaucer open Johnson's entries for words such as
coy, dame, and *donjon* (explained as 'The highest and strongest
tower of the castle, in which prisoners were kept'). They appear
too in illustration of specific senses, as under sense 4 of *defend* in
the French-derived meaning: 'To prohibit; to forbid [<*defendre*,
French]'. 'Where can you say, in any manner, age, / That ever
God *defended* marriage?', the accompanying citation from Chaucer's 'Wife of Bath's Tale' declares.[24]

It is by means of language, as Johnson would later stress, that
history is to be known.[25] Etymology, as he stated in 1747, would, in
this respect, constitute a further important aspect of the *Dictionary*'s
intended remit. In the *Plan*, this can prompt particularly confident
prognostications of futurity. Etymology, Johnson suggests, might
indeed act as prescriptive or proscriptive index, delineating the
borders of inclusion and exclusion for *Dictionary* and language
alike. 'By tracing...every word to its original, and not admitting,
but with great caution, any of which no original can be found', he
argued, 'we shall secure our language from being over-run with *cant*'
and 'crouded with low terms...of which therefore no legitimate
derivation can be shewn' (*Yale* XVIII.42). As Rosemary Sweet
confirms, a heightened concern for origins and legitimate descent
informed a range of disciplines in the eighteenth century. For
Johnson, as the previous chapter has explored, the 'Teutonick' and
Romance can be placed in firm opposition.[26] A range of entries
across the *Dictionary* celebrate the native lineage and the heritage of
words. 'This is the true Saxon meaning', Johnson notes, for instance,
under sense 2 of *wrack* (n.), explained as 'Ruin; destruction'. 'This
sense is truly Teutonick', he declares under sense 4 of *all* (adv.,
glossed as 'although'). 'A word now out of use, but truly English',

Johnson likewise writes under *long*, defined as 'By the fault; by the failure'.

Expectations that the derivable history of words might serve to delimit the boundaries of 'legitimate' speech instead enact a further series of departures. Johnson's early proposition that words without etymology might be excluded from *Dictionary* and language alike proved, in this respect, particularly fallible. 'Of this word, so common in the English language, it is very difficult to find the etymology', Johnson acknowledged, for example, under *put*. Far from being excluded, this was a word which produced one of Johnson's most densely detailed entries, enumerated across some sixty-five sense-divisions. Similar challenges were presented by words such as *stag*, *cattle*, or *callipers*, all of which were, in fact, included in the *Dictionary* and supported by appropriate evidence. 'Of this word I find no derivation'; 'A word of very common usage, but of doubtful or unknown etymology'; 'Of this word I know not the etymology', Johnson admits in the respective entries. 'Of this word I know not the original', he likewise writes under *hist*, defined as 'An exclamation commanding silence'.

As in Johnson's engagement with the complexities of meaning in Chapter 5, we can, in such instances, be forcefully reminded of the borders of human knowledge, alongside the limits of the lexicographer's power to provide the kind of certainties which might be desired. 'The etymology which I adopt is uncertain, and perhaps frequently erroneous', Johnson confesses in 1755 (*Yale* XVIII.99). Forced, in this respect, to negotiate still other divides between expectation and experience, Johnson can repeatedly foreground the difficulty of historical interpretation. He comments on what is not known and on what has not been found in the available historical evidence, as well as on what is—and is not—able to be deduced. 'I know not its original', Johnson declares under *frampold* (glossed as 'Peevish; boisterous; rugged; crossgrained'). 'This word, with all those of the same race, are of uncertain etymology', the entry for *bashful* confirms. *Brangle* ('Squabble; wrangle') is similar.

'Uncertainly derived', Johnson comments. 'I know not whence derived', Johnson categorically states for *jolt*. *Lower* offers similar puzzles, if little resolution: 'It is doubtful what was the primitive meaning of this word: if it was originally applied to the appearance of the sky, it is no more than to *grow low*, as the sky seems to do in dark weather: if it was first used of the countenance, it may be derived from the Dutch *loeren*, to look askance.'

Johnson's diction is marked by conjecture and iterated conditionals, as well as by familiar hedges such as 'seems' or 'perhaps'. 'Of this word the etymology is not known', he writes for *peacock*, adding: 'perhaps it is *peak cock*, from the tuft of feathers on its head; the peak of women being an ancient ornament: if it be not rather a corruption of *beaucoq*, Fr. from the more striking lustre of its spangled train'. The subjunctive ('if it be not rather') emphasizes rather than reduces the liminal spaces of knowledge in matters of linguistic history. Johnson hypothesizes rather than prescribes. The entry for *hurly-burly* offers no more resolution. 'I have been told that this word owes its original to two neighbouring families named *Hurly* and *Burly*, or *Hurleigh* and *Burleigh*, which filled their part of the kingdom with contests and violence', Johnson notes, for example, with some scepticism. Here, too, the subjunctive is prominent: 'If this account be rejected, the word must be derived from *hurl*, *hurly*, and *burly*, a ludicrous reduplication.' Similar uncertainties appear under *harangue*. 'The original of the French word is much questioned', he states: '*Menage* thinks it a corruption of *hearing*, English; *Junius* imagines it to be *discours au rang*, to a circle, which the Italian *arringo* seems to favour. Perhaps it may be from *orare*, or *orationare*, *orationer*, *oraner*, *aranger*, *haranguer*.'[27]

At other times, as in his entries for *pun* or *sleeveless*, Johnson simply appeals to the reader, posing etymological questions which remain, of necessity, open-ended and unresolved. 'I know not whence this word is to be deduced', he notes: 'to *pun*, is to grind or beat with a *pestle*; can *pun* mean an empty sound, like that of a mortar beaten, as *clench*, the old word for *pun*, seems only a

corruption of *clink*?' Lack of resolution under *sleeveless,* sense 2
('Wanting reasonableness; wanting propriety') is made particularly
plain. 'This sense, of which the word has been long possessed,
I know not well how it obtained', Johnson admits: '*Skinner* thinks
it properly *liveless* or *lifeless*: to this I cannot heartily agree, though
I know not what better to suggest. Can it come from *sleeve,* a knot,
or *skein,* and so signify *unconnected, hanging ill together*? or from
sleeve, a cover; and therefore means *plainly absurd*; foolish without
palliation?'

Distrust, as Johnson noted already in 1742, is perhaps 'a necessary
Qualification of a Student in History'.[28] This could, as the *Dictionary* often suggests, prove equally true in terms of lexicography,
emphasizing the need for independent enquiry, as well as diligent
'perusal' across a range of texts and sources. As Johnson realized, for
the writer engaged in history, distrust will serve to 'quicken his
Discernment of different Degrees of Probability, animate his Search
after Evidence and, perhaps, heighten his Pleasure at the Discovery
of Truth'.[29]

Such processes are, indeed, often transparent in the *Dictionary.*
'Mr. *Lye* observes that *gun* in Iceland signifies *battle*; but when *guns*
came into use we had no commerce with Iceland', as Johnson
comments, for example, under *gun,* here dispelling still other aspects
of historical fallacy in the rise of words. 'The French word *filer,* from
which some derive it, is of very late production, and therefore
cannot be its original', he likewise notes under *filch.* Johnson's
sceptical reading of etymology progressively undermines its viability
as linguistic censor in the ways which the *Plan* had once proposed.
'When words are restrained, by common usage, to a particular
sense, to run up to *etymology,* and construe them by dictionary, is
wretchedly ridiculous', as a citation from Collier's *View of the Stage*
(1698) declares, here under Johnson's entry for *etymology.* The
accompanying citation from Addison's *Spectator* No. 470 is equally
telling. As Addison pointedly observed, etymology, if used in this
way, inclines not to patterns of rational extrapolation but to the

ludicrous, such that *'Pelvis* is used by comick writers for a looking-glass, by which means the *etymology* of the word is visible, and pelvidera will signify a lady who looks in her glass'.

Usage on the margins: Obsolescence

Similar problems of certainty and closure appear at the either end of the temporal spectrum. Lexical obsolescence was, for instance, early isolated as a domain where prescriptive regulation should come into force, as in Swift's recommendation that words sanctioned by the kind of language society he advocates should not 'be afterwards antiquated'. As Swift added, forms 'long since antiquated' ought 'to be restored, on account of their Energy and Sound'.[30] Interventionist ideals of this kind were common. 'Obsolete words may be laudably revived, when either they are more sounding, or more significant than those in practice', Dryden had stated in a similar vein, suggesting a form of temporal language management by which the qualitative scrutiny of past and present might, in time, secure still other aspects of a perfected language state.[31] Desire—and other attendant visions of futurity—could be widely perceptible in this respect. Further endorsed in, say, Thomas Stackhouse's *Reflections on the English Language*,[32] such issues, as in Thomas Sheridan's work, assumed a marked topicality. It was, for instance, Chesterfield himself who was thereby invited to contemplate his demise into linguistic obscurity unless, as Sheridan advocated, appropriate measures for reform were secured by prescriptive and proscriptive redress.[33]

Johnson's attitudes to the past, and to patterns of change already completed, can be illuminating. As the 1747 *Plan* confirms, the *Dictionary* had, from the beginning, intended to include 'antiquated or obsolete words' when they were 'found in authors, who wrote since the accession of Elizabeth, from which we date the golden age of our language' (*Yale* XVIII.53). In terms of its projected role as reference book, such patterns of inclusion were regarded as particularly important. 'Of these many [words] might be omitted', Johnson acknowledged, 'but that the reader may require . . . that no difficulty should be left unresolved in books which he finds himself invited to read' (*Yale* XVIII.53). Entries such as *angel* offer apt illustration of the benefits of historical exegesis in this regard. An *angel*, Johnson explains under sense 5, was 'A piece of money anciently coined and impressed with an angel, in memory of an observation of Pope Gregory, that the pagan *Angli*, or English, were so beautiful, that, if they were christians, they would be *Angeli*, or *angels*'. 'The coin was rated at ten shillings', he adds in further elucidation. Similar is his explication of *bill* which, as in Shakespeare's *Richard II*, signifies 'a kind of weapon anciently carried by the foot, a battle axe'. *Termagant*, used in the eighteenth century to mean 'A scold; a brawling turbulent woman' also appears 'in *Shakespeare* to have been anciently used of men', as Johnson explains of other long-lost sense-divisions of the past.

Johnson's diction of 'anciently' and 'formerly' will, as here, con-firm the passing of time across a range of entries. At other points, he can nevertheless recur to the kind of interventionist precepts on language and time which writers such as Dryden and Swift had advanced. 'Agriculture, cultivation. An obsolete word, worthy of revival', Johnson notes, for instance, under *manurance*. *Opinion*, defined as 'To opine; to think', prompts similar considerations, even if Johnson's conclusions differ markedly. 'A word out of use, and unworthy of revival', he declares. *Scomm*, signifying 'A buffoon', elicits a parallel response. A more extensive comment under *hereout* (glossed as 'Out of this place') draws on some of the same concerns: 'All the words compounded of *here* and a preposition, except *hereafter*, are obsolete, or obsolescent; never used in poetry, and seldom in prose, by elegant writers, though perhaps not unworthy to be retained.'

Johnson's own sense of the historical perfectibility of discourse can, in such instances, clearly come to the fore. 'Obsolete words are admitted, when they are found in authours not obsolete, or when they have any force or beauty that may deserve revival' (*Yale* XVIII.86), as Johnson affirms in the 1755 'Preface' in words which clearly echo, and appropriate, Dryden's precepts. That English might benefit from the retention of *manurance* and compounds with *here* or, conversely, that it does not suffer from the loss of *opinion* used as a verb or of *scomm* is made plain. If the evaluative metalanguage of such entries offers glimpses of desire (and Johnson's sense of how English might indeed benefit from the processes of managed change), such examples are few and far between. The diction of time, and its passing, is, in contrast, pervasive. If some words and senses are rendered fully obsolete, others are seen to move, gradually, towards disuse. Obsolescence, like naturalization, is rendered a process as well as a state in which intervention is, in practice, rarely ventured.[34]

At one end of the spectrum of time and change, the facts of obsolescence are therefore presented as unequivocal. *County*, used to mean 'A count; a lord' is 'now wholly obsolete', Johnson states. 'This signification was anciently much in use, but is now wholly obsolete', he likewise affirms under *blend*, sense 3, defined as 'To pollute; to spoil; to corrupt' and illustrated by a citation from Spenser. *Acceptation* 'seems now wholly out of use', Johnson likewise explains, here with reference to its earlier sense as 'reception whether good or bad'. If *trustless*, defined as 'Unfaithful; unconstant; not to be trusted', is, to Johnson's mind 'a word elegant', this too is 'out of use'. Johnson does not proffer intervention. *Gride*, defined 'To cut; to make way by cutting', offers a parallel example. It is 'A word elegant, but not in use'. The longevity of *impartible*, by the same token, does not seem promising: 'Communicable; to be conferred or bestowed. This word is elegant, though used by few writers'.

Like *impartible*, words often seem to hover in the liminal territories of use, demonstrating the transitions that English, as a living language, will inevitably reveal. *Dealbation*, defined as 'The act of bleaching or whitening; rendering things white, which were not so before', is carefully described in 1755 as 'a word which is now almost grown into disuse'. *Nether* is similar. It 'is not now much in use',

Johnson writes. *Awful*, used to signify 'struck with awe; timorous, scrupulous', is likewise identified as a sense which, in mid-eighteenth century English, 'occurs but rarely'. 'Time', as Bacon stated, here in another citation which Johnson deploys on a number of occasions across the *Dictionary*, 'innovateth greatly, but quietly, and by degrees'.[35] In these terms, *adorement*, if not quite obsolete, is, Johnson records, hence 'scarcely used'; 'Now little in use', the entry for *goodly* in the sense 'Beautiful, graceful, fine' likewise explains. Across a wide range of entries, the *Dictionary* serves to prove the truth of Bacon's words. *Abolition*, as we are told with apparent equanimity, seems to be prompting the slow demise of *abolishment*: 'This is now more frequently used than *abolishment*'. *Absurdity* and *absurdness* are placed in similar processes of change; as Johnson notes, it is *absurdity* which 'is more frequently used'. 'A word almost obsolete', he likewise notes under *accoil*, defined as 'To fill up, in an ill sense; to croud, to stuff full'. *Scamble*, a word which tempts Johnson into further etymological scepticism (it 'has much exercised the etymological sagacity of *Meric Casaubon*; but, as is usual, to no purpose'), is 'scarcely in use'.

If, as in Johnson's 1755 'Preface', change is often seen as decay and degeneration, deploying popular tropes which construct the past as qualitatively superior to the present,[36] the *Dictionary* itself can operate in rather different ways. The diction of usage—and of 'custom' as a guide to currency or its converse—is, for example, often prominent in Johnson's imaging of the past. 'A word out of use', Johnson notes under *baigne*, meaning 'To drench; to soak'; 'A word no longer in use', he states for *guerdon* (defined as 'A reward; a recompense'). 'A word not in use', we are informed under *faithed*, glossed as 'Honest, sincere', and supported by a citation from *King Lear*. Use, rather than the aegis of the dictionary-maker, acts as determining factor in the longevity of words and the meanings that they hold. Usage is critical, dividing past and present across the *Dictionary* in calibrated patterns of presence and absence. The form *ope* 'is scarcely used but by old authors, and by them in the primitive not figurative sense', Johnson explains, for example, in his entry for *open* (adj.). Yet what 'old authors' do is necessarily distanced from the usage of later times. 'What makes a word obsolete, more than general agreement to forbear it?', Johnson demands (*Yale* XVIII.107–8).[37]

The extent to which the individual is able to revive the obsolete can, in such ways, prompt other forms of critical review. 'How shall it be continued, when it conveys an offensive idea, or recalled again into the mouths of mankind, when it has once become unfamiliar by disuse, and unpleasing by unfamiliarity?', Johnson queries in 1755 (*Yale* XVIII.108). That the dictionary-maker might be able to change 'general agreement', and make 'pleasing' what has become 'unpleasing' is, Johnson points out, unlikely. Whether unfamiliarity can be reversed is equally problematic. 'Orders are easily made, but they do not execute themselves', as Johnson reminded readers of the *Literary Magazine* in 1757.[38] As in Johnson's critical probing of academy discourses in his 'Life of Roscommon',[39] the mechanisms by which individual edict might secure universal agreement (as well as subsequent change) are by no means clear.

If Johnson can, on occasion, therefore seem to comply with popular prescriptive rhetoric, he can, as here, also point out its weaknesses. What was 'anciently' used cannot, in reality, easily be recovered into recent and current history—even if, as the *Dictionary* confirms, we may indeed come to know, and understand, how such words were used by the writers who lived when such terms were current. As Johnson explains under *advisement*, for example, this had indeed been used by 'old writers' to signify 'prudence and circumspection'. Yet, as he adds for the benefit of writers (and readers) in the present, this is a fact of history: 'It is now, in both senses, antiquated'. Similar is the use by 'old authors' of '*hight* ... for *named*, or was *named*', as the entry for *behight* confirms. 'Every age has its modes of speech and cast of thought', Johnson would stress in 1756 (*Yale* VII.52). Here he echoes the poet John Denham (*c.*1615–69) rather than Dryden, in other precepts which the

Dictionary, as under *mode*, had also ventured forth: 'There are certain garbs and *modes* of speaking, which vary with the times; the fashion of our clothes being not more subject to alteration than that of our speech.'

Lexicography, as Johnson came to explore across the years of writing the *Dictionary*, cannot therefore be an elixir, recovering dead words into life, however attractive such propositions might initially seem. Nor, by the same token, can the dictionary-maker be an alchemist whose words transmute the very nature of a living speech. 'When we see men grow old and die at a certain time one after another, from century to century, we laugh at the elixir that promises to prolong life to a thousand years', he writes in the 1755 'Preface' (*Yale* XVIII.104–5). Here, too, the reality of human experience is made to counter what one might, in other ways, hope and wish. Lexicography, Johnson makes plain, benefits from a similar perspective. 'Able to produce no example of a nation that has preserved their words and phrases from mutability', the dictionary-maker, as Johnson concludes, can 'with equal justice be derided, who . . . shall imagine that his dictionary can embalm his language, and secure it from corruption and decay' (*Yale* XVIII.105). If the diction of imagination once again comes to the fore, it is swiftly dispelled. The lexicographer, Johnson concludes, cannot 'change sublunary nature, and clear the world at once from folly, vanity, and affectation'.

Writing the present

'The present', Johnson wrote in August 1750, is in 'perpetual motion'. If the mutability of past states had been settled by time, the present offers no such resolution. Instead, it 'leaves us as soon as it arrives'; it 'ceases to be present before its presence is well perceived', being 'known to have existed' only by means of 'the effects which it leaves behind' (*Yale* III.223–4). History, in this sense, is made anew each day. As Johnson explored in the 1755 'Preface', language can, in fact, seem particularly resonant of qualities of this kind. Against fixity, we are instead reminded that 'words are hourly shifting their relations' (*Yale* XVIII.89) and prefixes 'are hourly united to new words as occasion requires' (*Yale* XVIII.87). As in Johnson's imaging of the 'intumescence of the tide'—or, indeed, the 'Sea of words'—language is characterized by the ceaseless nature of change itself (*Yale* XVIII.106; *Letters* I.92).

We tend prototypically, of course, to associate Johnson's *Diction-ary* with the language (and the writers) of the past. Nevertheless, as the *Dictionary* makes plain, the diction of the here and now, and of 'modern' as well as 'ancient', also frequently intervenes in the record of language which Johnson provides. Johnson writes, after all, for readers in his immediate present for whom the dictionary as refer-ence book must guide not only to the semantic nuances of the past, but also act as interpreter for current use. Johnson's definitions, as a result, will often span an arc of linguistic history. As in Johnson's entries for words deemed obsolete, we are, as we have seen, often returned to the present moment in the diction he deploys. To *descry*, for example, is 'To give notice of any thing suddenly discovered; as, the scout descried the enemy, that he gave notice of their approach'. If, as Johnson adds, 'This sense is now obsolete', he also draws attention to the relational patterns which history reveals: it 'gave occasion to those which are now in use'. *Debate* is similar. Given a meaning, in sense 2, of 'A quarrel; a contest', Johnson adds further information by which use in past and present divides: 'It is not used now of hostile contest'. 'This is now almost the only sense', Johnson writes in a similar mode for *prevent*, defined as 'To hinder; to obviate; to obstruct'. Its earlier senses by which it signified 'To preoccupy; to preengage' or 'to anticipate' have, he confirms, faded into disuse.

Johnson's iterated diction of 'now' can thereby place an entirely synchronic sense of language against earlier states which no longer exist. 'To judge rightly of the present we must oppose it to the past; for all judgment is comparative', as Johnson would stress in *Rasselas* (*Yale* XVI.112). Writing the history—and use—of words would, in this respect, prove no different. As in other aspects of the *Dictionary*, Johnson's temporal modifiers evoke the variability of a living tongue, and the operations of time which this reveals. 'It had anciently the preposition *with* before the person, to whom communication either of benefits or knowledge was made', Johnson writes, for example, under sense 3 of *communicate*. 'Now it has only *to*', he states, in contrast, under sense 4, providing appropriate illustration from writers such as Clarendon and Watts. A range of entries across the *Dictionary* elicit comments similar in kind. Past and present are juxtaposed under *inure*: 'It had anciently *with* before the thing practised, now *to*.' *Exile*, Johnson notes, 'seems anciently to have had the accent indifferently on either syllable' but, as he adds, 'now it is uniformly on the first'. *Neat*, in the sense 'Pure, unadulterated; unmingled' was 'formerly more extensive' but is 'now only used in the cant of trade'. Johnson's 'now' can insistently remind of the facts of change. Across the *Dictionary*, words expand and contract in sense and distribution.

What 'modern writers' do hence testifies to other changes at work in the native tongue, as Johnson's entry under *abet* makes clear: 'To push forward another, to support him in his designs by connivance, encouragement, or help. It is generally taken, at least by modern writers, in an ill sense'. Johnson's diction of the 'modern' can perhaps surprise. Yet, as under *abet*, usage, and its on-going forms make plain the shifts of connotation which remain at work. While *abet* moves from positive to negative, a move in the opposite direction characterizes the recent use of *accrue*. It means, Johnson notes, 'To be added, as an advantage or improvement, in a sense inclining to good rather than ill; in which meaning it is more frequently used by later authors'. Other words and senses are examined in ways which rely entirely on newly established shifts of use, such that, say, a *Methodist* is 'One of a new kind of puritans lately arisen'. *Magazine*—as Johnson's work on *The Gentleman's Magazine* confirmed—had, in recent years, likewise revealed new and significant developments in print culture: 'Of late this word has signified a miscellaneous pamphlet, from a periodical miscellany named the *Gentleman's Magazine*, by *Edward Cave*'.

'Modern English', at least in terms of Johnson's *Dictionary*, nevertheless perhaps appears most widely in Johnson's iterated emphasis on what 'we say' as a guide to English use. As under *withal*, Johnson can contrast past and present in these terms: 'it is sometimes used by writers where we now use *with*'. Johnson's invented examples, as we have seen,[40] take us towards his own language in use, and to the idioms and structures which characterized contemporary English of the eighteenth century. 'We *amend* a *bad*, but *improve* a *good* thing', as the entry for *improve* observes. 'We now say the *justice* of a cause, as well as of a judge', as Johnson likewise states under *justness*, here countering the strictly accurate distribution by which, as he notes, '*Justness* is properly applied to things, and *justice* to persons'. Here, too, language seems to be on the move.

The present can, of course, bring its own problems in terms of the determination of meaning, and the changes which might be at stake. As Johnson observed in *Rambler* 60, here in relation to human biography, 'If the biographer writes from personal knowledge', this brings with it concomitant 'danger', such that 'his interest, his fear, his gratitude, or his tenderness' might 'overpower his fidelity, and tempt him to conceal, if not to invent' (*Yale* III.323). Words—and the lexical biographies they reveal—can, at times, present the same problems. To write the past history of words is, in this respect, relatively easy. Seen from a distance, change can be viewed with equanimity. Closeup, it can be rather different, presenting, as we have seen in Chapter 5, other challenges for 'fidelity' by which 'interest', and the influence of negative language attitudes, can easily intervene. The processes of on-going history can elicit 'personal knowledge'—yet, as Johnson also illustrates, they can, at times, also bring 'fear'—and other aspects of resistance—into play.

What 'modern writers' do will not, in these terms, always meet with approval. As under *veil*, the inclusive 'we' can be conspicuous by its absence. 'To yield; to give place; to shew respect by yielding. In this sense, the modern writers have ignorantly written *veil*', Johnson writes, here adducing a practice which he evidently does not share. 'Modern corruption' seems to fare no better in Johnson's revised entry for *folk* in the fourth edition of 1773: 'it is properly a noun collective, and has no plural but by modern corruption'.[41] Similar is Johnson's evident distrust for the construction *to have rather*: 'this is, I think, a barbarous expression of late intrusion into our language, for which it is better to say *will rather*'.

The absence in English of those 'words more durable than brass' which Swift extols under *durable* in the *Dictionary* ('The glories of her majesty's reign ought to be recorded in words more *durable* than brass, and such as our posterity may read a thousand years hence')[42] can, in such ways, seem all too plain. While corruption is, as we have seen, often deployed to refer to the changes of external form by which language history can be manifest,[43] more negative connotations, resonant of the principle of decay and erroneous shift, can also emerge. As the *OED* notes, change can indeed often suggest decline in such uses: 'Change of language, a text, word, etc. from its correct or original condition to one of incorrectness, deterioration, etc'.[44] It is, as Johnson confirms, 'The means by which any thing is vitiated; depravation'.

Corruption, in Johnson's metalanguage, can hence be peculiarly double-edged. As under *alarum*, it is used to explain the visible change of form from the etymon or literal 'true meaning' ('corrupted, as it seems, from *alarm*'). Similar is *pore*, for which Johnson notes that 'I imagine *pore* to come by corruption from some English word'. Resistance in other entries is nevertheless transparent. '*From thenceforth* is a barbarous corruption', *thenceforth* (sense 2) likewise affirms in ways which withdraw approval from extensions of this kind. Similar is the comment he provides on the derivation of *embezzle*, and the changes of form that its own history might perhaps suggest: 'This word seems corrupted by an ignorant pronunciation from *imbecil*.' Johnson's entry for *you* offers a

188

particularly good example of the cross-currents of prescriptive and descriptive thinking in this respect. Johnson can introduce notions of correctness, and the idea of infelicitous change. Yet, by the same token, he can also record the salience of what is used in ways which—in terms of custom—counter the reservations he also feels compelled to advance. 'It is used in the nominative in common language, when the address is to persons; and though first introduced by corruption, is now established. In the following lines *you* and *ye* are used ungrammatically in the places of each other; but even this use is customary.'

We can, in such instances, be returned once more to the self-evident tensions of reason and desire, and the all too human engagement with words and what they mean. 'If the changes that we fear be thus irresistible, what remains but to acquiesce with silence, as in the other insurmountable distresses of humanity?', as Johnson demands in the 1755 'Preface'. Yet, as he offered in response, 'it remains that we retard what we cannot repel, that we palliate what we cannot cure. Life may be lengthened by care, though death cannot be ultimately defeated' (*Yale* XVIII.109). In Johnson's metaphor, the end-point is acknowledged—to *palliate* is, after all, as the *Dictionary* explains, merely 'To cure imperfectly or temporarily... to ease, not cure'.[45] 'Death', for words and man alike, will come when it will.[46] The course of change remains set. Nevertheless, it may yet be possible, Johnson suggests, to slow its progress, and perhaps to secure a temporary stay of execution for words and meanings whose tenure on life seems under threat. Hope is advanced, even as Johnson admits its fallibility. The *Dictionary*, as Johnson continues, is, after all, an enterprise which is, at heart, undertaken 'in hope of giving longevity to that which its own nature forbids to be immortal' (*Yale* XVIII.109).[47]

The lessons of history

Controlling time was, in fact, to assume an unexpected topicality across the *Dictionary*'s formation. It was Chesterfield moreover who appeared as architect of time's intended reform. Across Britain, in September 1752, time was brought into line with that of much of the rest of Europe;[48] the Julian calendar, used since 45 BC, was, as Chesterfield noted, 'corrected and amended' in favour of the Gregorian.[49] For this year alone, the second of September was followed by the fourteenth. Johnson's birthday, on 7 September under the old calendar, did not take place. Time, by Chesterfield's decree, was, in effect, standardized, establishing a new norm for the nation as a whole. As in the January issue of *The Gentleman's Magazine* (see Figure 5), time is seen as being redirected, here by Edward Cave in the guide of Sylvanus Urban, towards a newly improved and regulated path.

The affinities which were thereby generated between Chesterfield and Caesar would undoubtedly not have escaped Johnson's notice— nor would the consonances which this suggested with his own enterprise in which language, as we have seen, was also to be fixed, irrespective of time and the facts of current use. Caesar, in 45 BC, had directed time to run in a cycle of 365 and a quarter days. Chesterfield, in 1752, redirected it once more, implementing the diurnal patterns which we still observe. Yet, on closer examination, such patterns will, of course, reveal their own illusions in terms of human agency, and the responsiveness of time—or, indeed, language—to the dictates of the 'sublunary world'. If eleven days of September 1752 were apparently omitted, time itself had, in reality, continued seamlessly along its accustomed course, unimpeded and unaffected by Chesterfield's edict. That what had hitherto been 3 September was instead referred to as 14 September merely confirmed the arbitrariness of meaning, and the collective process by which the patterns of signification must be understood and used.

Illusions similar in kind, as Johnson explored, had long framed the dictionary-maker's attempt to control the workings of words in time. Edicts could be issued, and a perfected state of language eloquently set forth. As in the 1747 *Plan*, Chesterfield could be positioned as a modern Caesar, bringing language within his remit

Figure 5. *The Gentleman's Magazine* (1752), frontispiece. The Bodleian Libraries, The University of Oxford (Per. Bibl.2). Edward Cave, figured as Sylvanus Urban, is—as in the lines from Pope's *Essay on Man* which appear below the image—correcting 'old Time', and directing Time's course towards the shorter and improved path it will henceforth take.

191

of temporal control. A rhetoric of stasis, by which the mutable might be rendered immutable, remained prominent. Yet both time—and language—must, in reality, continue in a living language. In this respect, the fallible nature of human expectation emerges, as we have seen, as a widely prevalent Johnsonian theme. As he stressed a few years after completing the first edition of the *Dictionary*, 'If it be asked, what is the improper expectation which it is dangerous to indulge, experience will quickly answer, that it is such expectation, dictated not by reason but by desire.' It is 'expectation raised not by the common occurrences of life but by the wants of the Expectant ... Expectation that requires the common course of things to be changed, and the general rules of Action to be broken' (*Letters* I.203).

Language—and its own control—offered, of course, a range of timely lessons in this respect. As Johnson comprehensively explores, the ability of the dictionary-maker to change the 'common course of things' would, in reality, prove all too limited. Indeed, a lapse of half a century, as Johnson later confirmed to William Strahan, seems to be the boundary at which words once familiar will need to be glossed, and interpreted for readers for whom such forms are no longer part of their own living speech.[50] Publication of the *Dictionary* does not, as Johnson acknowledges, obviate such requirements; language and time moves on. 'There are, indeed, many truths which time necessarily and certainly teaches', as Johnson states in *Rambler* 50 (*Yale* III.271). Prime among these is, of course, that of temporality—and its ineluctable sway over human existence and its varied manifestations.

As in Johnson's later imaging of the dictionary as watch, time is, as he realizes, therefore integral both to lexicography and to the nature of language itself. 'Dictionaries are like watches', Johnson wrote to Francesco Sastres in 1784: 'the worst is better than none, yet even the best cannot be expected to go quite true' (*Letters* IV.379).[51] The pulse of time, and its on-going movement, governs the information that the watch, as time-piece, will reveal. Language, and its own temporal movement, is embedded in the role of the good dictionary as Johnson now perceives it. 'Running true', in sharp contradistinction to Johnson's imaging of the *Dictionary* in 1746–47, is made to engage with the dictionary-maker's ability to tell the time of language as it happens. Yet this, as Johnson had, of course, recognized in 1755, must also remain impossible. 'No dictionary of a living tongue ever can be perfect', the 'Preface' had affirmed (*Yale* XVIII.110). Even as the *Dictionary* was 'hastening to publication' (*Yale* XVIII.110), change was at work in the lexicon, moving beyond the forms which the dictionary-maker had set down.

8

The praise of perfection

By late spring in 1755, the *Dictionary* was, as Johnson's 'Preface' acknowledged, 'ended' if not 'completed' (*Yale* VIII.101). The diction of imperfection runs through his account of what he had achieved. 'The orthography and etymology, though imperfect, are not imperfect for want of care, but because care will not always be successful', he states. The examples, too, Johnson admits, will at times reveal but 'imperfect sense' (*Yale* XVIII.102). Even in terms of definition the same problems can emerge. 'He, whose design includes whatever language can express, must often speak of what he does not understand', as Johnson noted of other difficulties which had beset the writing of the *Dictionary* (*Yale* XVIII.110). 'Ignorance, pure ignorance' lay behind the erroneous definition of *pastern* which the *Dictionary* had provided. This was not, in fact, as the relevant entry explained 'The knee of an horse' but 'That part of the leg of a horse between the joint next the foot and the hoof', as the fourth edition of 1773 confirmed. Similar was *dab-chick* which, as Smollett observed, Johnson 'calls a chicken newly hatched; though in fact it is a water-fowl'.[1] As Johnson later commented, 'there are four or five hundred Faults' in the *Dictionary*. Correction, he estimated, 'would take...up three Months Labour, & when the Time was out, the Work would not be done'.[2]

Samuel Johnson and the Journey into Words. Lynda Mugglestone
© Lynda Mugglestone 2015. First published 2015 by Oxford University Press.

'Perfection', as Chesterfield had declared in 1754, is not, of course, 'to be expected from man'. Nevertheless, expectations that Johnson's *Dictionary* might prove exempt from this general truth were plain. In Chesterfield's calculated 'puff', Johnson's work, as we have seen, was firmly distinguished from the mere 'WORD-BOOKS' which English lexicography had hitherto produced. 'If we are to judge by the various works of Mr. Johnson, already published, we have good reason to believe that he will bring this as near to perfection as any one man could do', Chesterfield avers.[3] In what is clearly intended as another auspicious (and flattering) conjunction, the *Dictionary* is carefully aligned with 'those perfect productions, that now do so much honour' to Italy and to France.[4]

Johnson had, however, his own ideas about perfection. As in the *Plan,* it provides an example of the difficulties of determining meaning, as well as the problems which English, in particular, can pose in this respect. *Perfection,* Johnson notes, can, of course, be accorded a 'philosophical and exact sense'. Yet, he adds, this is 'of little use among human beings' (*Yale* XVIII.49). Instead, as in the *Dictionary, perfection* of this kind is made to pertain to realms beyond the 'sublunary' where lexicographers, of necessity, have their being alongside the works they produce.[5] Real perfection is an 'attribute of God' rather than man, sense 3 of *perfection* explains. The citation from Richard Hooker which Johnson includes under sense 1 ('The state of being perfect') was equally pertinent in this respect. Absolute perfection, Hooker stressed, is 'spiritual and divine, consisting in those things whereunto we tend by supernatural means . . . but cannot here attain'.

Other senses of *perfection* had come into existence though, as Johnson elaborates, such use was, by definition, 'loose and popular' rather than 'strict and critical' (*Yale* XVIII.49). It is by extensions of this kind that *perfection,* in other patterns of polysemy, can, as the *Dictionary* explains, signify 'something that concurs to produce supreme excellence' rather than being, in reality, perfect in and of itself.[6] Here, Johnson's prescriptive stance was plain. Such patterns of signification, he warned, 'ought to be distinguished'. To ally the fallibilities of what might pass, in human terms, for perfection with the true perfection the divine reveals will yield error in ways that extend far beyond semantics and the properties of words. Claims of human perfection, as in *Rambler* 14, instead all too easily turn towards hyperbole and exaggerated praise, evoking still other 'phantom[s]' in which 'fancy' and illusion rather than factual truth prevail (*Yale* III.74). The diction of 'The Vanity of Human Wishes' is again conspicuous. So, too, is that of Johnson's earlier 'Scheme'.

The praise of 'perfection', directed by Chesterfield to academies on the Continent and the dictionaries they produced, is subject to equally critical review. For Johnson, this easily exemplifies his 'loose and popular' sense, inclining, as in the entry for *hyperbole*, to the kind of 'rhetorick by which any thing is increased or diminished beyond the exact truth'. Chesterfield's praise confirms the kind of semantic 'licentiousness' which Johnson had earlier feared. *Perfection*, as the *Plan* had observed, is indeed 'often so much degraded from its original signification, that the academicians have inserted in their work *the perfection of a language*, and with a little more licentiousness might have prevailed on themselves to add *the perfection of a dictionary*' (*Yale* XVIII.49).[7]

While Johnson, as he acknowledged, had 'endeavoured well' in the long years of writing the *Dictionary*, he would therefore systematically distance his work from perfection, and the claims that might thereby be advanced (*Yale* XVIII.58).[8] Dictionary-making for Johnson remains an all too human process in which, as he reminds us, 'sudden fits of inadvertency will surprize vigilance, slight avocations will seduce attention, and casual eclipses of the mind will darken learning; and that the writer shall often in vain trace his memory at the moment of need, for that which yesterday he knew with intuitive readiness, and which will come uncalled into his thoughts to-morrow' (*Yale* XVIII.111). The achievements of the Académie Française or the Accademia della Crusca are, in a further corrective, also placed within schema of this kind. As the 1755 'Preface' makes plain, the *Dictionnaire* must, in reality, emblematize not perfection but its absence, and failure rather than success in terms of its stated remit to impose stasis and immutability on a living language. As we have seen, 'If the embodied cricks of *France*, when fifty years had been spent upon their work, were obliged to change its oeconomy, and give their second edition another form', then, as Johnson concludes, he too 'may surely be contented without the praise of perfection' (*Yale* XVIII.113).

Here, the *Dictionnaire* and Johnson's *Dictionary* are at one, united in what cannot be performed by human agency in the 'sublunary' world of words. Popular estimations of Johnson's work—and the perfection it must impose—had, of course, envisaged rather different conclusions. Chesterfield was by no means alone in the expectations he had advanced. 'This performance promised something so much like what all men of taste had long thought wanting to the purity, stability and perfection of our language', as William Shaw stated, recalling the appearance of Johnson's *Plan* of 1747 and the 'idea of an English dictionary' which it set out.[9] A *perfecter*, as the *Dictionary* explains, was 'One that makes perfect'. To *perfect* was 'To finish, to complete; to consummate'; it was 'to bring to its due state'. Yet, as Johnson indicated already in 1747, the 'due state' of English was, in reality, a product of its history, embedded in a narrative in which, against perfection, both chance and change were prominent. It 'did not descend to us in a state of uniformity and perfection, but was produced by necessity and enlarged by accident', he stressed (*Yale* XVIII.43). Imperfection was, as such, the natural condition of the native tongue; it reflected the vagaries of history and long use, rather than a system of ordered control.

That language can be perfected by lexicography was, as we have seen, therefore repeatedly placed in doubt. 'Every language has its anomalies, which, though inconvenient, and in themselves once unnecessary, must be tolerated among the imperfections of human things' (*Yale* XVIII.75), Johnson confirms in 1755. His diction is, yet again, placed in careful apposition to that which Chesterfield adopts in his letters to the *World*. Models of toleration divide. For Chesterfield, as Chapter 6 has explored, toleration was intentionally to be brought to an end by Johnson's work.[10] Johnson, in contrast, prescribes not closure but continuance, moving towards a far more reasoned apprehension of what dictionaries, and dictionary-makers, might achieve.

Perfection would, as a result, inform another set of journeys which have, conspicuously, not been taken. The endeavour 'to persue perfection' was, in effect, Johnson writes, to be 'like the first inhabitants of Arcadia, to chace the sun, which, when they had reached the hill where he seemed to rest, was still beheld at the same distance from them' (*Yale* XVIII.101). Such ambitions are futile and never-ending. Language, in this light, inevitably remains a realm of infinite possibilities which the lexicographer cannot circumscribe; there is, as Johnson was well aware, always more to be known and discovered. Obsolescence, like naturalization—or, indeed, toleration—cannot realistically be rendered a finite process. As in the narrative arc of *Rasselas*, language already proves a story for which a conclusion cannot be given, and matters neatly brought to an end.[11]

What we might assume to be indicative of perfection can demand equally careful reassessment. Stasis offers, as we have seen, a perfected state of language which is, as for Snell and Swift, almost utopian in its promise of a diction which will no longer fade into obsolescence and in which words, and meaning, will always stay the same. Such ideals are pervasive; an 'exemption from the change of seasons, and a perpetuity of spring' have indeed regularly been included 'among the felicities of the golden age', Johnson notes, for example, in *Rambler* 80, written in December 1750 (*Yale* IV.56). In such domains, he continues, 'the fancy may be amused with the descriptions of regions in which no wind is heard but the gentle zephir, and no scenes are displayed but vallies enamelled with unfading flowers, and woods waving their perennial verdure' (*Yale*

IV.56–7). The diction of 'unfading' flowers, and 'perennial' verdure can, of course, allure, offering a stereotype of felicity in which invariance and immutability are prime. Yet the dynamics of change and changelessness can prompt the kind of rational enquiry of received wisdom which, as for Fred Parker, underpins the nature of Johnsonian scepticism per se.[12] Utopias, as John Carey later warns, can easily become dystopias by a simple change of perspective.[13] The same proves true in Johnson's thinking. Invariance is merely a 'state of imaginary happiness', he observes (*Yale* IV.56). Granted such changelessness, the desire for variety would, he postulates, soon resurge: 'We should soon grow weary of uniformity', and the restrictions that this would, in reality, impose.

As Johnson concludes, he is by no means 'certain' that 'sufficient provision' has been made for 'that insatiable demand of new gratifications, which seems particularly to characterize the nature of man' (*Yale* IV.56–7). 'Uniformity must tire at last', even if 'it be uniformity of excellence', he stressed to similar effect in the 'Life of Butler' (*Yale* XXI.218). Language will, in reality, reveal similar disjunctions. Outside rhetorical ambitions for immutability, and a diction that will always stay the same, language as human artefact will instead respond to the desire for 'new gratifications', and the momentum that the 'nature of man' reveals. As Johnson repeatedly explored in the *Rambler*, the 'chair of instruction' can be notably uneasy, not least since 'whether any will submit to . . . authority' can be unclear (*Yale* IV.12). There are 'few things so liberally bestowed, or squandered with so little effect' as advice, he concludes (*Yale* IV.93). Edict and obedience will by no means necessarily coincide. Robert Lowth's refusal to sanction Johnson's recommended spelling for the printing of his *Life of William Wykeham* would, in this, by no means have surprised. 'Regardless I think I am right', Lowth insisted; the spelling *bulle* rather than Johnson's *bull* was, he instructed, to be used.[14] That neither Dodsley nor Chesterfield change their habitual forms in response to Johnson's work was similar. Even if, as Tieken Boon von Ostade contends, Hester Thrale adopts Johnson's favoured *-ick*, her spelling of *plumb, sower, chear-ful*, and countless other words remain unmodified by the example he provides.[15] As Johnson confirmed in his later revisions to the 'Life of Roscommon', even given 'the sanction of power', the 'present manners of the nation would deride authority, and therefore nothing is left, but that every writer should criticize himself'. Johnson's doubleness of perspective will, in this respect, move to include the dynamics of instruction and obedience, recommendation and dissent.

While change in material culture clearly requires new words and senses, so, too, as Johnson hence affirms, does the individual desire for self-expression. With no little irony, those who stressed the need for fixity can, from a different point of view, easily exemplify, as Johnson was aware, the 'demand for new gratification' in linguistic terms. Dryden, as we have seen, provides a prime example of such tensions across the *Dictionary*; if he extols stability, he also innovates in ways which repeatedly challenge the shared patterns of signification by which language is used and understood. Swift's creative neologisms in his letters (as well as elsewhere) likewise neatly undermine his advocacy of linguistic control while Chesterfield, too, as we have seen in Chapter 6, proves a conspicuous innovator, importing scores of new words and phrases across the borders he would, in principle, have Johnson defend.[16] Just as Johnson reminded Boswell in 1760, if experience is a means by which 'theory' is often contradicted, it also remains, as he added, the 'great test of truth' (*Life* V.454).

Such ideas prove, of course, staple elements of Johnsonian thinking. 'I know not any thing more pleasant, or more instructive', he writes to Bennet Langton in June 1758, 'than to compare experience with expectation', as well as to observe the differences between 'idea' and 'reality', and the 'hopes' and 'discoveries' which will thereby emerge (*Life* I.337). Received wisdom can, for Johnson, easily reveal its fallibilities, in terms of language as all else. As the 1755 'Preface' confirms, the rigidities of stasis as an image of perfection will inevitably share in similar processes. Johnson's diction in this respect is, indeed, firmly prescriptive. 'It must be remembered', he stresses, 'that while our language is yet living, ... words are hourly shifting their relations, and can no more be ascertained in a dictionary, than a grove, in the agitation of a storm, can be accurately delineated from its picture in the water' (*Yale* XVIII.89–90). Trying to 'embalm' that which is still alive is, as he suggests, likewise part of unreason and folly rather than legitimate endeavour. As Johnson makes plain, the *Dictionary* can explain and interpret but, like the 'Sea of words' to which Johnson also has recourse in 1755, language is defined by its fluidity, and its responsiveness to external conditions.

Just as in Johnson's later comments on Shakespeare, that such a writer should 'want a commentary' and 'that his language should become obsolete, or his sentiments obscure' can be a cause of regret. Nevertheless, as Johnson adds, it is 'vain to carry wishes beyond the condition of human things' (*Yale* VII.112). As in the *Dictionary*, Johnson instead presents a range of conditions for continued change rather than stasis in the native tongue. Lexicographical 'conquest', as we have seen, is firmly discounted (*Yale* XVIII.105), along with other unwarranted assumptions of the power the dictionary-maker might wield. In contrast, linguistic change and its mechanisms are carefully anatomized. Commerce and trade, as the 'Preface' notes, will therefore bring new words and meanings into play which 'will not always be confined to the exchange, the warehouse, or the port, but will be communicated by degrees to other ranks of the people, and be at last incorporated with the current speech' (*Yale* XVIII.106). Bacon's diction, and the salience of change 'by degrees', is again affirmed;[17] contact and the facts of linguistic diffusion will operate far outside the confines of a dictionary, and the meanings it might impose. Only a language 'secluded from strangers', as well as from the intellectual stimulus of books and learning, will, Johnson points out, be immune from conditions of this kind. English, as he observes, is necessarily remote from such conditions: 'No such constancy can be expected in a people polished by arts, and classed by subordination, where one part of the community is sustained and accommodated by the labour of the other' (*Yale* XVIII.106).

As Johnson's wider discussion of lexical change in the 'Preface' explores, such mutability is, however, equally to be seen part of the advancement of knowledge, reifying the discoveries which gradually come to light. Language reflects, he stresses, the flow of ideas, and the flux of experience and thought: 'Those who have much leisure to think, will always be enlarging the stock of ideas, and every increase of knowledge, whether real or fancied, will produce new words, or combinations of words' (*Yale* XVIII.106). Innovation and renovation cannot, in reality, be stilled. Nor, in truth, would one want to remain constantly at one with the ideas, and the knowledge of the past. Language, culture, and knowledge change in symbiosis. As 'various sciences' are cultivated, the 'language is amplified', Johnson confirms (*Yale* XVIII.107). In a further rejoinder to Swift's 'petty treatise', he stresses moreover that 'gain' cannot exist without loss: 'When the mind is unchained from necessity, it will range after convenience; when it is left at large in the fields of speculation, it will shift opinions; as any custom is disused, the words that expressed it must perish with it; as any opinion grows popular, it will innovate speech in the same proportion as it alters practice' (*Yale* XVIII.106). Bound to the cycles of budding and falling away, language is seen as fundamentally regenerative. Johnson can, in such considerations, emerge, as Hanks argues, as a thoroughly 'modern' lexicographer.[18]

In Johnson's 'Preface', written in reality, as we have seen, as a conclusion to his endeavours, we end therefore with a firm attempt to see things as they are. The journey into words is complete; travel, as he would later stress to Thrale, here proves its utility, disabusing those who journey of the fallacies and fictions with which they once set out.[19] 'Nothing tends so much to enlarge the mind as *travelling*', a citation from Isaac Watts confirms under *travel* in the *Dictionary*. Whether literal or metaphorical, 'A man not enlightened by *travel* or reflexion, grows as fond of arbitrary power, to which he hath been used, as of barren countries, in which he has been born and bred', Addison affirms in a further quotation which places lack of knowledge and assumptions of unreasonable power in a similar context. As in *Rambler* 137, heroism in the world of words is made, in the end, to reside in discovery and knowledge, in the endeavour to 'conquer new regions in the intellectual world', as well as to 'find [one's] way through the fluctuations of uncertainty, and the conflicts of contradiction'. If dictionary-making is a battle, what is to be defeated is, at best, that which remains unknown in the 'unexplored abysses of truth' (*Yale* IV.362). For the lexicographer, heroism and drudgery can unite, even if the 'sea of words' must, of necessity, remain unstilled.

Johnson's metaphors of circumnavigation are, in this, particularly apposite. He returns, in essence, to where he began. The state of language remains unchanged by his endeavours, even if, in 'ascertaining' and 'settling', he has removed ambiguity and obscurity from countless words and senses. If Locke's 'conduit' of understanding is thereby facilitated,[20] the policies of eradication which were outlined at various points of the *Plan* are not sustained; as we have seen, Johnson's policy of branding can fade into metalinguistic comments which, for most words, attempt to engage with the contexts in which they are used, and the prosodies they reveal. We are perhaps by no means consoled by Johnson's stress on the imperfectability of human discourse—nor indeed by his careful elision of those 'supplemental satisfactions' which rose-tinted images of the future (and prescriptive redress) so often bring. 'Whether to see life as it is, will give us much consolation, I know not', as Johnson later admitted to Langton. Yet, as he added, 'the consolation which is drawn from truth, if any there be, is solid and durable; that which may be derived from errour must be, like its original, fallacious and fugitive' (*Life* I.339).

The critics on the shore
'A man of lively fancy no sooner finds a hint moving in his mind, than he makes momentous excursions to the press, and to the

world', Johnson had reflected in *Rambler* 2, written in March 1750. The essay offers a careful account of the ease which such 'wantoning in common topics' and 'the indulgence of hope' offers the writer. To say what is expected brings a guarantee of praise, Johnson acknowledged; 'A train of sentiments generally received enables him to shine without labour' and, indeed, 'to conquer without a contest' (*Yale* III.9). Nevertheless, as Johnson adds, 'What is new is opposed, because most are unwilling to be taught' (*Yale* III.14). The writer's journey can, in such circumstances, be marked by its own felicity: 'we may believe authors... more inclined to pursue a track so smooth and so flowery, than attentively to consider whether it leads to truth' (*Yale* III.10).[21]

Johnson's journeys into words are, of course, as he states to Garrick and Moore, characterized by difficulty rather than felicity, and 'danger' rather than the untroubled passage he envisages in 1750. Johnson, as he states to Warton, has 'wandered' (*Letters* I.92); habits of excursion, as we have seen, can, during the *Dictionary*'s formation, take him far from his intended course and the 'settled path' which might perhaps be followed. Other difficulties, as he writes to Warton, nevertheless wait on the metaphorical 'shore' (*Letters* I.92). Approaching land, he, too, must, like Florio, pass the strictures of those '*Lande-Critikes, monsters of men*'.[22] Johnson, as we have seen, foresaw further possibilities of attack and defence.[23]

Johnson's estimation of the conflicted reception that the *Dictionary* might meet proved, in fact, remarkably accurate. Early comment, as we have seen in Chapter 2, had already ventured a range of criticisms; Chesterfield, Taylor, as well as Johnson's other critical readers, all intentionally guided the dictionary into markedly more prescriptive (and proscriptive) domains. In later comment too, Johnson's presumed patterns of consonance—or, indeed, departure—from the kind of 'common topics' which featured in popular language attitudes could be a matter of critical import. Johnson, for instance, easily conquers without a contest in Garrick's celebratory sonnet 'Upon Johnson's *Dictionary*'. Garrick's oppositional discourse extended the martial imagery Johnson had used in the *Plan*. Wielding 'pen' rather than 'sword', Johnson is deemed to have defeated the French Academy in what becomes a paean to national honour as realized by lexicography. 'Well-arm'd like a hero of yore', Johnson's achievements are given unqualified praise: he 'has beat forty *French*, and will beat forty more'.[24]

A lengthy review, probably by John Hawkesworth, which appeared in Cave's *Gentleman's Magazine* in April 1755 meanwhile carefully engaged with perfection and lexicography in ways which Johnson would have appreciated: 'let not any... depreciate, for trivial imperfections, a work in which perfection was not possible to man', Hawkesworth wrote.[25] Yet, like Garrick, Hawkesworth set English against French, assimilating Johnson's work into the kind of academy discourses which the 'Preface', as we have seen, consummately rejects. Johnson, he writes, 'alone has effected in seven years, what the joint labour of forty academicians could not produce to a neighbouring nation in less than half a century'.[26] That Johnson had, in effect, created a *de facto* academy swiftly passed into popular folk-linguistics, and the history of English.

As for Sheridan, Johnson's *Dictionary* was seen as the 'cornerstone' by which 'our language' might be fixed[27] while, by April 1757, a writer in the *London Chronicle* commends the way in which Johnson had 'supplied the Want of an Academy', and 'performed Wonders towards Fixing our Grammar, and Ascertaining the determinate Meaning of Words'. While words are known 'to be in their own Nature of a very unstable and fluctuating Quality', Johnson's endeavours, the writer continued, have prevented the obsolescence of eighteenth-century English, while time itself has been defeated. The *Dictionary* is a '*monumentum aere perennius*', the writer declared: 'To his Labours it may hereafter be owing that our Drydens, our Addisons, and our Popes shall not become as obsolete and unintelligible as Chaucer.'[28] The *Dictionary* is made to fulfil Swift's desiderata, irrespective of Johnson's self-evident reservations in this respect. Johnson's authority in spelling is similarly commended.

As Nares noted in 1784, this 'has nearly fixed the external form of our language'; Johnson is commended for the reforms he instituted, and the remedies for 'unsettled orthography' which he has introduced.[29] Johnson 'fix'd the standard of that wavering tongue', Richard Graves declared in 1786.[30]

There were, of course, detractors. Ironically, these can at times prove more perceptive about what Johnson had, in reality, achieved. Adam Smith, reviewing Johnson's work in the *Edinburgh Review* commented negatively, for example, on the reticence which the *Dictionary* often demonstrates in proscriptive and prescriptive terms. While Johnson has 'extended his views much farther' than earlier lexicographers, 'we cannot help wishing, that that the author had trusted less to the judgment of those who may consult him, and had oftener passed his own censure upon those words which are not of approved use, tho' sometimes to be met with in authors of no mean name'.[31] While Johnson, as we have seen, scrutinized both 'suffrage' and dictatorship, his agency should, as Smith contends, clearly have been used to better effect.

Johnson's interest in citations, and the 'testimony' these provide, can meet similar censure. His evidence is 'too profuse', Thomas Edwards declares: 'His needless number of authorities is intolerable.' They range, too, as we have seen, far outside the accepted canons of correctness: 'I am more angry that his Authors are often of no authority', Edwards exclaimed. Authority, he argued, should be embodied in the dictionary-maker, not relegated to a range of minor writers and the evidence they provide. Johnson's methodology was, from this point of view, deemed entirely awry; the proper territory of the dictionary-maker was, as Edwards stressed, surely far more prescriptive. The empirical forays Johnson had made should have been restricted to canonical writers whose correctness was guaranteed. Yet, to Edward's disapproval, 'L'estrange, Peacham Brown Mortimer and twenty others, who either are not known, or known have no character for writing correctly' were all produced as witnesses to English in use.[32] As in Chapter 3, Johnson's juxtapositions of Mortimer and Pope, or Raleigh and Milton, could readily discomfit popular expectation: 'Those bad words of Brown and L estrange should, I think, have a mark of reprobation put upon them least they should from this Dictionary be again brought into use', Edwards concludes.[33] If Chesterfield had, as Edwards notes, promised 'implicite obedience' to his 'chosen Dictator', this was, however, 'a much higher complement' than he himself felt, as a result, able to give to Johnson's *Dictionary*.[34]

Johnson's failure to reform and fix English spelling, and his tolerance of variant forms, encounters similar censure. Edwards had early offered a number of recommendations to Johnson in this respect (which Johnson had politely refused).[35] Charles Lucas's *Essay on Waters*, written in Lucas's reformed spelling, would in this light offer an intentional corrective to Johnson's perceived deficits.[36] Deferring too often to 'custom', Johnson had, Lucas suggested, failed to prescribe a new standard by which words might be used. A range of other schemes for regulation and control likewise continued to appear. Smollett, as in the *Critical Review*, would, for example, seize other opportunities by which linguistic purity might be instilled on a language which still seemed all too mutable. As both Basker and Hanley note, Smollett's directives present a far more stringent insistence on correctness, and the reformist agenda that good usage should observe.[37] Irrespective of Johnson's cautions on the illusions of power that academies present, ambitions for the autocratic reform of language remained open to further endeavour and individual decree. Writing Johnson's biography, Arthur Murphy both cited—and resisted—Johnson's claims in this respect. Johnson's verdict 'surely is not conclusive', Murphy contends; the 'standard of the best writers' will provide 'the authority of superior genius' which others should observe.[38] Across the eighteenth century and into our own, Johnson's *Dictionary* can be made a monument to what it had not performed, and to what—as Johnson stressed—remained, of necessity, beyond human reach.

Appendix: 1755–73

For a dictionary, there can, in reality, be no last words. As Johnson realized in 1755, even if *Z* is reached, the destination once proposed remains as distant as before. Revising the *Dictionary* for the fourth edition in 1773, Johnson was, as a result, forced to confront once more what lexicography had, and had not achieved. As Reddick confirms, this was to be yet another venture for the *Dictionary* as commodity.[1] Two earlier editions had been published without substantial intervention and change; a second folio edition (1755–56) was published weekly in individual sections to make it more affordable. A compact and cheaper edition, with authority names but not accompanying quotations, also appeared in 1756, aimed at 'common readers' who might not be able to afford the elegance (and commodiousness) of the full text.[2] The third edition, as Catherine Dille has shown, reveals some interesting processes of revision, but is still essentially the 'same' text.[3] The fourth edition, which has been thoroughly discussed by Reddick, represents therefore the only wide-ranging reassessment which Johnson carried out.

The suggestion for a new edition again came from the booksellers.[4] Johnson began work in 1771, being paid £300 (the equivalent of some £30,000 today). Peyton and Alexander McBean, two of his former amanuenses, returned to their work. Writing to Boswell, Johnson was nevertheless again dismissive of what he had been able to achieve. Imperfection necessarily remained. 'A new edition of my great Dictionary is printed, from a copy which I was persuaded to revise; but having made no preparation, I was able to do very little', he commented in February 1773 (*Letters* II.8–9). If the dictionary is 'great', this is in terms of size (Johnson's sense 1: 'Large in bulk or number') rather than convictions of its quality or power to effect change.[5] 'Some superfluities I have expunged, and some faults I have corrected, and here and there have scattered a remark; but the main fabrick of the work remains as it was.' As he added, 'I had looked very little into it since I wrote it, and, I think, I found it full as often better, as worse, than I expected.'

In Johnson's revisions, the text is often corrected, such that typographical errors in the first edition disappear in the fourth; an *observer* in 1755 had, for example, been defined as 'One who looks vigilantly on persons on things; close remaker'. The missing *r* in *remake* was added in 1773, giving the semantically accurate 'remarker'.[6] New 'excursions into books' have also been made,[7] while evidence from the processes of revision confirms that Johnson also returned to the 'transcripts' collected for the *Dictionary* of 1755. As Reddick notes, citations from the Bible, Milton, Young, and William Law—whose *Serious Call to a Devout and Holy Life* (1729) Johnson first read as an undergraduate in 1728–29—are all prominent in the changes Johnson incorporated.[8] New entries also appear, from the specificity of *stibiarian*, defined as 'a violent man; from the violent operation of antimony' and given as 'obsolete', to core lexis such as *stewpan*; 'A pan used for stewing', Johnson explains. *Reckoning-book*: 'A book in which money received and expended is set down', and *intenable* provide other additions. 'Indefensible', Johnson noted of *intenable*, constructing his own examples of use: 'as, an *intenable opinion*; an *intenable fortress*'. A *hedge-creeper* in, another new entry, is 'one that skulks under hedges for bad purposes'.

Other entries such as those under *lest* and *might* (n.) reveal a wide-ranging reassessment, imposing new structures and sense-divisions in ways that reveal Johnson's changed apprehension of both sense and meaning. *Lest* had, for example, been cursorily treated in 1755. 'That not' comprised the whole of its definition. Two quotations, from the Bible and Addison, had documented its use. In 1773, *lest* is instead given two sense-divisions which comment on usage in far greater detail, as well as an extended array of supporting evidence.[9] *Mighty* was another word that clearly offered far more scope for Johnson's acts of reinterpretation. The two senses of the first edition ('Powerful; strong', and 'Excellent, or powerful in any act') are now revised to twelve, none of which matches precisely those given in 1755. Twenty-one citations are variously used in illustration, in contradistinction to the four on which the first edition had relied. Johnson's revisions for *to discover* are likewise worthy of note. The three senses deemed adequate in 1755 are now revised to nine, allowing scope for meanings such as 'To detect; to find though concealed' (Johnson's new sense 7) or 'To find things or places not known before' (sense 8) to be documented and evidenced in full.

Definitions prove similarly mutable. As under *flammability*, Johnson's aims of 'perspicuity' and clarity prompt the expansion which sense 1 now reveals: 'The quality of admitting to be set on fire' as in 1755 becomes, in 1773, 'The quality of admitting to be set on fire, so as to blaze'. *Favouredly* is expanded with similar specificity. The definition 'Always joined with *well* or *ill*, in a fair or foul sense' is modified by an additional phrase, making the circumstances of use plain: 'with good or bad appearance'. Similar is the new attention given to *nigh*. Defined in five words in 1755 ('not at a great distance'), the revisions of 1773 offer a careful anatomisation of sense and use: 'Not at a great distance, either in time or place, or course of events: when it is used of time, it is applied to time future'. Other improvements appear under *bald*. Given as merely 'Wanting hair' in 1755, 'want' had hovered ambiguously between the sense of absence or lack, and that of desire. 'Wanting hair; despoiled of hair by time or sickness', the fourth edition instead eloquently explains. The careful rephrasing of the 1755 definition of *slowworm* offers other ways in which 'nearer and nearer approaches' to perfection 'may be made', as Johnson declares in the 'Advertisement' to the 1773 edition (*Yale* XVIII.375). 'The blind worm; a small viper, venomous, but scarcely mortal', Johnson had noted in 1755. The revised definition reveals a shift in both factual accuracy and nuance: 'The blind worm; a large viper, not mortal, scarcely venomous'.

Across a range of entries, Johnson likewise amplifies the 'colours' of words, adding a new sense under *drive* (v.) in order to explain that 'To *drive*, in all its senses, whether active or neuter, may be observed to retain a sense compounded of violence and progression'. *Hanker*, defined in 1755 as 'To long importunately; to have an incessant wish', now gains the stylistic qualification: 'It is scarcely used but in familiar language'. *Notable*, in the sense 'Remarkable; memorable; observable' is further explained by the comment: 'it is now scarcely used, but in irony'. As under *run* (v.), Johnson's processes of attention in this respect are marked. A new sense 13 completes the entry, serving as an overview for what has gone before: 'This is one of the words which serves for use when other words are wanted, and has therefore obtained a great multiplicity of relations and intentions; but it may be observed always to retain much of its primitive idea, and to imply progression, and, for the most part, progressive violence.' *Run* in 1755 had 15 senses; here, too, Johnson has reconsidered and revised.

Such longer reflective comments appear at a range of points in 1773, confirming other aspects of the difficult journey into words, and the challenges of lexicography in which, as the 'Advertisement' for the fourth edition also confirmed, 'perfection is unattainable' (*Yale* XVIII.375). Johnson's thoughtful exposition of *with* and its complex patterns of use in a new sense 18 is, for example, typical. New patterns of doubt and uncertainty are

prominent, alongside new consideration of the patterns of 'common...
speech': 'This preposition might perhaps be exemplified in many more
relations, for its use is very frequent, and therefore very lax and various.
With and *by*, it is not always easy to distinguish, nor perhaps is any
distinction always observed. *With* seems rather to denote an instrument,
and *by* a cause: thus, *he killed his enemy* with *a sword*, but *he died* by *an
arrow*. The arrow is considered rather as a cause, as there is no mention of
an agent. If the agent be more remote, *by* is used; as, *the vermine which he
could not kill* with *his gun, he killed* by *poison*.' As Johnson adds, 'If these
two propositions be transposed, the sentence, though equally intelligible,
will be less agreeable to the common modes of speech.'

Other changes meanwhile return us to the complexities of power and
powerlessness, and of conquest and control. While the 1773 'Preface' retains
its stress on the inevitability of change, and the futility of endeavours to 'lash
the wind', and 'enchain syllables', as well as of railing against the 'intumescence of the tide', the *Dictionary* can, at times, comes perilously close to the
stereotypes of 'the vice of age' (and the 'severity and censoriousness' which
this comports) which Johnson had explored in *Rambler* 50 (*Yale* III.272).
'Every old man complains of the growing depravity of the world, of the
petulance and insolence of the rising generation', Johnson had noted (*Yale*
III.269); the old, he added, often tell a narrative of decline, seeing change as
degeneration, and variation as loss, such that the 'discipline and sobriety of
the age in which his youth was passed' is celebrated, while the present can be
seen as out of step.

Revising the *Dictionary* can therefore remind not only of mutability—of
words, meanings, or the forms they might assume—but equally of time itself,
and its relentless passing. If, as under *lesser* and *latter*,[10] Johnson can confirm
the salience of custom, its force, in other entries, can prompt regret. Change
can be negatively positioned, as under *brasing* ('Made of brass'). In 1755, the
entry had appeared without metalinguistic comment. Johnson now, however,
reflects on the intervening years, and the sense of degeneration which time
has wrought. It 'is now less properly written according to the pronunciation
brazen', he points out. The phrasal structures of verbs which, in 1755, often
served to confirm Johnson's close attention to patterns of usage can gain
similar correctives. As Johnson notes, for example, under *call*, this means, in
essence, 'To stop without intention of staying'. Yet usage has expanded in
potentially undesirable ways: 'This meaning probably rose from the custom of
denoting one's presence at the door by a *call*; but it is now used with great
latitude. This sense is well enough preserved by the particles *on* or *at*; but is

forgotten, and the expression made barbarous by *in.*' New forms of vicious-ness likewise emerge. As under *according* (sense 3), Johnson notes that 'The following phrase is, I think, vitious', here with reference to Swift's use of 'according as'. Similar additions appear under *accrue* (sense 4), *deal* (sense 5), and *fore* (sense 2).

Johnson can revise entries and the limits of 'toleration' in tandem. If the state of language is different in 1773 so, too, is Johnson's stance in entries such as these. *Fruitive* reveals another example of heightened prescriptive sensibilities. 'Enjoying; possessing; having the power of enjoyment. A word not legitimate', Johnson states. Conspicuous, too, is Johnson's diction of the 'unauthorised', even when set against 'authorities' which, of necessity, document the use in question. 'One who studies or describes insects', the 1755 entry for *insectologer* had noted. 'A word, I believe, unauthorised', Johnson adds in 1773, suggesting a somewhat different attitude to his supporting evidence from William Derham's *Physico-Theology* of 1713: 'The insect itself is, according to modern insectologers, of the ichneu-mon-fly kind.' Similar shifts appear in the revision of *relate* ('To vent by words. Unauthorised') or that of *scout*, here in a new sense 2: 'To ridicule; to sneer. This is a sense unauthorised, and vulgar', Johnson states, in ways which render the negative sense of 'vulgar' particularly marked. The change is not approved, nor is evidence provided.

Time, too, prompts revision in other ways. If, as Johnson comments to Sasstres, the dictionary is a watch (*Letters* IV.379), his changing sense of the past is equally apparent across the 1773 edition. *Scantly* is 'obsolete', Johnson now notes, though he had used it in defining *scarcely* in 1755. Further comments on what is 'not in use' attend Johnson's entries for words such as *daft* (adj.), and *dag*, *daub* ('to play the hypocrite'), *depriv-ation* (sense 3: 'Defamation; censure; a sense not now in use'), *despiteous* ('Malicious; furious. A word now out of use'), or *disadvantageable*, defined as 'Contrary to profit; producing loss. A word not used'. Similar are the revisions he appends to *liegeman*, or *limp* in the sense 'vapid, weak', or *lore* ('Lost; destroyed'), together with a wide range of other similar emend-ations.[11] If the *Dictionary* is enlarged and corrected as Johnson's 1772 poem 'Post Lexicon Anglicanum Auctum et Emendatum' (*Yale* VI.271–4) confirms, the text is, as a range of critics have already stressed, often more conservative—revealing new endeavours to 'palliate what we cannot cure' in ways which return us once more to the conflicts of the *Plan*, and the all too natural—if unrealizable—hopes by which immutability, invariance, and perfection are framed in terms of language.

Notes

Preface

1. See *Rambler* 158, in *The Rambler* III–V. In *The Yale Edition of the Works of Samuel Johnson*, (eds.) W. J. Bate and Albrecht B. Strauss (New Haven and London: Yale University Press, 1969): V.80. All further text references are to this edition.
2. Lawrence Lipking, *Samuel Johnson: The Life of an Author* (Cambridge, Mass.: Harvard University Press, 1998): 243.
3. Paul Fussell, *Samuel Johnson and the Life of Writing* (London: Chatto and Windus, 1972): 8.
4. James Boswell, *Boswell's Life of Johnson; Together with Boswell's Journal of a Tour to the Hebrides and Johnson's Diary of a Journey into North Wales*, (ed.) George Birkbeck Hill, rev. and enlarged L. F. Powell, 2nd edn., 6 vols. (Oxford: Clarendon Press, 1971): I.2. Henceforth referred to, in the text, as *Life*.
5. See Kevin Hart, *Samuel Johnson and the Culture of Property* (Cambridge: Cambridge University Press, 1999): 20. As Hart adds, 'To think of anyone as a monument, even for a second or two, is to realise that a doubling has taken place. A monument tells us than an individual has been made into more than himself, made sublime or even a spectacle.'
6. Christopher Smart, 'Some Thoughts on the English Language', *The Universal Visiter and Memorialist* (January, 1756): 4.
7. See Samuel Johnson, *Johnson on the English Language*. In *The Yale Edition of the Works of Samuel Johnson*, (eds.) Gwin J. Kolb and Robert DeMaria, Jr. (New Haven, Conn. and London: Yale University Press, 2005): XVIII.38. All further text references are to this edition.
8. Jonathan Swift, *A Proposal for Correcting, Improving and Ascertaining the English Tongue in a Letter to the Most Honourable Robert, Earl of Oxford and Mortimer, Lord High Treasurer of Great Britain* (London: Benjamin Tooke, 1712): 37.
9. Samuel Johnson, *The Letters of Samuel Johnson*, (ed.) Bruce Redford, 5 vols. (Oxford: Clarendon Press, 1992–94): I.92 and I.100. Subsequent references to this edition are cited parenthetically in the text.

10. See Thomas Tickell, *A Poem to His Excellency the Lord Privy-Seal, on the Prospect of Peace* (London: Jacob Tonson, 1713): 19.
11. See further Chapter 1.
12. Arthur Murphy, *An Essay upon the Life and Genius of Samuel Johnson, LL.D.* (London: T. Longman, B. White, 1792): 74.
13. Walter Jackson Bate, *The Achievement of Samuel Johnson* (New York: Oxford University Press, 1955): vii.
14. See Marina Dossena, '"The Cinic Scotomastic"? Johnson, His Commentators, Scots, French, and the Story of English', *Textus. English Studies in Italy* (Issue: *Samuel Johnson's* Dictionary *and the Eighteenth-Century World of Words*, (ed.) Giovanni Iamartino and Robert DeMaria, Jr.) 19 (2006): 51–68.
15. See Allen Reddick, *The Making of Johnson's Dictionary, 1746–1773*, rev. edn. (Cambridge: Cambridge University Press, 1996), and Allen Reddick (ed.), *Samuel Johnson's Unpublished Revisions to the Dictionary of the English Language* (Cambridge: Cambridge University Press, 2006).
16. Thomas Edwards to Daniel Wray, 23 May 1755, *The Correspondence of Thomas Edwards* (Bodleian Library, Oxford, MS Bodl. 1012): 208.

Chapter 1

1. Samuel Johnson, *A Dictionary of the English Language; in which the Words are Deduced from their Originals and Illustrated in their Different Significations by Examples from the Best Writers* (London: J. and P. Knapton, T. and T. Longman, C. Hitch and L. Hawes, A. Millar, and R. and J. Dodsley, 1755). Unless otherwise stated, all references to the *Dictionary* are to this edition.
2. Murphy (1792): 74.
3. William Shaw and Hester Lynch Piozzi, *William Shaw, Memoirs of the Life and Writings of the Late Dr. Samuel Johnson; Hester Lynch Piozzi, Anecdotes of the Late Samuel Johnson, LL.D.*, (ed.) Arthur Sherbo (London: Oxford University Press, 1974): 121 (henceforth 'Shaw (1974)').
4. See William Shakespeare, *The Winter's Tale*, Act 4, Scene IV: 'A cause more promising / Than a wild dedication of yourselves / To unpath'd waters, undream'd shores.'
5. Johnson took out the lease on Gough Square in 1747 though work on the dictionary began one year earlier. See James L. Clifford, *Dictionary*

Johnson: Samuel Johnson's Middle Years (London: Heinemann, 1980): 15. One motivation for the move, Clifford suggests, was the desire to be near the printers.

6. Clifford (1980): 25 and 16.

7. John Baret, *An Alvearie or Triple Dictionarie: in Englische, Latin, and French* (London: Henry Denham, 1574). *Alvearie*, as the *OED* explains, derives from classical Latin *alveārium*, 'beehive'. As Baret explains in his opening address 'To the Reader', 'for the apt similitude betweene the good scholers and diligent Bees in gathering their wax and hony into their Hiue ... I called then their Aluearie'. See James Sledd, 'Baret's *Alvearie*, an Elizabethan Reference Book', *Studies in Philology* 43 (1946): 147–63.

8. [Stephen Skinner], *Gazophylacium Anglicanum: Containing the Derivation of English Words* (London: E. H. and W. H., 1659). As the *OED* confirms, a *gazophylacium* is 'The box in which offerings to the Temple were received; a strong-box or treasure chest'. See *Oxford English Dictionary Online, gazophylacium* (n.) [henceforth *OED Online*].

9. On lexical biography and the *OED*, see Lynda Mugglestone '"Life-Writing": The Lexicographer as Biographer in the *Oxford English Dictionary*'. In R. W. McConchie, Teo Juvonen, Mark Kaunisto, Minna Nevala, and Jukka Tyrkkö (eds.), *Selected Proceedings of the 2012 Symposium on New Approaches in English Historical Lexis (HEL-LEX 3)* (Somerville, Mass.: Cascadilla Proceedings Project, 2013): 14–26. On the dictionary as watch, see further pp. 192–3.

10. On later representations of this idea, see e.g. the lecture the 'World of Words and its Explorers' which James Murray (then editor-in-chief of the first edition of the *Oxford English Dictionary*) gave to the London Institute in 1903 (Murray Papers, Bodleian Library), and also John Considine, *Adventuring in Dictionaries: New Studies in the History of Lexicography* (Newcastle: Cambridge Scholars Publishing, 2010).

11. Ephraim Chambers, *Some Considerations Offered to the Publick, Preparatory to a Second Edition of Cyclopaedia: or, An Universal Dictionary of Arts and Sciences* (London: 1735): 2. On Johnson's use of Chambers's *Considerations* as source-text in the *Dictionary*, see *Yale* XVIII.xxiii–iv.

12. Ephraim Chambers, *Cyclopædia: or, an Universal Dictionary of Arts and Sciences*, 2 vols. (London: James and John Knapton, 1728): I.i.

13. Thomas Blount, *Glossographia: or A Dictionary, Interpreting all Such Hard Words...as are Now Used in Our Refined English Tongue* (London: Thomas Newcomb, 1656): sig.A3r.

14. Blount (1656): sig.A2r.

15. See *Dictionary* (1755), *gravel* (v.), sense 2. 'William the Conqueror, when he invaded this island, chanced at his arrival to be *gravelled*; and one of his feet stuck so fast in the sand, that he fell to the ground', as an illustrative citation from William Camden confirms.

16. Thomas Blount, *A World of Errors Discovered in The New World of Words, or, General English Dictionary, and in Nomothetes, or, The interpreter of Law-words and Terms* (London: Abel Roper, John Martin, and Henry Herringman, 1673): sig.A2r. 'Must this then be suffered?', Blount's opening sentence demands. Phillips introduced some important changes, but Blount's contentions are supported by later analysis. See e.g. Ian Lancashire, 'Johnson and the Seventeenth-Century Glossographers', *International Journal of Lexicography* 18 (2005): 157.

17. John Florio, *A Worlde of Wordes, or Most Copious, and Exact Dictionarie in Italian and English* (London: Edward Blount, 1598): sig.a5v. Florio's earlier identity as travel writer (and translator), in his *A Shorte and Briefe Narration of the Two Nauigations and Discoueries to the Northwest Partes called Newe Fraunce* (London: H. Bynneman, 1580), undoubtedly influenced the metaphors he deploys.

18. Alexander Pope and William Warburton (eds.), *The Works of Shakespear*, 8 vols. (London: J. and P. Knapton, S. Birt, et al, 1747): II.227, n.

19. Pope and Warburton (eds.) (1747): I.xxv.

20. Florio (1598): sig.a5v.

21. See Alvin Kernan, *Printing Technology, Letters, & Samuel Johnson* (Princeton: Princeton University Press, 1987).

22. On the cultural history of Grub Street, see further Pat Rogers, *Grub Street: Studies in a Subculture* (London: Methuen, 1972).

23. See James A. H. Murray, *The Evolution of English Lexicography* (Oxford: Clarendon Press, 1900): 6–7: 'the English Dictionary, like the English Constitution, is the creation of no one man, and no one age' but a 'growth that has slowly developed itself adown the ages' and, for a wider discussion of these ideas, Henri Béjoint, *Tradition and Innovation in Modern English Dictionaries* (Oxford: Clarendon Press, 1994).

24. On the 'lacrimae lexicographi' as trope, see Paul Korshin, 'Johnson and the Renaissance Dictionary', *Journal of the History of Ideas* 35 (1974): 306.

25. Johnson provided careful attribution: 'A small wear or dam, where wheels are laid in a river for catching of fish. *Phillips's World of Words*', he noted under *burrock*. 'A forge in an iron mill, where the iron is wrought into complete bars, and brought to perfection. *Phillips's World of Words*', the entry for *chafery* confirms. These entries were among the first parts of the *Dictionary* to be set in type and confirm Johnson's long-standing familiarity with Phillips's work. As Fleeman notes, the sections of the *Dictionary* covering *A-Carry* had been set by December 1750. See David Fleeman, 'Dr. Johnson's *Dictionary*, 1755'. In Kai Kin Yung (ed.), *Samuel Johnson 1709–84* (London: The Herbert Press, 1984): 39–40.

26. Johnson was originally contracted to produce the *Dictionary* in three years.

27. Jack Lynch, 'The Ground-Work of Style: Use, Elegance, and National Identity in Johnson's *Dictionary*', Unpublished paper delivered on 29 September 1996 at NEASECS in Worcester, Mass. (1996): 1, available at http://andromeda.rutgers.edu/~jlynch/Papers/dict.html.

28. Howard Weinbrot, *Aspects of Samuel Johnson: Essays on his Arts, Mind, Afterlife, and Politics* (Newark, N.J.: University of Delaware Press, 2005): 18.

29. See *Dictionary* (1755), *track* (n.), sense 2.

30. Anne Fisher, *An Accurate New Spelling Dictionary, and Expositor of the English Language*, 6th edn. (London: G. G. and J. Robinson, 1788). As she stressed, on p. ii, 'though the I and J, and also the U and V, are four distinct and different letters, both in name, shape, and sound; yet they have been ever blended and confounded in Dictionaries, to the great entanglement of youth'.

31. Samuel Richardson to Thomas Edwards, 21 April 1753. In Samuel Richardson, *Selected Letters of Samuel Richardson*, (ed.) John Carroll (Oxford: Clarendon Press, 1964): 226.

32. The degree of Master of Arts by diploma was awarded to Johnson on 20 February 1755. He did not become 'Dr. Johnson' until 1765, when he was awarded a Doctor of Laws by Trinity College, Dublin.

33. The text was in Latin, and the version given here derives from Boswell's account (*Life* I.282). John Hawkins gives a slightly different version in which Johnson has 'for the adorning and settling of his native language,

compiled, and being about to publish an English Dictionary' been granted the degree. See John Hawkins, *The Life of Samuel Johnson, LL.D.*, (ed.) O. M. Brack, Jr. (Athens, Ga.: University of Georgia Press, 2009): 207.

34. On Chesterfield as Johnson's patron, see further Chapter 2.

35. John Barrell, *English Literature in History, 1730–80: An Equal, Wide Survey* (London: Hutchinson, 1983). On Johnson and slavery, see James Basker, '"To the Next Insurrection of the Negroes": Johnson, Race, and Rebellion', *Age of Johnson* 11 (2000): 17–51.

36. Janet Sorensen, *The Grammar of Empire in Eighteenth-Century British Writing* (Cambridge: Cambridge University Press, 2000): 89.

37. See Samuel Johnson, *Poems*. In *The Yale Edition of the Works of Samuel Johnson*, (ed.) E. L. McAdam, Jr., with George Milne (New Haven, Conn. and London: Yale University Press, 1964; repr. 1975): VI: 90. All further text references are to this edition.

38. Thomas Sprat, *The History of the Royal-Society of London, for the Improving of Natural Knowledge* (London: J. Martyn, 1667): sig.A2v 'Epistle Dedicatory'. Johnson reviewed Thomas Birch's two-volume *History of the Royal Society*, in which he confirms his reading of Sprat, in the *Literary Magazine* in 1756.

39. See Daniel Carey, 'Compiling Nature's History: Travellers and Travel Narratives in the early Royal Society', *Annals of Science* 54 (1997): 269–92. See also Judy Hayden, *Travel Narratives, the New Science, and Literary Discourse, 1569–1750* (Burlington, Vt.: Ashgate, 2012). As Hayden (pp. 8–17) explores, Bacon and Sprat both link geographical and intellectual exploration, especially under the aegis of the Royal Society.

40. Johnson's 'Life of Admiral Drake' appeared in *The Gentleman's Magazine* 10 (1740), and is reproduced in Samuel Johnson, *Early Biographical Writings of Dr. Johnson*, (ed.) David Fleeman (Farnborough: Gregg International, 1973): 36–66.

41. On Johnson's involvement with the serialization of Anson's circumnavigation, see Carl Carlson, *The First Magazine; a History of the Gentleman's Magazine, with an Account of Dr. Johnson's Editorial Activity and of the Notice given America in the Magazine* (Providence, R.I.: Brown University, 1938). For the text of Anson's journey, see Richard Walter and Benjamin Robins, *A Voyage Round the World in the Years MDCCXL, I, II, II, IV by George Anson*, (ed.) Glyndwr Williams (London: Oxford University Press, 1974). On the disjunction

of Anson's own hopes and expectations, with the reality of his ventures, see also Glyndwr Williams, *The Prize of all the Oceans: the Triumph and Tragedy of Anson's Voyage Round the World* (London: Harper Collins, 1999).

42. See e.g. Walter and Robins (1974): 100: 'The coast from Cape *Blanco* to *Terra del Fuego*, and thence to Streights *Le Maire*, we were in some measure capable of correcting by our own observations'; the improved map was able now to provide information 'much nearer the truth than what has hitherto been done'.

43. See Thomas Curley, *Samuel Johnson and the Age of Travel* (Athens, Ga.: University of Georgia Press, 1976): 117.

44. See *Dictionary* (1755), *sea* (n.), sense 1 and *land* (n.), sense 2.

45. See *Dictionary* (1755), *sea* (n.), sense 4.

46. W. H. Auden, *The Enchafèd Flood, or, The Romantic Iconography of the Sea* (London: Faber and Faber, 1951): 18.

47. Andrew Varney, *Eighteenth-Century Writers in their World. A Might Maze* (Basingstoke: Macmillan, 1998): 8–9.

48. See Johnson's image of the activity required in 'beat[ing] the track of the alphabet' (*Yale* XVIII.26), and also *Dictionary* (1755), *beat*, (adj.), sense 10: 'to tread a path'; sense 11: 'To make a path by marking it with tracks'.

49. On the difficulties of finding one's way at sea, see also Johnson's *Account of an Attempt to Ascertain the Longitude at Sea, by an Exact Theory of the Variation of the Magnetical Needle* (London; R. Dodsley, 1755), formally by Zachariah Williams but, in reality, written by Johnson and with an Italian translation by Giuseppe Baretti.

50. See further pp. 164–5, 168–70.

51. See p. 52. Johnson discusses these lines in his 'Life of Prior'. See Samuel Johnson, *The Lives of the Poets, The Yale Edition of the Works of Samuel Johnson*, (ed.) John H. Middendorf, vols. XXI–XXIII (New Haven, Conn. and London: Yale University Press, 2010): XXII.705. All further text references are to this edition.

52. See Donald J. Greene, 'Pictures to the Mind: Johnson and Imagery'. In *Johnson, Boswell and Their Circle: Essays presented to Laurence Fitzroy Powell in Honour of his Eighty-Fourth Birthday* (Oxford: Clarendon Press, 1965): 137–58.

53. Cited in Steven Lynn, *Samuel Johnson After Deconstruction: Rhetoric and the Rambler* (Carbondale, Ill.: Southern Illinois University Press, 1992): 24.

54. Joseph Spence, *Observations, Anecdotes, and Characters of Books and Men: Collected from Conversation*, (ed.) James M. Osborn (Oxford: Clarendon Press, 1966): I.187 No.432, March 1743.

55. Locke's influence is, as DeMaria stresses, often perceptible across the Dictionary. See Robert DeMaria, 'The Theory of Language in Johnson's *Dictionary*'. In *Johnson after Two Hundred Years*, (ed.) Paul Korshin (Philadelphia: University of Pennsylvania Press, 1986): 159-74. Locke is cited over three thousand times in the *Dictionary*.

56. Chambers (1728): xxi.

57. See e.g. Curley (1976); Thomas Jemielity, 'Dr. Johnson and the Uses of Travel', *Philological Quarterly* 31 (1972): 488-59; Thursten Maxwell Moore, *Samuel Johnson and the Literature of Travel* (Unpublished Ph. D. Dissertation, Ann Arbor: University of Michigan, 1966).

58. 'Alas...how few books are there of which one ever can possibly arrive at the last page?', Johnson rhetorically demanded, 'Was there ever yet any thing written by mere man that was wished longer by its readers, excepting Don Quixote, Robinson Crusoe, and the Pilgrim's Progress?', cited in Robert DeMaria, Jr., *Samuel Johnson and the Life of Reading* (Baltimore, Md., London: Johns Hopkins University Press, 1997): 7.

59. [John Newbery], *The World Displayed: Or, A Curious Collection of Voyages and Travels Selected from the Writers of all Nations*, 20 vols. (London: J. Newbery, 1759-61): I. Johnson's resistance to colonialism, and the politics of incursion, is particularly marked in his accompanying 'Introduction', in ways which also sit uneasily against his imagined acts of power in 1747. 'The *Europeans* have scarcely visited any coast, but to gratify avarice, and extend corruption; to arrogate dominion without right, and practice cruelty without incentive', as Johnson writes. Discovery can, in this light, also have a negative edge, while the discriminatory practices of the 'civilised' upon the 'native' are overtly condemned: 'We are openly told, that they had the less scruple concerning their treatment of the savage people, because they scarcely considered them as distinct from beasts; and indeed the practice of all the *European* nations, and among others of the *English* barbarians that cultivate the southern islands of *America* prove, that this opinion, however absurd and foolish, however wicked and injurious, still continues to prevail. Interest and pride harden the heart, and it is vain to dispute against avarice and power' (p. xiv). See also Robert D. Spector, *Samuel Johnson and the Essay* (London: Greenwood Press, 1997): 120-2. As Spector notes (p. 120), Johnson's 'Introduction' provides

'some of the most insightful eighteenth-century commentary on the cruelties and hypocrisies of colonialism'.

60. See Brian Hanley, *Samuel Johnson as Book Reviewer: A Duty to Examine the Labors of the Learned* (Newark, N.J.: University of Delaware Press; London: Associated University Presses, 2001).

61. See *Dictionary* (1755), *travel* (n.), sense 4. This stands interestingly against Moore's assertion (1966: 68) that 'There is no evidence in his writings that he considered travel writing to be a distinct literary genre (though it was a recognisable type).'

62. See Samuel Johnson, *Rasselas and Other Tales*, (ed.) Gwin J. Kolb, *The Yale Edition of the Works of Samuel Johnson* (New Haven and London: Yale University Press, 1990): XVI. All further text references are to this edition.

63. On Johnson's use of this trope in writing the *Dictionary*, see further Lynda Mugglestone, 'Writing the *Dictionary of the English Language*: Johnson's Journey into Words', in Howard D. Weinbrot, and William Freeman Vilas (eds.), *Samuel Johnson: New Contexts For a New Century* (Sa Marino, Ca.: Huntington Library Press and University of California Press, 2014): 131–42 [henceforth cited as Mugglestone (2014a)].

64. Samuel Johnson, *A Voyage to Abyssinia*. In *The Yale Edition of the Works of Samuel Johnson*, (ed.) Joel L. Gold (New Haven, Conn. and London: Yale University Press, 1985): XV.3.

65. See Fred Parker, *Scepticism and Literature: An Essay on Pope, Hume, Sterne, and Johnson* (Oxford: Oxford University Press, 2003): 7, on this role of travel in Johnson's work: 'Both his principal travel books—the fictional *Rasselas* and the *Journey to the Western Islands*—make much of the disparity between expectation and actuality; many of his essays advance some cogent general proposition which is then promptly modified under review.' See also Francis Hart, 'Johnson as Philosophic Traveler: The Perfecting of an Idea', *ELH* 36 (1969): 679–95.

66. See further Chapter 3. 'Imagines' plays a similar critical role in the *Dictionary*.

67. Robert DeMaria, Jr., *Johnson's Dictionary and the Language of Learning* (Oxford: Oxford University Press, 1986a): 87.

68. See *Dictionary* (1755), *opinion* (n.), sense 1. '*Opinion* is a light, vain, crude and imperfect thing, settled in the imagination, but never arriving at the understanding, there to obtain the tincture of reason', as an illustrative citation from Ben Jonson confirms.

69. Gwin J. Kolb and James H. Sledd, 'Johnson's *Dictionary* and Lexico-graphical Tradition', *Modern Philology* 50 (1953): 173.
70. See Greene (1965): 140–1.
71. Lipking (1998): 121.

Chapter 2

1. For recent references to Johnson in this role, see e.g. Michael Leap-man, 'What's so funny about gout?', *The Daily Telegraph* (2 October 2012).
2. Jack Lynch, 'Disgraced by Miscarriage: Four and a Half Centuries of Lexicographical Belligerence', *The Journal of the Rutgers University Libraries* 62 (2006): 36. On the dictionary before Johnson, see also DeWitt T. Starnes and Gertrude E. Noyes, *The English Dictionary from Cawdrey to Johnson, 1604–1755*, 2nd edn. (Amsterdam and Philadel-phia: J. Benjamin, 1991) and Henri Béjoint, *The Lexicography of English* (Oxford: Oxford University Press, 2010).
3. [Samuel Johnson], 'Preface'. In Richard Rolt, *A New Dictionary of Trade and Commerce, compiled from the Information of the most Eminent Merchants, and from the Works of the Best Writers on Com-mercial Subjects* (London: T. Osborne and J. Shipton, 1756): n.p.
4. On the eighteenth-century dictionary as commodity, see also Lynda Mugglestone, 'The Battle of the Word-Books: Competition, the "Com-mon Reader", and Johnson's *Dictionary*'. In Freya Johnston and Lynda Mugglestone (eds.), *Samuel Johnson: The Arc of the Pendulum* (Oxford: Oxford University Press, 2012): 140–53.
5. Reddick (1996): 16.
6. Murray Pittock, *Inventing and Resisting Britain: Cultural Identities in Britain and Ireland, 1685–1789* (Basingstoke: Macmillan, 1997): 5.
7. Philip Gove, 'Notes on Serialization and Competitive Publishing: John-son and Bailey's Dictionaries, 1755', *Proceedings of the Oxford Biblio-graphical Society* 5 (1938): 305–22. The 1755 edition of Bailey was edited by Joseph Nicol Scott, and modelled closely on Johnson's work.
8. J[ohn] K[ersey], *A New English Dictionary: or, a Compleat Collection of the Most Proper and Significant Words Commonly Used in the Lan-guage* (London: Henry Bonwicke and Robert Knaplock, 1702): title page. 'Kersey's work in this and in his subsequent compilations was a turning point in English lexicography', Sidney Landau notes in

Dictionaries: The Art and Craft of Lexicography, 2nd edn. (Cambridge: Cambridge University Press, 2001): 44.

9. George Snell, *The Right Teaching of Useful Knowledg, to Fit Scholars for Som Honest Profession* (London: John Stephenson, 1649): 38.

10. Snell (1649): 40.

11. William Bray (ed.), *Diary and Correspondence of John Evelyn F.R.S.* (London: George Bell, 1887): III.159–60. On the history of language academies in England, see B. S. Monroe, 'An English Academy', *Modern Philology* 8 (1910): 107–22.

12. See Mary Segar, 'Dictionary-making in the Early Eighteenth Century', *Review of English Studies* 7 (1931): 210–13, and, on Tonson, see Reddick (1996): 17. Thomas Brereton also advertises subscriptions for a work with a closely similar title—*A Compleat and Standard Dictionary of the whole English Language, after the Method of the celebrated One of the French Academy, in Four Volumes*—in his journal *The Critick* in February 1718. See further p. 56–7.

13. Segar suggests that Philips inherited Addison's materials. See Segar (1931): 210–11. On Philips, see also John Considine, 'Ambrose Philips and *Little Preston*', *Notes and Queries* n.s. 60 (2013): 70–1.

14. On Henley and the Earl of Orrery, see further Monroe (1910): 13.

15. Monroe (1910): 10 ff. See also James Basker, 'Minim and the Great Cham: Smollett and Johnson on the Prospect of an English Academy'. In J. Engell (ed.), *Johnson and his Age* (Cambridge, Mass. London: Harvard University Press, Harvard English Studies vol. 12, 1984): 137–61.

16. Swift (1712): 9.

17. John Dryden, *Fables Ancient and Modern: Translated into verse, from Homer, Ovid, Boccace, & Chaucer* (London: Jacob Tonson, 1700).

18. Swift (1712): 42. His proposals closely echo Snell in terms of the need for stability and the desire to communicate across time. See e.g. Snell (1649): 40 who advocates linguistic stability such that 'posteritie may bee abel to read and understand, what was written by their Elders, that lived five hundred years before'.

19. Jonathan Swift, *Gulliver's Travels, The Cambridge Edition of the Works of Jonathan Swift*, (ed.) David Womersley (Cambridge: Cambridge University Press, 2012): XVI.12.

20. Swift (1712): 34 and 15.

21. Hawkins (2009): 105.

22. Reddick (1996): 13.

23. [Dodsley, Robert], 'Review of *The Plan of a* DICTIONARY *of the* English *Language*', *The Museum: Or, the Literary and Historical Register* 3 (1747): 389.
24. [Dodsley] (1747): 387.
25. Hawkins (2009): 105.
26. This referred to the use of *prodigious* as an interjection expressing astonishment or dismay which was an innovation in early eighteenth-century usage. *OED* first attests its use in Colley Cibber's comedy *The Double Gallant: or, The Sick Lady's Cure* (1707): 'Prodigious! how some Women can muddle away their Money upon Houswifry.' See *OED Online, prodigious* (adj. and int.), sense 2b.
27. Samuel Ford (1717–93) was Johnson's first cousin who matriculated at Trinity College, Oxford in 1736.
28. Hawkins (2009): 17.
29. On Dodsley and Johnson, see Lois Spencer, 'Robert Dodsley and the Johnsonian Connexion', *The New Rambler* 18 (1977): 1–18.
30. Harry M. Solomon, *The Rise of Robert Dodsley: Creating the New Age of Print* (Carbondale, Ill.: Southern Illinois University Press, 1996): 88 and 90. On Dodsley's career as publisher, see also Ralph Straus, *Robert Dodsley: Poet, Publisher & Playwright* (London: John Lane, 1910). Dodsley purchased the copyright to Johnson's poem 'The Vanity of Human Wishes', and his play *Irene*, during the *Dictionary*'s production.
31. See Robert Dodsley, *The Correspondence of Robert Dodsley, 1733–1764*, (ed.) James E. Tierney (Cambridge: Cambridge University Press, 1988): 97 and n. 1.
32. See e.g. James Buchanan's *Linguæ Britannicæ vera Pronunciatio: or, a New English Dictionary* which Millar published in 1757. Buchanan's distinctive focus on pronunciation, and the detailed provision of a 'standard' accent for all, made his work a potentially profitable venture.
33. George Justice, *The Manufacturers of Literature. Writing and the Literary Marketplace in Eighteenth-Century England* (Newark, N.J.: The University of Delaware Press, 2002): 15.
34. See *Dictionary* (1755), *scheme* (n.), senses 1 and 2.
35. Fussell (1972): 158. Many of Johnson's *Rambler* essays, he adds, 'are either openly or covertly about the insufficiency of preconcerted "schemes" or plans to deal with the actual occasions of life'.
36. See *Yale* XVIII.378–427. The original is now part of the Hyde Collection at the Houghton Library at Harvard University.

37. See Pat Rogers, *The Samuel Johnson Encyclopaedia* (Westport, Conn.: Greenwood Press, 1996): 392–3.
38. On variation and eighteenth-century spelling, see further Chapter 4.
39. Variability of this kind is, in fact, often retained in the *Dictionary* so that under *drive* (v.), Johnson notes, without stigmatization, that it has the 'preterite *drove*' which was 'anciently *drave*', as well as variant past participles in '*driven*, or *drove*'.
40. Johnson cites Davies's 'Nosce Teipsum' (1599) in corroboration: 'And shuns it though *for thirst she dye*' (*Yale* XVIII.401).
41. The same reader, interestingly, asks 'whether Custom is not ye Chief Rule of Language' (*Yale* XVIII.403). 'Custom' is presumably intended in a narrower rather than broader sense, inclining to its role as corrective model in ways which exclude that by which *to die for* is used.
42. See Manfred Görlach, 'A New Text Type: Exercises in Bad English'. In F. Austin and C. Stray (eds.), *The Teaching of English in the Eighteenth and Nineteenth Centuries. Essays for Ian Michael on his 88th Birthday, Paradigm* 2 (2003): 5–14.
43. See Johnson's 'Life of Dr. Boerhaave' which he wrote for the *Gentleman's Magazine* in 1739 (reproduced in Fleeman (1973): 25–35), and also Richard Schwartz, *Samuel Johnson and the New Science* (Madison, Wis.: University of Wisconsin Press, 1971): 70. As Schwartz notes, 'all the elements of Johnson's methodology are here in the works and principles of Boerhaave: the ordered study, diligent observation and experimentation, the application of reason to data which results in synthesis'.
44. By 1755, *plough* is given as Johnson's preferred headword, though *plow* appears in a range of definitions, e.g. *break* (sense 27): '*To break ground. To plow*'; *coulter* (n.) 'The sharp iron of the plow which cuts the earth, perpendicular to the share'; *ear* (v.) 'To plow; to till'; *earth-board* (n.), 'The board of the plow that shakes off the earth', as well as in etymologies (see e.g. Johnson's gloss of Latin *aro* ('to plow') under *arable*; *earsh* (n.) (from *ear*, 'to plow')), and citations (see e.g. *depth* (n.) sense 4; *edge* (n.) sense 2). On Johnson's spelling, see Noel Osselton, 'Informal Spelling Systems in Early Modern English: 1500–1800'. In N. F. Blake and Charles Jones (eds.), *English Historical Linguistics: Studies in Development* (Sheffield: CECTAL, University of Sheffield, 1984): 123–37, and also Chapter 4 this volume.
45. On Johnson's revisions, see further *Yale* XVIII.8.

46. Elizabeth Hedrick, 'Fixing the Language: Johnson, Chesterfield, and the *Plan of a Dictionary*', *ELH* 55 (1988): 427.
47. Dodsley, as he commented, 'had a property in the Dictionary, to which his Lordship's patronage might have been of consequence' (*Life* I.264).
48. Dodsley confirms Chesterfield's status as Johnson's patron in *The Museum* in 1747: 'The great Importance and general Usefulness of such a Body of Language, appeared so clearly to the noble Person to whom this Plan is addressed, that he signified a Willingness of becoming its Patron, from that unaffected Flow of public Spirit, which has ever animated his Conduct.' See [Dodsley] (1747): 385.
49. Reddick (1996): 18.
50. See *Dictionary* (1755), antonomasia (n.): 'A form of speech, in which, for a proper name, is put the name of some dignity, office, profession, science, or trade; or when a proper name is put in the room of an appellative. Thus a king is called his majesty; a nobleman, his lordship.'
51. Johnson's revisions at this stage of the text add further examples. See e.g. *Yale* XVIII.482, where 'By your opinion' is emended to read 'by your Lordship's opinion'.
52. See *Ausonius*, (ed.) Jeffrey Henderson, (trans.) Hugh G. Evelyn-White (London and Cambridge: Harvard University Press, Loeb Classical Library 96, 1919): 8, I.iv 'Prefatory Pieces'. See also *Yale* XVIII.55.
53. As *OED* confirms, *cynosure* has been used in English from 1596, *zenith* since late Middle English. On loanwords and the *Dictionary*, see further Chapter 6.
54. Johnson is often cautious about the value of imagination. As he pointed out in the 'Life of Butler', 'Imagination is useless without knowledge: nature gives in vain the power of combination, unless study and observation supply materials to be combined' (*Yale* XXI.219).
55. On perfection and the *Dictionary*, see further Chapter 8.
56. Cited in John Wilson Croker, *Johnsoniana, or, Supplement to Boswell* (Philadelphia: Carey and Hart, 1842): 312.
57. David Mallet, *Amyntor and Theodora: or, the Hermit* (London: Paul Vaillant, 1747): iii.
58. Mallet (1747): iii–iv.
59. W. S., 'The Signification of Words now Varied', *Gentleman's Magazine* 19 (1749): 66.
60. Dodsley also issued 1,500 copies of the Plan (free of charge) in March 1755.

61. [Philip Dormer Stanhope, Lord Chesterfield], Letter to *The World* No. 100 (28 November 1754a): 602 (henceforth referred to as [Chesterfield] (1754a)). Edited by Moore, the *World* was printed by Dodsley in Pall-Mall 'where letters to the author are taken in'.

62. [Chesterfield] (1754a): 600.

63. The date at which Johnson composed the 'Preface' remains unknown. Fleeman (1984: 41) suggests, probably rightly, that it was not composed before late December 1754—and therefore after reading Chesterfield's letters to the *World*.

64. Lipking (1998): 31.

65. On the breakdown of the relationship with Chesterfield, see Paul Korshin, 'The Johnson–Chesterfield Relationship: A New Hypothesis', *PMLA* 85 (1970): 247–59, and Howard Weinbrot, 'Johnson's *Dictionary* and *The World*: The Papers of Lord Chesterfield and Richard Owen Cambridge', *Philological Quarterly* 50 (1971): 663–9.

66. See Shaw (1974): 121 and Murphy (1792): 74.

67. Johnson's revisions in March 1755 to ll. 159–60 of 'The Vanity of Human Wishes' (by which the injunction to 'mark what ills the scholars life assail / Toil, envy, want, the garret, and the jail' is emended to '... Toil, envy, want, the patron, and the jail' (*Yale* VI.99 and n.) is equally indicative of this change.

68. See Johnson's 1755 'Preface': 'to enchain syllables, and to lash the wind, are equally the undertakings of pride, unwilling to measure its desires by its strength' (*Yale* XVIII.105).

Chapter 3

1. See *OED Online, excursion* (n.), sense 5: '*spec.* A journey or "trip" undertaken for the sake of pleasure or health. In recent use often: a pleasure-trip taken by a number of persons'. This sense was not in use when Johnson wrote.

2. See *Dictionary* (1755), *excursion* (n.), sense 2.

3. See p. 220, n.39.

4. Clifford (1980): 48.

5. Robert James, *A Medicinal Dictionary, including Physic, Surgery, Anatomy, Chymistry and Botany, together with a History of Drugs*, 3 vols. (London: T. Osborne, 1743–5). See Allen T. Hazen, 'Samuel Johnson and Dr. Robert James', *Bulletin of the Institute of the History of Medicine* 4 (1936): 456–7, and also James Gray and T. J. Murray, 'Dr. Johnson and Dr. James', *Age of Johnson* 7 (1996): 213–45; O. M. Brack,

and Thomas Kaminski, 'Johnson, James, and the *Medicinal Dictionary*', *Modern Philology* 81 (1984): 378–400 As Johnson comments (*Life* 3.22): 'My knowledge of physick...I learnt from Dr. James, whom I helped in writing the proposals for his Dictionary and also a little in the Dictionary itself.'

6. Thomas Kaminski, *The Early Career of Samuel Johnson* (New York: Oxford University Press, 1987): 173.

7. Miller (1691–1771) was responsible for the botanical entries in Bailey's *Dictionarium Britannicum* and published his highly successful *Gardeners Dictionary* in 1732 (it was in its sixth edition by 1752; a fourth edition of Miller's abridged version also appeared in 1754). See Hazel Le Rougetel, 'Miller, Philip (1691–1771)'. In *Oxford Dictionary of National Biography Online* [*ODNB Online*].

8. On Johnson's use of Cowell, see J. T. Scanlan, 'Johnson's *Dictionary* and Legal Dictionaries'. In Iamartino and DeMaria (eds.) (2006): 87–106.

9. Hill's account is considerably more expansive. Johnson shortens and tightens to good effect. See John Hill, *A History of the* Materia Medica. *Containing Descriptions of all the substances used in Medicine* (London: T. Longman, C. Hitch, and L. Hawes, 1751): 831–4.

10. Jack Lynch, 'Johnson's Encyclopaedia'. In Jack Lynch and Anne McDermott (eds.), *Anniversary Essays on Johnson's* Dictionary (Cambridge: Cambridge University Press, 2005): 129–46.

11. Stephen Skinner's *Etymologicon Linguae Anglicanae* (1671) remained a significant resource for etymological information. Johnson frequently makes reference to it.

12. Some, of course, were in existence but absent from Johnson's collection of citations and the headwords under which these were filed. See e.g. *deceptive*: 'Having the power of deceiving' for which Johnson merely adduces '*Dict.*'. Johnson's own definition of *jugglingly*: 'In a deceptive manner' conversely illustrates its use.

13. Johnson's examples locate *perusal* in the act of careful reading, as in Bacon's: 'The petitions being thus prepared, do you constantly set apart an hour in a day to *peruse* those petitions?' See e.g. *OED, peruse* (v.), sense 3(c) (trans.): 'To examine in detail; to scrutinize, inspect, survey, oversee; to consider, to take heed of. Now also: to look over briefly or superficially; to browse'. On Johnson's use of *peruse*, and perusal as process, see DeMaria (1997): 10.

14. See Korshin (1974): 303. The *Dictionnaire* of the Académie Française preferred invented examples as a further safeguard for correctness. See Anthony Cowie, 'Examples and Collocations in the French *Dictionnaire de langue*'. In Marie-Hélène Corréard (ed.), *Lexicography and Natural Language Processing: A* Festschrift *in Honour of B. T. S. Atkins* (Grenoble: Euralex, 2002): 73–90.

15. Thomas Nashe's *Christ's Teares over Jerusalem* (1593) is the likely source of Cockeram's entries for words such as *decurtate* ('To shorten'), *creditor-crazed* (glossed 'Banquerout'), and *dreriment* ('Sorrow, heaviness'). See J. A. Riddell, 'The Beginning: English Dictionaries of the First Half of the Seventeenth Century', *Leeds Studies in English 7* (1974): 117–53.

16. On Addison, see Segar (1931): 210–11. For Brereton's dictionary project, see *The Critick* (17 February 1718). See Page Life, 'Brereton, Thomas (1690/91–1722)'. In *ODNB Online*.

17. [Thomas Wilson], *The Many Advantages of a Good Language to any Nation: with an Examination of the Present State of our Own: as also, an Essay towards Correcting Some Things that are Wrong in it* (London: J. Knapton et al., 1724): 34 and 32.

18. [Wilson] (1724): 41–2.

19. An early ambition to make the quotations he collected 'useful to some other end than the illustration of a word' (*Yale* XVIII.94) foundered, as Johnson explained, in other gaps which necessarily appeared between 'design' and 'execution'.

20. Spence (1966) I.170–1, Nos. 389–90, dated 5–7 April 1744.

21. Spence (1966) I.187–8, Nos. 435–37, dated 1734; No. 438, dated 1–7 May 1730.

22. Spence (1966) I.170, No. 388, dated December 1743.

23. Robert DeMaria, Jr., 'North and South in Johnson's *Dictionary*'. In Iamartino and DeMaria (eds.) (2006): 13.

24. See *Dictionary* (1755), *toast* (n.), sense 3.

25. See *Dictionary* (1755), *exemplary* (adj.), sense 1.

26. Davies was, however, frequently used. See pp. 59, 69.

27. Lipking (1998): 117.

28. Deidre Lynch, '"Beating the Track of the Alphabet": Samuel Johnson, Tourism, and the ABCs of Modern Authority', *ELH* 57 (1990): 377. Lynch's contention that 'these quotations register the outcome of Johnson's retreat from a documentary engagement with the real'

(p. 378) remains problematic in the light of available evidence on his processes of reading and annotation.

29. Shaw (1974): 14.
30. See *Dictionary* (1755), *feast* (n.), senses 1 and 3.
31. Hawkins (2009): 105 and 219.
32. Hawkins (2009): 126.
33. See Johnson (1973): 30.
34. Hawkins (2009): 108.
35. See Reddick (1996: 204) for a list of Johnson's marked-up books. This excludes, however, the recent discovery of Johnson's marked-up copy of George Chapman's translation of Homer's *Odyssey* (London: Nathaniel Butter, 1634), with annotations for the *Dictionary* covering some 40 pages.
36. Matthew Hale, *The Primitive Origination of Mankind, Considered and Examined According to the Light of Nature* (London: William Godbid, 1677). Bound with Johnson's annotated copy of Robert Burton's *The Anatomy of Melancholy*, 8th edn. (London: Peter Parker, 1676), this was presented to the Bodleian Library by the *OED* lexicographer Charles Onions. It originally belonged to the Philological Society.
37. See Alan Cromartie, 'Hale, Sir Mathew (1609–1676)'. In *ODNB Online*.
38. See also Daisuke Nagashima, 'How Johnson read Hale's *Origination* for his *Dictionary*; A Linguistic View', *Age of Johnson* 7 (1996): 247–90.
39. Johnson's first assistant was Francis Stewart who was employed from 1746; the others were Alex and William McBean, V. J. Peyton, Robert Shiels, and Mr Maitland. See Eugene Thomas, 'Dr. Johnson and his Amanuenses', *Transactions of the Johnson Society* (1974a): 20–30, and also Eugene Thomas, 'A Bibliographical and Critical Analysis of Johnson's Dictionary' (Unpublished diss., University of Wales 1974). On the making of the *Dictionary*, see further James H. Sledd and Gwin J. Kolb, *Dr. Johnson's Dictionary: Essays in the Biography of a Book* (Chicago: University of Chicago Press, 1955).
40. See *Dictionary* (1755), *transcript* (n.): 'A copy; any thing written from an original'.
41. As Reddick suggests, individual amanuenses made use of different marks as they moved through the text. See further Anne McDermott, 'The Compilation Methods of Johnson's Dictionary', *Age of Johnson* 16 (2005): 1–20, and also Reddick (1996): 38–9; Thomas (1974a): 23–4.
42. Robert DeMaria Jr., *The Life of Samuel Johnson* (Oxford: Blackwell, 1993): 115.

43. Obvious omissions include *colloquial*, a word Johnson uses in the 'Preface' and the 'History' (see Yale XVIII.107, 210), as well as *literary, notable, athlete, amorphous*, and *irritable. Shoulderblade*, omitted in the first edition, gained a new entry in 1773. Many similar examples could be given.

44. W. K. Wimsatt Jr., 'Johnson's Dictionary'. In Frederick W. Hilles (ed.), *New Light on Dr. Johnson* (New Haven, Conn.: Yale University Press, 1959): 70.

45. Johnson's copy of Isaac Watts, *Logick: or, The Right Use of Reason in the Enquiry after Truth*, 8th edn. (London: T. Longman and T. Shewell, 1745) is in the British Library.

46. The citation was nevertheless omitted from the *Dictionary*.

47. This appears in the *Dictionary* under *pencil* (n.), sense 2: 'A black lead pen, with which cut to a point they write without ink'.

48. DeMaria (1997): xii.

49. See *OED Online, visive* (adj.). Seventeen quotations from seventeenth-century English appear.

50. See Johnson's note under *store-house* (n.): '*Stôr*, in old Swedish and Runick, is *much*, and is prefixed to other words to intend their signification; stor, Danish; *stoor*, Islandick, is *great*. The Teutonick dialects nearer to English seem not to have retained this word.'

51. Burton links Xerxes and the excesses of human ambition, as well as the corrective power of the sea, in ways which also resonate with Johnson's 'The Vanity of Human Wishes'. See further p. 17.

52. See *Dictionary* (1755), *plastick* (adj.): 'Having the power to give form'. Johnson likewise underlines *intellective* on pp. 1 and 3 of Hale.

53. See A. S. McGrade, 'Hooker, Richard (1554–1600)'. In *ODNB Online*: 'There are more citations of Hooker in the first volume of Samuel Johnson's Dictionary that of any other [prose] author, save Locke', McGrade affirms.

54. See *OED Online, complicatedness* (n.).

55. Johnson's patterns of omission were also influenced by the constraints of space. He attempted, as we know, to curtail the scale of the *Dictionary* once he had finished A–C, in the interests of completing the work within two volumes. See Fleeman (1984): 39–40. A number of incomplete cross-references link entries in A and B to forms or explanations which do not appear in later sections of the text.

56. *Dictionary* (1755), *beemol* (n.). No definition is provided.

57. *Dictionary* (1755), *conduce* (v.a.): 'To conduct; to accompany in order to shew the way'.

58. For similar entries, see e.g. *cursorary* (adj); *fract* (v.); *blandish* (v.).

59. On Johnson's dislike of Hobbes's principles, see O. M. Brack and Robert E. Kelley (eds.), *The Early Biographies of Samuel Johnson* (Iowa City: University of Iowa Press, 1974): 82. Johnson also resisted Pope's recommendation of Bolingbroke, whose appearances in the *Dictionary* are by no means commendatory. See e.g. *Gallicism*, *owe* (sense 5), *irony*.

60. See further pp. 163, 165.

61. It is nevertheless clear that his use of Raleigh was far wider than these specified domains suggest. See further pp. 75–6.

62. Noel Osselton, 'On the History of Dictionaries'. In R. K. K. Hartmann (ed.), *Lexicography; Principles and Practice* (London: Academic Press, 1983): 13–21.

63. See e.g. DeMaria (1986a), Reddick (1996), Lynch (1990).

64. See pp. 119, 125–6.

65. See e.g. *Dictionary* (1755), *prejudice* (v.), sense 3. Johnson cites Henry Pemberton's 1746 *Dispensatory of the Royal College of Physicians* (London: T. Longman and T. Sherwell): 82.

66. Other uses appear under e.g. *investigate*, sense 2; *laconick* (adj.); *monument*; and *modernism* (n.). Similar evidence from the letters of Arbuthnot to Pope appears under *despisable* ('I am extremely obliged to you for taking notice of a poor old distressed courtier, commonly the most *despisable* thing in the world'). Pope's correspondence had been published in Warburton's edition of Pope's works in 1751.

67. See e.g. Johnson's entries for *batter* (v.), *brad* (n.), *chump* (n.), *crank* (n.).

68. On Johnson's 'excursions' into writers before Sidney, see especially Chapter 7.

69. Spence (1966) I.170, No. 389, dated 5–7 April 1744.

70. See Allen Walker Read, 'The Contemporary Quotations in Johnson's Dictionary', *ELH* 2 (1935): 246–51; Reddick (1996): 33, and also W. K. Wimsatt, Jr. and Margaret H. Wimsatt, 'Self-Quotations and Anonymous Quotations in Johnson's Dictionary', *ELH* 15 (1948): 60–8.

71. Ingrid Tieken Boon van Ostade, 'Samuel Richardson's Role as Linguistic Innovator; A Sociolinguistic Analysis'. In Ingrid Tieken Boon van Ostade and John Frankis (eds.), *Language Usage and Description:*

Studies Presented to N.E. Osselton on the Occasion of his Retirement (Amsterdam: Rodopi, 1991): 47–58.

72. W. R. Keast, 'The two *Clarissas* in Johnson's *Dictionary*'. *Studies in Philology* 54 (1957): 429–39.

73. Lipking (1998): 117. Lipking's discussion is, however, restricted to Johnson's use of male writers.

74. See Peter Sabor, 'Women Reading and Writing for *The Rambler*'. In Tiffany Potter (ed.), *Women, Popular Culture, and the Eighteenth Century* (Toronto: University of Toronto Press, 2012): 167–84.

75. This was, Hanley (2001: 203) notes, 'the only time [Johnson] bothered to review a novel'. Johnson certainly wrote the 'Dedication' to Lennox's *Female Quixote*. On Johnson's support for Lennox and possible co-authorship, see Clifford (1980): 40–3 and 90–2, and Jaclyn Geller 'The Unnarrated Life: Samuel Johnson, Female Friendship, and the Rise of the Novel Revisited'. In Philip Smallwood (ed.), *Johnson Revisioned. Looking Before and After* (Cranbury, N.J.: Rosemont Publishing, 2001): 83.

76. Robert Cawdrey, *A Table Alphabeticall Contayning and Teaching the True Writing and Vnderstanding of Hard Vsuall English Words* (London: Edmund Weauer, 1604): title-page.

77. [Chesterfield] (1754a): 603. Chesterfield's ironic commendation of female lexical ingenuity served to damn with faint praise: 'When this happy copiousness flows, as it often does, into gentle numbers, good Gods! how is the poetic diction enriched, and the poetical licence extended.' See further pp. 85–6, and also Charlotte Brewer, '"A Goose-Quill or a Gander's"? Female writers in Johnson's *Dictionary*', in Johnston and Mugglestone (eds.) (2012): 120–39.

78. [Richard Owen Cambridge], Letter to *The World* No. 102 (12 December 1754): 612. As he states, 'It would be no less an error to imagine that they wanted a repository for their words after they have worn them out, than that they wished for a wardrobe to preserve their cast-off fashions. Novelty is their pleasure; singularity and the love of being before-hand is greatly flattering to the female mind.'

79. Samuel Johnson, *An Account of the Life of Dr. Samuel Johnson, from his Birth to his Eleventh Year, Written by Himself. To which are added, Original Letters to Dr. Samuel Johnson by Miss Hill Boothby* (London: Richard Phillips, 1805): 78.

80. Brewer (2012) identifies some twenty citations from Lennox in the *Dictionary*.

81. See James Basker, 'Myth upon Myth: Johnson, Gender, and the Misogyny Question', *Age of Johnson* 8 (1997): 175–88, and also Isabel Grundy, 'Samuel Johnson as Patron of Women', *Age of Johnson* 1 (1987): 59–77. Grundy argues for Johnson's positive patronage of women writers within a community of authors. Johnson's decision to provide female testimony in the *Dictionary*, thereby moving away from the paradigms of male authority: female instruction which hitherto dominated English lexicography is clearly of interest in this context.
82. See George Birkbeck Hill (ed.), *Johnsonian Miscellanies* (Oxford: Clarendon Press, 1897): II.252–3.
83. Johnson refers to Robert Lowth's *Short Introduction to English Grammar* (London: A. Millar; R. and J. Dodsley, 1762). Lowth's discussion (p. 30) of gender and nouns was brief: 'Some few Substantives are distinguished as to their Gender by their termination: as, *prince, princess*; *actor, actress*; *lion, lioness*; *hero, heroine.*'

Chapter 4

1. See *OED Online, dictionary* (n.).
2. See Cawdrey (1604): A4^v.
3. Johnson's interest in order is, in many ways, prototypical of eighteenth-century thought. 'Intellectual historians have traditionally characterized the Enlightenment as a time when the rage for order dominated institutions and texts as well as thought', J. Douglas Canfield observes in *Rhetorics of Order/Ordering Rhetorics in English Neoclassical Literature* (Newark: University of Delaware Press, 1989): 13. See also Lawrence Lipking, *The Ordering of the Arts in Eighteenth-Century England* (Princeton: Princeton University Press, 1970) and, with specific reference to order and the world of words, Lynda Mugglestone, 'Ranging Knowledge by the Alphabet: The Literature of Categorization and Organization 1700–1830'. In Robert DeMaria, H. Chang, and S. Zachar (eds.), *A Companion to British Literature. Vol. III: Long Eighteenth-Century Literature 1660–1835* (Chichester: Wiley-Blackwell, 2014): 207–22 [henceforth Mugglestone (2014b)].
4. Chambers (1728): i.
5. [Chesterfield] (1754a): 601.
6. [Philip Dormer Stanhope, Lord Chesterfield]. Letter to *The World* No. 101 (5 December 1754b): 606.
7. See McDermott (2005), and also Reddick (1996): 25–54.
8. W.S. (1749): 66.

9. See Reddick (1996): 38–9.
10. See also Johnson's comment that 'In making this collection, I trusted more to memory, than, in a state of disquiet and embarrassment, memory can contain' (*Yale* XVIII.99).
11. See *OED Online, clip* (v.), sense 1b.
12. Extant proofs of *OED1* frequently bear the signs of physical reduction for both citation and definition. Space costs money, as Johnson's printers were equally conscious. Expansive citations were not desirable. See Lynda Mugglestone, *Lost for Words. The Hidden History of the Oxford English Dictionary* (London and New York: Yale University Press, 2005).
13. Johnson's reference is to his first amanuensis, Francis Stewart who was hired in 1746 but died before the *Dictionary* was complete.
14. See Wimsatt (1959): 75.
15. See *Dictionary* (1755), *pencil* (n.), sense 2.
16. See *Dictionary* (1755), *rabbit* (n.): 'A company of scholars, going to catch conies, carried one with them which had not much wit, and gave in charge, that if he saw any, he should be silent for fear of scaring of them; but he no sooner espied a company of *rabbits*, but he cried aloud, *ecce multi cuniculi*; which he had no sooner said, but the conies ran to their burrows; and he being checked by them for it, answered, who would have thought that the *rabbits* understood Latin?'
17. See p. 43.
18. [Chesterfield] (1754a): 601.
19. [Chesterfield] (1754a): 601–2.
20. See Barrell (1983) and also Adam Beach, 'Standardizing English, Cultural Imperialism, and the Future of the Literary Canon', *Texas Studies in Literature and Language* 43 (2001): 117–41. Sorensen (2000): 76 ff., explores a similar point of view.
21. Donald Greene, *The Politics of Samuel Johnson*, 2nd edn. (Athens, Ga. and London: University of Georgia Press, 1990): 79.
22. John Locke, *An Essay Concerning Human Understanding*, (ed.) Peter Nidditch (Oxford: Oxford University Press, 1975): 402.
23. See *Yale* VI.109–10 for the details of Johnson's composition and revision.
24. On Johnson's interest in common law and the basis of good governance, see further Chapter 5, and also Tom Bingham, *Dr. Johnson and the Law, and Other Essays on Johnson* (London: Inner Temple and Johnson's House Trust, 2010), and Edward McAdam, *Dr. Johnson and the English Law* (Syracuse, N.Y.: Syracuse University Press, 1951).

25. Chesterfield to his son (4 October 1752). See Stanhope, Philip Dormer [Lord Chesterfield], *Letters Written by the Earl of Chesterfield to his Son*, 5th edn., 4 vols. (London: Eugenia Stanhope, 1774): III.372.

26. John A. Vance, *Samuel Johnson and the Sense of History* (Athens, Ga.: University of Georgia Press, 1984): 87–9 and 139. As Lipking notes (1998: 107), analogies with Caesar frequently invoke a sense of 'vaulting ambition' in Johnson's writing.

27. [Samuel Johnson], 'Review of *Memoirs of the Court of Augustus*', *Literary Magazine* 1 (1756): 42.

28. 'Government is...necessary' for 'the happiness of society', Johnson emphasizes in Sermon 24. See Samuel Johnson, *Sermons*. In *The Yale Edition of Samuel Johnson*, (eds.) Jean Hagstrum and James Gray (New Haven, Conn. and London: Yale University Press, 1978): XIV.250. The sermon as a whole (*Yale* XIV.249–60) provides a careful examination of good government.

29. See Greene (1990).

30. See Cowie (2002).

31. [Samuel Johnson], 'Life of the Earl of Roscommon', *The Gentleman's Magazine* 18 (1748): 214. See also Charles Batten, 'Samuel Johnson's Sources for "The Life of Roscommon"', *Modern Philology* 2 (1974): 184–9, and Carl Neimeyer, 'The Earl of Roscommon's Academy', *Modern Language Notes* 49 (1934): 432–7. As Batten confirms, Fenton was one of Johnson's main sources for the 'Life'.

32. On Johnson's revisions to the 'Life' of Roscommon, see further Chapter 8.

33. See pp. 39–40.

34. In *Rambler* 51 (written in September 1750), Johnson makes plain the need for reference models against the vagaries of personal spelling. As Cornelia (who is staying with an 'old lady' in the country) remarks: 'I once ventured to lay my fingers on her book of receipts [recipes], which she left upon the table.' However, she 'was not able to make use of the golden moments; for this treasury of hereditary knowledge was so well concealed by the manner of spelling used by her grandmother, her mother, and herself, that I was totally unable to understand it, and lost the opportunity of consulting the oracle, for want of knowing the language in which its answers were returned' (*Yale* III.277).

35. Lipking (1998): 134.

36. David Crystal, *Spell it Out: the Singular Story of English Spelling* (London: Profile Books, 2012): 189. On Johnson's influence in this respect, see further pp. 200–1.

37. See *Dictionary* (1755), *reasonable* (adj.), sense 3.
38. On Johnson's resistance to spelling reform, see further pp. 107–9.
39. Benjamin Martin, *Lingua Britannica Reformata: Or, A New English Dictionary* (London: J. Hodges, 1749): vi. On orthographical diversity in eighteenth-century dictionaries, see further Lynda Mugglestone, 'Registering the Language—Dictionaries, Diction, and the Art of Elocution'. In Raymond Hickey (ed.), *Eighteenth-Century English: Ideology and Change* (Cambridge: Cambridge University Press, 2010): 317–19.
40. Buchanan (1757): 16.
41. See also pp. 200–1.
42. As so often in Johnson, it is important to read with the semantics of eighteenth-century English in mind. *Dubious* is orientated towards uncertainty, rather than the negative and condemnatory associations it later gained. See *Dictionary* (1755), *dubious* (adj.), senses 1–3.
43. See also the entries for *intireness/entireness*.
44. The spelling in citations will, however, typically represent printers' spelling rather than the practice of different writers per se; textual accidentals were regularly normalized in the process of translation from script to print.
45. See equally Greene's account (1990: 145) of Johnson's habits in his political writings 'to inform the reader of the facts, to point out aspects of an argument that may not be obvious to him, to encourage him to do his own thinking'. Hanley (2001: 14) makes a similar point on Johnson's practice as book reviewer.
46. This is not always true of the fourth edition where spellings in citations can be 'molested' in favour of a corrected norm. This is, however, likely to represent a form of compositorial intervention. See e.g. the changes of *authour* to *author* in the citation from Addison's *Spectator* No. 289 under *brickdust* (n.) or of *smoak* to *smoke* in citations under *bedstead* and *wreath*. Such emendations are irregular.
47. See *Dictionary* (1755), *goal* (n.s.), sense 4: 'It is sometimes improperly written for *gaol*, or *jail*'.
48. A similar pattern appears in Johnson's comments on contemporary variation in pronunciation. See e.g. *gazette* ('accented indifferently on the first or last syllable').
49. See equally the entry for *–im*, extended in the 4th edition of the *Dictionary* 1773 to include Johnson's comment on the changing currents of use: 'What is *im* in Latin, when it is not negative, is often *em* in

French; and our writers, as the Latin or French occurs to their minds, use *im* or *em*: formerly *im* was more common, and now *em* seems to prevail.'

50. See also his comment (*Yale* XVIII.78) that 'some words, such as *dependant, dependent; dependance, dependence*, vary their final syllable, as one or another language is present to the writer'.

51. On modality as a marker of prescription, see Robin Straaijer, 'Deontic and Epistemic Modals as Indicators of Prescriptive and Descriptive Language in the Grammars by Joseph Priestley and Robert Lowth'. In Ingrid Tieken Boon van Ostade and Wim van der Wurff (eds.), *Current Issues in Late Modern English* (Bern: Peter Lang, 2009): 57–88.

52. For *chirurgeon* and Johnson's private spelling, see e.g. *Letters* I.193: 'I ... am glad that the Chirurgeon at Coventry gives him so much hope'; *Letters* II.19: 'I think the London Chirurgeons use it'; *Letters* III.280: 'Mrs. Lennox has just been with me to get a Chirurgeon to her Daughter'.

53. Roger Lass, 'Introduction'. In Roger Lass (ed.), *The Cambridge History of the English Language. Vol. III: 1476–1776* (Cambridge: Cambridge University Press, 2000): 11. See likewise Lass's contention that 'By Pope's time most of modern orthography is in place, and only minor matters like <-c> rather than <-ck> ... remain to be sorted out.'

54. For Vivian Salmon, such patterns characterize Johnson's private spellings alone: 'Even Johnson was content to use such unconventional forms as *enervaiting, peny*.' See Vivian Salmon, 'Orthography and Punctuation'. In Lass (ed.) (2000): 52. Johnson's private letters confirm a high level of variability in this respect.

55. See Ingrid Tieken Boon van Ostade, *An Introduction to Late Modern English* (Edinburgh: Edinburgh University Press, 2009): 42.

56. See e.g. *Letters* I.105. 'We walked uncovered into the chapel' and 'The Chappell is about thirty eight feet long' occur in the same paragraph.

57. See Thrale, Hester Lynch (1951). *Thraliana: The Diary of Mrs. Hester Lynch Thrale, Later Mrs. Piozzi, 1776–1809*, (ed.) Katherine C. Balderston, 2nd edn., 2 vols. (Oxford: Clarendon Press): I.401.

58. Textual variation of this kind can productively be compared with Gwin Kolb's account of orthographical variation in the 'Fair Copy' and the print text of the 1747 *Plan* in which variations such as *ancient/antient, authour/author, crowd/crouded* also appear. As Kolb concludes, 'Neither version, despite the presence in the fair copy of passages in Johnson's hand, yields unambiguous clues as to Johnson's personal

preferences (if, indeed, he had any strong predilections) in spelling.'
See Gwin J. Kolb, 'Establishing the text of Dr. Johnson's *Plan of a
Dictionary of the English Language*'. In W. H. Bond (ed.), *Eighteenth-
Century Studies In Honor of Donald F. Hyde* (New York: The Grolier
Club, 1970): 85.

59. Other interesting patterns of variation exist, for instance, in *vicious/
vitious, achieve/atchieve* (and related words), and *-or/-our* (see e.g.
terror/terrour, author/authour, horror/horrour).

60. See e.g. George Harris, *Observations upon the English Language. In a
Letter to a Friend* (London: Edward Withers, 1752). Harris appropri-
ates the diction of Johnson's *Plan* ('Change in Language is of itself an
Evil, and ought not to be attempted, but for great Advantage') in order
to advance ways by which such 'advantage' might be achieved, such
that *sovereign* and *foreign* ought to be spelled without <g>, while words
like *genuine, sanguine,* and *libertine* should lose their final *-e*. Harris
also advocates a wide range of etymological spellings in the interests of
propriety. If Chesterfield required an orthographical dictator, Harris
would, in a range of ways, been a safer guide.

61. Johnson's review of Charles Lucas's *An Essay on Waters* (in the
Literary Magazine 6 of August 1756) indicates similar reservations in
terms of the imposition of individual linguistic reform and the wilful
re-ordering of the written word. Lucas's text was printed using an
orthographical system of his own devising. Johnson was not convinced.
As he pointed out (p. 167), Lucas, in disregarding the precedent of
usage, has merely 'been induced by an affected fondness for analogy
and derivation, to disfigure his pages with new modes of spelling…
and may dispose many to conclude too hastily, that he has very little
skill in questions of importance, who has so much leisure to lavish
upon trifles'.

Chapter 5

1. Spence (1966) I.375, No. 954.
2. See further p. 8.
3. Henry Fielding, *The History of Tom Jones, a Foundling* (London:
A. Millar, 1749): II.85.
4. Thrale (1951): I.467.
5. Spence (1966): I.375.
6. Snell (1649): 39–40.
7. See p. 49.

8. See further pp. 20–1.

9. See *Dictionary* (1755), *think* (v.), sense 7: 'To judge; to conclude'.

10. Chris Pearce, 'Recovering the "Rigour of Interpretative Lexicography":
Border Crossings in Johnson's *Dictionary*'. In Iamartino and DeMaria
(eds.) (2006): 33–51.

11. Donald Siebert, '*Bubbled, Bamboozled*, and *Bit*: "Low Bad" Words in
Johnson's *Dictionary*', *Studies in English Literature 1500–1900* 26
(1986): 485.

12. Suzanne Romaine, 'Introduction'. In Suzanne Romaine (ed.), *The
Cambridge History of the English Language*. Vol. IV: *1776–1997* (Cambridge: Cambridge University Press, 1998): 7–8.

13. Kolb and Sledd (1953): 172.

14. See Anne McDermott, 'Johnson the Prescriptivist? The Case for the
Defense' (2005). In Lynch and McDermott (eds.) (2005): 113–28 and
Geoff Barnbrook, 'Johnson the Prescriptivist: the Case for the Prosecution' (2005a). In Lynch and McDermott (eds.) (2005): 92–112.

15. R. K. K. Hartmann (1979). 'Who Needs Dictionaries?'. In R. K. K.
Hartmann (ed.), *Dictionaries and Their Users* (Exeter: University of
Exeter): 1–2. On the 'fuzziness' of description and prescription as
lexicographical interface, see further Mugglestone (2015).

16. See McDermott (2005): 117.

17. See *Dictionary* (1755), *animadversion* (n.).

18. Matthew Hodgart, *Samuel Johnson and his Times* (London:
B. T. Batsford, 1962): 47 and 48.

19. Harold Allen, 'Samuel Johnson: Originator of Usage Labels'. In
Mohammad A. Jazayery (ed.), *Linguistics and Literature/Sociolinguistics
and Applied Linguistics* (The Hague: Mouton, 1979): IV.198.

20. On the history of usage labels in English lexicography, see e.g. Allen
(1979): 193–200; Geoff Barnbrook, 'Usage notes in Johnson's *Dictionary*', *International Journal of Lexicography* 18 (2005b): 189–201; and
Noel Osselton, 'Usage Guidance in Early Dictionaries of English',
International Journal of Lexicography 19 (2006): 99–105.

21. See also Pearce (2006) on Johnson's structuring of his entries in this
respect.

22. Johnson's reference is to his final citation, taken from the *London
Dispensatory*: 'To this is added a vinous bitter, warmer in the composition
of its ingredients than the watry infusion; and, as gentian and lemon-peel
make a bitter of so grateful a flavour, the only care required in this
composition was to chuse such an addition as might not *prejudice* it.'

23. See *Dictionary* (1755), *whence* (adv.), senses 1 and 4.
24. As in Straaijer's analysis of proscriptive methods, 'ought' acts as a signal of both remediation and imposed change. See Straaijer (2009): 62.
25. Hawkins (2009): 165.
26. On Johnson's theory and practice of criticism, see especially Philip Smallwood, *Johnson's Critical Presence: Image, History, Judgement* (Aldershot: Ashgate, 2004).
27. See p. 96.
28. See *Dictionary* (1755), *redolent* (adj.).
29. See Locke (1975): 476. On the pervasiveness of Locke as critical thinker in the *Dictionary*, see also Elizabeth Hedrick, 'Locke's Theory of Language and Johnson's *Dictionary*', *Eighteenth-Century Studies* 20 (1987): 422–44, and DeMaria (1986a, b).
30. See Locke (1975): 510. Locke is also 'clipped' and condensed, for the purposes of lexicography: 'Language being the great Conduit, whereby men convey their Discoveries, Reasonings, and Knowledge, from one to another, he that makes an ill use of it, though he does not corrupt the Fountains of Knowledge, which are in Things themselves, yet he does, as much as in him lies, break or stop the Pipes whereby it is distributed to the publick use and advantage of Mankind.'
31. Crystal (2012): 193.
32. See e.g. entries in *OED1* for words such as *burgle, enormity*, and *transpire*, where similar processes of resistance are plain. See James A. H. Murray, Henry Bradley, William A. Craigie, and Charles T. Onions (eds.), *A New English Dictionary on Historical Principles* (Oxford: Clarendon Press 1884–1928).
33. Joan Beal, *English in Modern Times 1700–1945* (London: Arnold, 2004): 90.
34. On Johnson and the meaning of *buxom*, see further Allen Reddick, 'So What's Wrong with "Buxom"? Samuel Johnson, Poetical language, and Semantics'. In *Selected Proceedings of the 2012 Symposium on New Approaches in English Historical Lexis* (HEL-LEX 3), (eds.) R. W. McConchie et al. (Somerville, Mass.: Cascadilla Proceedings Project, 2013): 159–65.
35. See e.g. *OED1, agnail*: '*Hang-nail*, given by Halliwell as a dialect word, is evidently like the Sc. equivalent *anger-nail* (anger = irritation, inflammation), a corruption of *ang-nail*'. Similar instances can be found in *boar-thistle*, given as a corruption of *bur-thistle*, or *hand-saw* as a corruption of *heron-saw*. A dead metaphor, corruption refers

to the observable disparity between etymon and current use. See e.g. Johnson's etymological comment that *jauntiness* is 'corrupted from *gentil*', or his comments on *kickshaw* on p. 124. Like other words, *corruption* has, however, its own polysemies. See e.g. Johnson's entry for *you*, and also pp. 188–9.

36. See Fussell (1972): 148.

37. The reference is to Horace's *Ars Poetica* ll. 71–2. See *Yale* XVIII.xxx.

38. On conflicts of this kind in Johnson, see also Daisuke Nagashima, *Johnson the Philologist* (Osaka: Kansai University, 1988), especially ch. 5: 'Johnson the Linguistic Agonistes'.

39. This figure includes, however, a wide range of register-based comments, which draw attention to stylistic appropriacy. See further pp. 132–9.

40. McDermott (2005): 122.

41. See e.g. *Dictionary* (1755), *sure* (adj.), sense 6: 'To be SURE. Certainly. This is a vitious expression: more properly *be sure*'; *good*, sense 5: 'the expression is, I think, vitious'. For Johnson's use of 'vicious' as marker in the 4th edn., see p. 213.

42. Siebert (1986): 485.

43. On Johnson and observation as critical practice, see especially Ian Donaldson, 'Samuel Johnson and the Art of Observation', *ELH* 53 (1986): 779–99.

44. Johnson's use of 'ought', as in comparable instances in contemporary grammars, can also operate as another form of hedging. On the different properties of *ought* in prescriptive writing, see Straaijer (2009): 62, and for similar assessments in relation to the grammarian Robert Lowth, see Ingrid Tieken Boon van Ostade, *The Bishop's Grammar: Robert Lowth and the Rise of Prescriptivism in English* (Oxford: Oxford University Press, 2011).

45. This explains, in practice, other 'bad' words in the *Dictionary*. See e.g. *huswife* (n.)

46. Giovanni Iamartino, 'Pragmatically Speaking in Early Modern English: Usage Notes and Labels in Johnson's *Dictionary*'. In Gabriella Di Martino and Maria Lima (eds.), *English Diachronic Pragmatics* (Napoli: CUEN, 2000): 263–82.

47. On gender and labelling, see Brewer (2012).

48. On Johnson's wider interest in the world of trade and commerce, see John H. Middendorf, 'Dr. Johnson and Mercantilism', *Journal of the History of Ideas* 21 (1960): 63–83.

49. See further Siebert (1986): 488.

50. On Johnson's close interest in the principles of stylistic decorum, see William Edinger, *Johnson and Detailed Representation: The Significance of Classical Sources* (Victoria, B.C.: University of Victoria, 1997).

51. 'A word may be in conversational or even epistolary use for ten or twenty years before it attains to the dignity of literature': see James A. H. Murray, 'Thirteenth Annual Address of the President to the Philological Society', *Transactions of the Philological Society* (1884)19: 517.

52. See also Johnson's comments in the 'Life of Cowley': 'words being arbitrary must owe their power to association, and have the influence, and that only, which custom has given them' (*Yale* XXI.76). As Locke had stressed, '*Words* by long and familiar use ... excite in Men certain *Ideas*, so constantly and readily, that they are apt to suppose a natural connexion between them. But that they *signify* only Men's peculiar *Ideas*, and that *by a perfectly arbitrary Imposition* is evident.' See Locke (1975): 408.

53. See *Dictionary* (1755), *bounce* (v.), sense 3. Johnson's use of such 'familiar' diction within his definitions is also worthy of note.

54. This has often been taken as strongly proscriptive (see e.g. Beal 2004: 45).

55. Kate Wild. 'Vulgar and Popular in Johnson, Webster and the *OED*'. In Eliswndra Bernal and Janet DeCesaris (eds.), *Proceedings of the XIII Euralex International Congress* (Barcelona: Documenta Universitaria, 2012): 1209–14.

56. Johnson's argument is centred on decorum, and the matching of style and sense, as he elaborates in a closely similar passage in the 'Life of Cowley' (*Yale* XXI.76).

57. See *OED Online*, *scrounge* (v.). Evidence provided in the relevant entry in September 2014 traces usage to 1909.

58. See Julie Coleman, *A History of Cant and Slang Dictionaries*. Vol I: *1557–1784* (Oxford: Oxford University Press, 2004). Johnson's entry for *micher* provides useful illustration. This is, he notes, still 'retained in the cant language for an indolent, lazy fellow'.

59. See Shaw and Piozzi (1974): 68.

60. DeMaria (1997): 25.

Chapter 6

1. Johnson uses *contribution* in a specifically military sense. See *Dictionary* (1755), *contribution* (n.), sense 3: 'That which is paid for the support of an army lying in a country'. On the circumstances of this exchange, see further Reddick (1996): 59–60.

2. See further pp. 87–8.

3. Patrick Hanks, 'Johnson and Modern Lexicography', *International Journal of Lexicography* 18 (2005): 246. As Hanks stresses in his comprehensive review of Johnson's practice, 'A detailed study of Johnson's policy and practice with regard to foreign borrowings would be a welcome addition to the literature.'

4. Sir Thomas Browne, *Certain Miscellany Tracts* (London: Charles Mearne, 1683): 134. The quotation is taken from Browne's Tract VIII: 'Of Languages, and particularly of the Saxon Tongue'. As Johnson commented (see Johnson (1973): 442), Browne 'discourses with great learning, and generally with great justness, of the derivation and changes of languages'.

5. John Wilkins, *An Essay towards a Real Character, and a Philosophical Language* (London: Samuel Gellibrand, 1668): 6.

6. John Dryden, 'The Dedication to the *Aeneis* to the *Earl of Mulgrave*'. In *The Poems of John Dryden*, (ed.) Kinsley (1958): III.1060.

7. See Donald Bond (ed.), *The Spectator* (Oxford: Clarendon Press, 1965): II.149–50.

8. Bond (ed.) (1965) II: 149.

9. [Chesterfield] (1754a): 602–3.

10. [Chesterfield] (1754a): 603: 'Mr. Johnson's labours will now, and, I dare say, very fully, supply that want, and greatly contribute to the farther spreading of our language in other countries.'

11. [Chesterfield] (1754a): 601.

12. See Jeremy Black, *Natural and Necessary Enemies, Anglo-French Relations in the Eighteenth Century* (London: Duckworth, 1988): 48. On French ambitions for a British invasion, see also Linda Colley, *Britons: Forging the Nation, 1707–1837* (London: Pimlico, 2003): 3–4. As Johnson's letters confirm, French invasion remained a threat. See e.g. *Letters* III.180–1: 'The battle, whenever it happens, will be probably of greater consequence than any battle in our time. If the French get the better we shall perhaps be invaded, and must fight for ourselves upon our own ground.'

13. See e.g. [Cambridge] (1754). A range of other texts across the mid-eighteenth century give expression to fears of this kind: see e.g. Simon Smith and Richard Munn, *The Danger of Great Britain and Ireland Becoming Provinces to France* (London: J. Roberts and R. Davis, 1746).

14. The 'Seven Years War' formally began in May 1756, ending with the Peace of Paris in 1763.

15. On Johnson and translation, see further pp. 162–3.
16. See e.g. John, Earl Wycombe to his father in 1784: 'It has puzzled me very much to find out why you should suppose that three weeks residence in Paris should have converted me at once into a macaroni, an epicure, and a coxcomb' (cited in Jeremy Black, *The British Abroad: The Grand Tour in the Eighteenth Century* (Stroud: Sutton, 2003a): 189). Black also illuminatingly cites John Wesley's comments in 1784 to Robert Jones: 'If you go abroad, I would by no means advise you to go to France. That is no place to save expense: But it is the only place to make your sons coxcombs, and your daughters coquettes.'
17. Hannah Grieg, *The Beau Monde: Fashionable Society in Georgian London* (Oxford: Oxford University Press, 2013). On French and fashionable socio-cultural identities, see also Jeremy Black, *France and the Grand Tour* (Basingstoke: Palsgrave Macmillan, 2003b). With a certain irony given his stance on naturalization, Chesterfield provides the first use of *bon ton* in the *OED*, in a letter dated 1 December 1747: 'Leipsig is not the place to give him that *bon ton*, which I know he wants.' See *OED Online, bon* (adj.). On Chesterfield and lexical innovation, see pp. 165–6.
18. See e.g. John Gascoigne, *Joseph Banks and the English Enlightenment: Useful Knowledge and Polite Culture* (Cambridge: Cambridge University Press, 1994): 205 ff., and Joan Beal, '"À la Mode de Paris": Linguistic patriotism and Francophobia in 18th-Century Britain'. In Carol Percy and Mary Catherine Davidson (eds.), *The Languages of Nation: Attitudes and Norms* (Bristol: Multilingual Matters, 2012): 141–54.
19. Johnson echoes Phillips (1658) in many of these statements. However, as Clement Hawes notes, Johnson can also turn a 'skeptical gaze' on the restrictive nature of 'Anglocentric antiquarianism' during the dictionary years. See e.g. *Rambler* 177 (*Yale* V.171). See Clement Hawes, 'Johnson's Cosmopolitan Nationalism'. In Smallwood (ed.) (2001): 53.
20. John Cannon, *Samuel Johnson and the Politics of Hanoverian England* (Oxford: Oxford University Press, 1994): 237.
21. See Henry Felton's *A Dissertation on Reading the Classics, and Forming a Just Style* (London: Jonah Bowyer, 1713): 98–9. The original citation reads: 'In *English* therefore, I would have all *Gallicisms* (for Instance) avoided, that our Tongue may be sincere, that we may keep to our own Language, and not follow the *French* Mode in our Speech, as we do in our Cloaths.'

22. See *Dictionary* (1755), *Latinism* (n.): 'A Latin idiom; a mode of speech peculiar to the Latin'; *Grecism*: 'An idiom of the Greek language'.
23. See *Dictionary* (1755), *bank* (n.).
24. For similar uses of *we*, see e.g. *fall*, sense 6; *sevennight*; *lancepesade*.
25. Paul Rastell, 'What Do We Mean by *We*?', *English Today* 19 (2003): 53: 'There is a connotation of implicit approval of those covered by *we* and disapproval of the non-*we*, which may have disturbing overtones.'
26. As Wimsatt confirms, Dryden's translation of (and Preface to) Charles Alphonse De Fresnoy's *De Arte Graphica* (1695), referred to as *Dufresnoy* in the *Dictionary*, is 'the prose work of Dryden by far the most frequently quoted'; it was the source of a range of 'Gallicisms', as under *perfectionate, prejudice, prevention*, and *serve*. See W. K. Wimsatt, Jr., 'Samuel Johnson and Dryden's "Du Fresnoy"', *Studies in Philology* 48 (1951): 26. On *flatter*, see further p. 165.
27. April McMahon, *Understanding Language Change* (Cambridge: Cambridge University Press, 1999): 201.
28. See Johnson's 'Life of Dryden' which identifies loans of this kind as a form of social pretension: '[Dryden] had a vanity, unworthy of his abilities; to shew...the rank of the company with whom he lived, by the use of French words, which had then crept into conversation: such as "fraischeur" for "coolness", "fougue" for "turbulence",...none of which the language had incorporated or retained. They continue only where they first stood, perpetual warnings to future innovators' (*Yale* XXI.489).
29. See e.g. *Letters* II.348 and II.349.
30. See Samuel Richardson, *Clarissa* (1747) II. xii. 66: 'Faulty morals deservedly...bring down rank and birth to the *Canaille*.' See *OED Online, canaille* (n.). *Canaille* remained without citational evidence in Johnson's *Dictionary*.
31. Isabel Balteiro, 'Prescriptivism and Descriptivism in the Treatment of Anglicisms in a Series of Spanish-English Dictionaries', *International Journal of Lexicography* 24 (2011): 280.
32. Balteiro (2011): 300.
33. See *Dictionary* (1755), *ch*. Johnson contrasts 'words purely English, or fully naturalized' in which <ch> has the 'sound of *tch*' with the sound of *sh* it has in some non-naturalized French words. He makes a similar point for the realisation of <ch> with /k/ for Greek-derived words such as *cholerick*.
34. See *Dictionary* (1755), *merely* (adv.).

35. See *Dictionary* (1755), *ae*.
36. See *Dictionary* (1755), *oe*: 'This combination of vowels does not properly belong to our language, nor is ever found but in words derived from the Greek, and not yet wholly conformed to our manner of writing.'
37. See *Dictionary* (1773), *defoedation*.
38. See pp. 55, 178 for Johnson's use of Skinner. As Johnson explained (*Yale* XVIII.81), Skinner 'probably examined the ancient and remoter dialects only by occasional inspection into dictionaries...*Skinner* always presses forward by the shortest way.'
39. *OED* confirms early uses in translations of Homer and Virgil, alongside its use by Milton, Cowley, and John Fryer. Use in the first half of the eighteenth century is, however, sparsely documented. See *OED Online*, *verdant* (adj.).
40. This citation was slightly 'clipped' in the *Dictionary*. Johnson's version reads: 'The sublime rises from the nobleness of thoughts, the magnificence of the words, or the harmonious and lively turn of the phrase; the perfect sublime arises from all three together.'
41. See *Dictionary* (1755), *yet* (adv.), sense 4.
42. *OED* notes the use of *mensal* in Irish English, and as a term in Scottish history from 1607 designating 'land set aside to supply food for the table'. *OED* also records Richardson's use in *Clarissa*, providing antedatings from Blount's *Glossographia*, and the 1440 *Promptorum Parvolorum*. See *OED Online*, *mensal* (adj.), sense 1 and (n.) sense 2.
43. *Trait*, for Johnson, confirms Warburton's unwarranted 'rage of gallicism' in editing Shakespeare's *Antony and Cleopatra*; Warburton emended 'tricks' to 'traits' in Enobarbus's aside to Cleopatra (IV. ii.14): ''Tis one of those odd traits which sorrow shoots / Out of the mind'. Johnson, editing Shakespeare in 1765, restores 'tricks'. See equally Thrale (1951): I.168 where Thrale's decision to underline *trait* (in an entry for 10 November 1777) confirms its still unassimilated status: 'Johnson as he was just in every Thing, was scrupulously so in giving Characters of living people, but he had not great Opportunities of knowing them...his want of Sight or hearing often made him liable to lose such *Traits* as would have changed his Opinions had they come within his reach.'
44. See *OED Online*, *trait* (n.).
45. See e.g. Johnson's entry for *cate* (1773) which makes its quantitative sense particularly clear: 'This is scarcely read in the singular.'

46. See e.g. *OED1, bise:* 'In mod.Eng. only an alien French word.' 'Alien' or 'imperfectly naturalized' words are designated in *OED1* by ||, enabling their categorization in tabular form for each section of the *Dictionary*. A total of 399 'aliens' appear in the volume covering D, and 319 in E.
47. *OED Online, Gallicism* (n.). The (unrevised) definition derives from the relevant fascicle of *OED1*, published in 1898: 'An idiom or mode of expression belonging to the French language, esp. one used by a speaker or writer in some other language; also, in generalized sense, free use of French idiom, "Frenchy" kind of diction.'
48. A similar point can be made for Johnson's use of regional designations such as 'Scottish' which mark out geographically restricted patterns of use against the unmarked national variety. See e.g. *laird* which is given as 'The lord of a manor in the Scottish dialect' or *tyke* which 'in Scottish still denotes a dog, or one as contemptible and vile as a dog'.
49. Philip Durkin, *Borrowed Words. A History of Loanwords in English* (Oxford: Oxford University Press, 2014): 10.
50. See Dryden's *Aeneis*, Book 6, l. 668: 'Dishonest, with lop'd Arms, the Youth appears'. In *The Poems of John Dryden*, (ed.) Kinsley (1958): II.1218. See *Dictionary* (1755), *dishonest* (adj.), sense 3.
51. On Johnson as translator, see further pp. 162–3, and also J. L. Abbott, 'No "Dialect of France": Samuel Johnson's Translations from the French', *University of Toronto Quarterly* 35 (1967): 129–40.
52. Johnson's negative comment on Caxton's translation, in *Idler* 69 (*Yale* II.215), offers further illustration of this stance: Caxton 'printed nothing but translations from the French, in which the original is so scrupulously followed, that they afford us little knowledge of our own language; tho' the words are English, the phrase is foreign'.
53. See Dryden, 'The Ninth Book of the *Aeneis*'. In *The Poems of John Dryden*, (ed.) Kinsley (1958): III.1320, l. 1095.
54. See *OED Online, falsify* (v.).
55. See 'Mr. Locke's Second Reply to Edward, Bishop of Worcester'. In John Locke, *The Works of John Locke*, 12th edn., 13 vols. (London: C. and J. Rivington, 1824): IV.279.
56. Thomas Gilmore, 'Johnson's Attitudes Towards French Influence on the English Language', *Modern Philology* 78 (1981): 243–60.
57. See e.g. the reported conversation in *Life* I.186: 'ADAMS. But, Sir, how can you do this in three years? JOHNSON. Sir, I have no doubt that I can do it in three years. ADAMS. But The French Academy, which consists of forty members, took forty years to compile their Dictionary.

JOHNSON. Sir, thus it is. This is the proportion. Let me see; forty times forty is sixteen hundred. As three to sixteen hundred, so is the proportion of an Englishman to a Frenchman.'

58. As Gilmore (1981: 245) notes, Johnson's 'use of italics seems quite inconsistent and even, at times, careless': 'For two long stretches in the *E*'s and *I*'s, Johnson (or his printer) seems largely to have forgotten to use italics for words that elsewhere in the alphabet would have been set in this type.'

59. [Daniel Defoe], 'The True-Born *Englishman*'. In *The True-Born Englishman and Other Poems*, (ed.) W. R. Owens (London: Pickering & Chatto, 2003): I.100 and 96, ll. 372–3 and 194.

60. See *Dictionary* (1755), *cimeter* (n.). Rafael Bluteau's *Vocabulario Portuguez, e Latino* was first published in 1712; a two-volume *Supplement* followed in 1727–8.

61. Johnson's awareness of the potential inaccuracy of his etymologies was plain. See e.g. his comment (*Yale* XVIII.83): 'Our knowledge of the northern literature is so scanty, that of words undoubtedly *Teutonick* the original is not always to be found ... I have therefore inserted *Dutch* or *German* substitutes, which I consider not as radical but parallel, not as the parents, but sisters of the *English*.'

62. Johnson was learning Spanish with Giuiseppe Baretti in 1773, Italian from 1776, and Dutch in 1767. See also Johnson's decision in 1755 to write a 'Dedication' to Baretti's *Introduction to the Italian Language* (London: A. Millar, 1755).

63. Johnson's diary entries regularly refer to his extensive reading in Greek. See e.g. *Yale* I.147 and I.108.

64. *Clarissa* was translated into French, German, and Dutch by 1755. See *Letters* I.93 n. 6.

65. See *Yale* I.58: 'Of this Prayer there is no date, nor can I tell when it was written; but I think it was in Gough-square, after the Dictionary was ended.'

66. Johnson's restricted abilities in French provide another enduring—if erroneous—stereotype.

67. *Letters* II.31: 'Of dear Mrs Salusbury I never expect much better news ... *de pis en pis* is the natural and certain course of her dreadful malady.'

68. Johnson adduced William Temple's 1690 *Essays: Upon Ancient and Modern Learning* in qualified support. As *OED* confirms under *rapport* (n.), 'The quot[ation]s. show that Johnson was mistaken in supposing that Temple was the introducer and sole user of the word.' Temple was

part of the process of naturalization, not its actuation. *Prime* (v.) 'To lay the first colours on a painting', deemed a 'Gallicism' by Johnson, is subject to similar change.

69. See *Dictionary* (1755), *flatter* (v.), sense 3. As *OED Online* notes (*flatter* (v.), sense 8: 'To "caress", gratify (the eye, ear, etc.)). Johnson describes this as "a sense purely Gallick"; but it occurs in his own writings, and is now established.'

70. See *OED Online, correction* (n.), sense 8.

71. See *Life* I.86n. ('I own it pleased me to find amongst them one trait of the manners of the age in London, in the last century') and *Life* I.118: '[Johnson] however indulged himself in occasional little sallies, which the French so happily express by the term *jeux d'esprit*, and which will be noticed in their order, in the progress of this work.' Addison, in a further conflict of principles and practice, provides the *OED*'s first evidence (1712: *Spectator* No. 305, para 16: 'Whether any such Relaxations of Morality, such little *jeux d'esprit*, ought not to be allow'd in this intended Seminary of Politicians'; see *OED Online, jeu d'esprit* (n.)), as well as the *OED*'s first evidence of *toujours* in 1711. See *OED Online, toujours* (adv.).

72. [Cambridge] (1754): 615.

Chapter 7

1. Swift (1712): 8.

2. Swift (1712): 34.

3. See e.g. Thomas Stackhouse, *Reflections on the Nature and Property of Languages in General, and on the Advantages, Defects, and Manner of Improving the English Tongue in Particular* (London: J. Batley, 1731): 188. Sheridan's ambitions to 'lay the foundation for regulating and refining our speech, till it is brought to a degree of perfection...and afterwards of fixing it in that state to perpetuity, in a sure and settled standard' are explored in his *Course of Lectures on Elocution: together with Two Dissertations on Language* (London: W. Strahan, 1762): 259.

4. See *Dictionary* (1755), *fancy* (n.), sense 2.

5. See Paul Aikon, 'Johnson and Time Criticism', *Modern Philology* 85 (1988): 543–57.

6. Jonathan Swift to Alexander Pope, July 23, 1737. On Johnson's use of epistolary writing as linguistic evidence, see further pp. 75, 89.

7. See *Dictionary* (1773), *witticism*. As in the corresponding entry in 1755, Johnson provides supporting evidence from writers such as L'Estrange

and Addison, though he adds evidence of Dryden's lexical inception: 'A mighty witticism, pardon a new word', taken from Dryden's Preface to *The State of Innocence and the Fall of Man* (1674). On *fraischeur*, see further pp. 149–50. See also e.g. *Dictionary* (1755), *passivity*, which is given as 'an innovated word', i.e. a neologism, without further comment.

8. As Johnson notes, here too expectation and reality will, for many entries, diverge: 'This is specious, but not always practicable' (*Yale* XVIII.91).

9. Johnson echoes Bacon in his imaging of change occurring 'by degrees'. See further p. 182.

10. Catherine Parke, *Samuel Johnson and Biographical Thinking* (Columbia, Mo.: University of Missouri Press, 1991). For Parke, however, space rather than time is given as the *Dictionary*'s central concern: 'The chief characteristic of the dictionary is mass and the way it fills space with a single, if complex, subject.... While the dictionary recognises the relationship between time and language, it aims to give an extensive, spatial account of the language that, by its breadth, and by the accumulating force of its examples, aims to combat time with space' (p. 54). See also Johnson's interest in documenting the 'primitive [i.e. "original"] ideas of... words which are therefore set first, though without examples, that the figurative senses may be commodiously deduced' (*Yale* XVIII.92).

11. [Dodsley] (1747): 388.

12. See [Chesterfield] (1754a): 599: 'I heard the other day with great Pleasure from my worthy friend Mr. Dodsley, that Mr. Johnson's English dictionary, with a grammar and history of our language, will be published this winter.'

13. [Chesterfield] (1754a): 603.

14. On Johnson's sources for the 'History', see Robert DeMaria Jr., 'Johnson's Extempore History and Grammar of the English Language'. In Lynch and McDermott (eds.) (2005): 77–91, and also *Yale* XVIII.115–19. The links to Warton's *Observations* are explored in more detail in Gwin Kolb and Robert DeMaria, 'Thomas Warton's Observations on the *Faerie Queene* of Spenser, Samuel Johnson's *History of the English Language*, and Warton's *History of English Poetry*: Reciprocal Indebtedness?', *Philological Quarterly* 74(3) (1995): 327–35.

15. Christopher Vilmar, 'The Authoritative Samuel Johnson', *The Cambridge Quarterly* 38 (2009): 166.

16. Johnson probably used Christopher Rawlinson's edition of Alfred's translation. See *Yale* XVIII.115.

17. Thomas Warton, *Observations on the* Faerie Queene *of Spenser* (London: R. and J. Dodsley, 1754): 227.

18. See *Dictionary* (1755), *deduce* (v.), sense 1.

19. See *Dictionary* (1755), *rasure* (n.), sense 2. Given as deriving from Latin *rasura*, it signifies 'A mark in a writing where something has been rubbed out'.

20. See e.g. Johnson's self-evident censure of imagination and fancy in his comments on the work of other lexicographers, as under *alloo* ('It is commonly imagined to come from the French *allons*'; *prowl* ('Of this word the etymology is doubtful: the old dictionaries write *prole*, which the dreamer *Casaubon* derives from προαλὴζ, ready, quick').

21. On Johnson and modern English, see further pp. 184–8.

22. See Ludmilla Minaeva, 'Quotations in the Dictionary: the Pros and Cons'. In Anna Braasch and Claus Povlsen (eds.), *Proceedings of the Tenth Euralex International Congress* (Copenhagen: Center for Sprogteknologi, 2002): 624: 'Johnson did not cite writers prior to the 16th C.'

23. See further p. 136–7.

24. For Johnson's use of Chaucer in the *Dictionary*, see also e.g. *dredge* (n.); *drotchel* (n.); *erke* (n.); *fond* (n.); *glitterand*; *grin* (n.); *harlot* (n.); *huggermugger* (n.); *kerchief* (n.); *pallet* (n.); *portass* (n.); *quaint* (adj.); *rote* (n.); *round* (v.); *scall* (n.) [added in 1773]; *shall* (v.); *sneap* (v.); *spick* (adj.); *tackle* (n.); *truantship* (n.); *welkin* (n.); and *wrench* (n.). As Kolb and DeMaria confirm (*Yale* XVIII.184), Johnson used the 1721 edition of Chaucer's *Works* edited by John Urry.

25. See Johnson's often-cited comment (in Boswell's *Tour of the Hebrides*), that 'There is no tracing the connection of ancient nations, but by language; and therefore I am always sorry when any language is lost, because languages are the pedigree of nations.'

26. See e.g. Rosemary Sweet, *Antiquaries: The Discovery of the Past in Eighteenth-Century Britain* (London: Hambleden, 2004): 192: 'The dominance of Rome and classical antiquity over the cultural imagination for the eighteenth century became less secure and the identification of the English nation with its specifically Saxon or Teutonic origins became more pronounced.' Johnson's comments on 'Saxon' and 'Teutonick' reveal considerable interest in the historical—and linguistic—origins of nationhood.

27. Edward Lye edited Franciscus Junius's *Etymologicum Anglicanum* in 1743; Johnson used it extensively in investigating the problems of etymological descent. As in the 1755 'Preface', Junius's work is made to share Johnson's metaphor of the lexicographical journey: 'the learning of *Junius* is often of no other use than to show him a track by which he may deviate from his purpose' (*Yale* XVIII.81).

28. [Samuel Johnson], 'Account of the Conduct of the Dutchess of Marlborough', *The Gentleman's Magazine* 12 (1742): 129. As Vance stresses, this represents 'Johnson's first major expression of his interest in historiography—the philosophy behind a proper understanding and evaluation of historical documents'. See John Vance, 'Johnson's Historical Reviews'. In Prem Nath (ed.), *Fresh Reflections on Samuel Johnson* (Troy, N.Y.: Whitston, 1987): 64.

29. [Johnson] (1742): 129.

30. Swift (1712): 34, 31.

31. Dryden's discussion of lexical obsolescence appears in the 'Dedication' to *The Satires of Decimus Junius Juvena* (1693). In *The Poems of John Dryden*, (ed.) Kinsley (1958) II: 610–11: 'in my Opinion, Obsolete Words may then be laudably reviv'd, when either they are more Sounding, or more Significant than those in practice: And when their Obscurity is taken away, by joining other Words to them which clear the Sense; according to the rule of *Horace*, for the admission of new Words. But in both cases, a Moderation is to be observ'd, in the use of them: For unnecessary Coynage, as well as unnecessary Revival, runs into Affectation; a fault to be avoided on either hand.' See also Johnson's use of this citation in the *Dictionary* (1755), under *obsolete* (adj.); *laudably* (adv.); *practice* (n.); *sounding* (adj.); and in *Dictionary* (1773) under *coinage*.

32. See e.g. the close echo of Swift in Stackhouse (1731): 192: 'no words, who which this Society may give a Sanction (whatever new ones they may think proper to receive), shall ever be antiquated'.

33. Sheridan was quick to proffer his own assistance in matters of fixing language with Chesterfield's support. Chesterfield, as Sheridan states, is 'so discerning a judge' and 'the proper person to be addressed on such an occasion'. This, he adds, 'will be confirmed by the general voice of the nation. To prove this, it is only necessary to mention what the scheme is: "A design to revive the long lost art of oratory, and to correct, ascertain, and fix the English language".' See Thomas Sheridan,

British Education or, the Source of the Disorders of Great Britain
(London: J. and R. Dodsley, 1756): v.
34. For naturalization as process, see pp. 158–60.
35. See e.g. *Dictionary* (1755), *innovation* (n.). Bacon's words are taken
    from his *Essay* 24 (1625): 'Of Innovations': 'It were good, therefore,
    that men in their innovations would follow the example of time itself;
    which indeed innovateth greatly, but quietly, by degrees scarce to be
    perceived.'
36. On readings of change as decay, see e.g. David Lowenthal, *The Past is a
    Foreign Country* (Cambridge: Cambridge University Press, 1995), 87
    ff., and, with particular reference to Johnson, Jack Lynch, '"The
    Ground-work of stile": Johnson on the History of the Language',
    Studies in Philology 97 (2000): 454–72.
37. Johnson's convictions of obsolescence are not always accurate. That
    jeopardy is 'a word not now in use' is, for example, easily contravened
    by Johnson's own use in the definition of *peril* (n.): 'Danger; hazard;
    jeopardy'. The declared obsolescence of *dell* ('A pit; a valley; a hole in
    the ground; any cavity in the earth') is similarly problematic.
38. [Samuel Johnson], 'A Reply to a Paper in the Gazetteer of May 26,
    1757', *Literary Magazine* 14 (1757): 255.
39. See p. 96.
40. On Johnson's use of nosism in the *Dictionary*, see further pp. 187–8.
41. As here, Johnson's fourth edition can reveal great prescriptive interest
    in the revisions which are imposed. See further Chapter 8.
42. Swift's words are taken from p. 37 of his 1712 *Proposal*.
43. See p. 188, and also Johnson's entries (discussed above) for words such
    as *harangue* and *peacock*.
44. See *OED Online*, *corruption* (n.), and also pp. 243–4.
45. See *Dictionary* (1755), *palliate* (v.), sense 3.
46. On Johnson's thinking in this respect, see also Graham Nicholls, '"The
    Race with Death". Samuel Johnson and the Sense of an Ending',
    Transactions of the Johnson Society (1975): 17–25.
47. See also Johnson's entry, and supporting evidence, for *immortality* in
    Dictionary (1755).
48. Full implementation of the Gregorian calendar took some time. Russia
    and Estonia adopted it only in 1918; Turkey officially adopted it in
    1927. It has not yet been adopted in Ethiopia.
49. On calendar reform and the eighteenth century, see especially Robert
    Poole, *Calendar Reform in Early Modern England* (London: University

College London Press, 1998). As Poole notes, Lord Chesterfield's Bill was drawn up in 1749.

50. See *Letters* II.130–1: 'In fifty years almost every book begins to require notes either to explain forgotten allusions and obsolete words.'

51. On Johnson's *Dictionary* and the metaphor of time, see further Lynda Mugglestone, 'The Dictionary as Watch', *The New Rambler. Journal of the Johnson Society of London* 2007–8. (2010): 70–7.

Chapter 8

1. Cited in Basker (1984): 152. The definition was emended to 'A water-fowl', in the second 'corrected' edition of the abridged version of the *Dictionary*, published in 1760. The first edition, uncorrected in this respect, was published in 1756. See Samuel Johnson, *A Dictionary of the English Language... Abstracted from the Folio Edition*, 2nd edn., 2 vols. (London: J. Knapton, C. Hitch, and L. Hawes et al., 1756).

2. Thrale (1951): I.165.

3. [Chesterfield] (1754a): 600.

4. [Chesterfield] (1754a): 600–1.

5. On Johnson and the 'sublunary' in terms of the *Dictionary*, see further *Yale* XVIII.105.

6. See *Dictionary* (1755), *perfection* (n.), sense 2.

7. As Johnson's *Dictionary* confirms, licentiousness of this kind is characterized by the absence of 'just restraint'. See *Dictionary* (1755), *licentiousness* (n.).

8. On Johnson's use of perfection in relation to the *Dictionary*, see also *Yale* XVIII: xx, xxvi–ii.

9. Shaw (1974): 76.

10. See pp. 144, 163–6.

11. See *Rasselas*, ch. XLIX: 'The conclusion, in which nothing is concluded' (*Yale* XVI.175).

12. See Parker (2003).

13. John Carey (ed.), *The Faber Book of Utopias* (London: Faber, 1999): xii: 'a dystopia is merely a utopia seen from another point of view'. As he stresses, utopian readings act as a careful mirror of a society's hopes and anxieties.

14. Robert Lowth to Robert Dodsley, 3 November 1757. See Dodsley (1988): 304.

15. Johnson's 'sowces his Plumb Pudden with melted Butter', Thrale comments (1951: I.186). See also Tieken Boon van Ostade (2009): 109;

on Thrale's spelling, see also Thrale (1951), where spellings such as *joulting, turneps, secrecy, cheerful, compleat, sower ('sour') poyson, alledge* confirm a wide range of contemporary variation.

16. Chesterfield's expressed desire for orthographical certainty is, in a similar way, by no means matched by the realities of his own practice.

17. See further p. 182.

18. See Hanks (2005).

19. See p. 20.

20. See p. 124.

21. On truth against received wisdom as an object of in quiry, see e.g. p. 122.

22. See p. 9.

23. See p. 9.

24. [David Garrick], 'Upon JOHNSON's *Dictionary*', *The Gentleman's Magazine* 25 (1755): 190. The Académie Française had, by convention, forty 'immortels' as members.

25. [Hawkesworth, John], 'Some Account of a Dictionary of the ENGLISH LANGUAGE, by SAMUEL JOHNSON A.M.', *The Gentleman's Magazine* 25 (1755): 150.

26. [Hawkesworth] (1755): 150.

27. Sheridan (1756): 376.

28. 'To the Admirers of Shakespeare', *The London Chronicle: Or, Universal Evening Post* (12–14 April 1757): 358.

29. Robert Nares, *Elements of Orthoepy: Containing a Distinct View of the Whole Analogy of the English Language so far as it relates to Pronunciation, Accent, and Quantity* (London: T. Payne, 1784): 270–1, 268. Nares nevertheless proposes additional rules where Johnson seems too liberal. See Nares (1784): 273 ff.

30. Richard Graves, *Lucubrations: Consisting of Essays, Reveries, &c. in Prose and Verse* (London: J. Dodsley, 1786): 217.

31. [Adam Smith], 'Review of *A Dictionary of the English Language* by Samuel Johnson', *The Edinburgh Review* 1 (1755): 61–2.

32. Edwards to Daniel Wray, 23 May 1755; 16 June 1755. In *Correspondence*: 208, 211. On Edwards as a critic of Johnson, see further Vedder M. Gilbert, 'The altercations of Thomas Edwards with Samuel Johnson', *JEGP* 11 (1952): 326–5.

33. Edwards to Daniel Wray, 16 June 1755. In *Correspondence*: 211.

34. Edwards to Daniel Wray, 5 May 1755. In *Correspondence*: 206, 211.

35. Edwards's *An Account of the Trial of the Letter y alias Y* (London: W. Owen 1753) was published, anonymously, in 1753.

36. See p. 241, n. 61.
37. See Basker (1984) and Hanley (2001).
38. See Murphy (1792): 117–19.

Appendix

1. See pp. 30, 33.
2. The first edition cost £4 and ten shillings.
3. Catherine Dille, 'The *Dictionary* in Abstract: Johnson's Abridgements of the *Dictionary of the English Language* for the Common Reader'. In Lynch and McDermott (eds.) (2005): 198–211. See also Robert De-Maria and Gwin Kolb, 'The Preliminaries to Dr. Johnson's *Dictionary*: Authorial Revisions and the Establishment of the Texts', *Studies in Bibliography* 48 (1995): 121–34.
4. See Thrale (1951): I.165: 'The Booksellers set him about it soon after however, & he went chearfully enough to his Business.'
5. See e.g. *Dictionary* (1755), *great* (adj.), sense 2: 'Having any quality in high degree'; sense 6: 'Of large power'; sense 7: 'Illustrious; eminent'.
6. Not all 'corrections' improve. The citation from *King Lear* which appeared under *dowered* in 1755 ('Will you with those infirmities she owes, / Unfriended, new-adopted to our hate, / Dower'd with our curse') gains, for example, the erroneous emendation 'new-adapted' (though 'adopted' remains under *new* in first and fourth editions alike.
7. See also Allen Reddick, 'Johnson beyond Jacobitism: Signs of Polemic in the "Dictionary" and the "Life of Milton", *ELH* 64 (1997): 983–1005 which gives a useful account of Johnson's methodology in terms of sources and collection for the 4th edition.
8. As Reddick (1997) notes, Johnson's revisions 'involve a disproportionate number of sources of a particular politico-theological kind', in ways which can suggest an ideological conservatism (and one which is, at times, also mirrored in the linguistic stance which can be assumed). See Reddick (1997): 985–6.
9. 'This particle may be sometimes resolved into *that not*, meaning prevention or care lest a thing should happen', Johnson notes under sense 1; 'It sometimes means only *that*, with a kind of emphasis', he adds under sense 2. See *Dictionary* (1773), *lest* (conj.).
10. See p. 128.
11. See e.g. Johnson's revisions to *hask*; *haught*; *heart-robbing*; *hest* ('command'; 'injunction'); *hence* (v.); *hospital*, sense 2 ('a place for shelter or entertainment'); *missay* (v.); *miswent* ('to go wrong').

References

Primary sources

Ausonius (1919). ed. Jeffrey Henderson, trans. Hugh G. Evelyn-White (London and Cambridge: Harvard University Press, Loeb Classical Library vol. 96).

Bailey, Nathan (1721). *An Universal Etymological English Dictionary* (London: E. Bell, J. Darby, A. Bettesworth et al.); 13th edn. (1747).

Baret, John (1574). *An Alvearie or Triple Dictionarie: in Englische, Latin, and French* (London: Henry Denham).

Baretti, Giuseppe (1755). *An Introduction to the Italian Language* (London: A. Millar).

Blount, Thomas (1656). *Glossographia: or A Dictionary, Interpreting all Such Hard Words ... as are Now Used in Our Refined English Tongue* (London: Thomas Newcomb).

Blount, Thomas (1673). *A World of Errors Discovered in The New World of Words, or, General English Dictionary, and in Nomothetes, or, The Interpreter of Law-words and Terms* (London: Abel Roper, John Martin, and Henry Herringman).

Bond, Donald (ed.) (1965). *The Spectator*, 5 vols. (Oxford: Clarendon Press).

Boswell, James (1971). *Boswell's Life of Johnson; Together with Boswell's Journal of a Tour to the Hebrides and Johnson's Diary of a Journey into North Wales*, (ed.) George Birkbeck Hill, rev. and enlarged L. F. Powell, 2nd edn., 6 vols. (Oxford: Clarendon Press).

Bray, William (ed.) (1887). *Diary and Correspondence of John Evelyn F.R.S.*, 4 vols. (London: George Bell).

Browne, Thomas (1683). *Certain Miscellany Tracts* (London: Charles Mearne).

Buchanan, James (1757). *Linguæ Britannicæ vera Pronunciatio: or, a New English Dictionary* (London: A. Millar).

Burton, Robert (1676). *The Anatomy of Melancholy*, 8th edn. (London: Peter Parker)

[Cambridge, Richard Owen] (1754). Letter to *The World* no. 102 (12 December): 611–16.

Cawdrey, Robert (1604). *A Table Alphabeticall Contayning and Teaching the True Writing and Vnderstanding of Hard Vsuall English Words* (London: Edmund Weauer).

Chambers, Ephraim (1728). *Cyclopædia: or, an Universal Dictionary of Arts and Sciences*, 2 vols. (London: James and John Knapton); 5th edn. 1742.

Chambers, Ephraim (1735). *Some Considerations Offered to the Publick, Preparatory to a Second Edition of Cyclopaedia: or, An Universal Dictionary of Arts and Sciences* (London).

Cockeram, Henry (1623). *The English Dictionarie: or, An Interpreter of Hard English Words* (London: Nathaniel Butler).

Defoe, Daniel (2003). *The True-Born Englishman and Other Poems*, (ed.) W. R. Owens (London: Pickering & Chatto).

[Dodsley, Robert] (1747). 'Review of *The Plan of a DICTIONARY of the English Language*', *The Museum: Or, the Literary and Historical Register* 3: 385–90.

Dodsley, Robert (1988). *The Correspondence of Robert Dodsley, 1733–1764*, (ed.) James E. Tierney (Cambridge: Cambridge University Press).

Dryden, John (1700). *Fables Ancient and Modern: Translated into verse, from Homer, Ovid, Boccace, & Chaucer* (London: Jacob Tonson).

Dryden, John (1958). *The Poems of John Dryden*, (ed.) James Kinsley, 4 vols. (Oxford: Oxford University Press).

Dyche, Thomas and Pardon, William (1740). *A New General English Dictionary; Peculiarly Calculated for the Use and Improvement of Such as are Unacquainted with the Learned Languages*, 3rd edn. (London: Richard Ware).

[Edwards, Thomas] (1753). *An Account of the Trial of the Letter y alias Y* (London: W. Owen).

Edwards, Thomas. 'The Correspondence of Thomas Edwards' (Bodleian Library, Oxford, MS Bodl. 1012).

Felton, Henry (1713). *A Dissertation on Reading the Classics, and Forming a Just Style* (London: Jonah Bowyer).

Fielding, Henry (1749). *The History of Tom Jones, a Foundling*, 2 vols. (London: A. Millar).

Fisher, Anne (1788). *An Accurate New Spelling Dictionary, and Expositor of the English Language*, 6th edn. (London: G. G. and J. Robinson).

Florio, John (1580). *A Shorte and Briefe Narration of the Two Nauigations and Discoueries to the Northweast Partes called Newe Fraunce* (London: H. Bynneman).

Florio, John (1598). *A Worlde of Wordes, or Most Copious, and Exact Dictionarie in Italian and English* (London: Edward Blount).

Foote, Samuel (1753). *The Englishman in Paris. A Comedy* (London: Paul Vaillant).

[Garrick, David] (1755). 'Upon JOHNSON's *Dictionary*', *The Gentleman's Magazine* 25: 190.

Glossographia Anglicana Nova (1707). (London: Daniel Brown, Tim Goodwin).

Graves, Richard (1786). *Lucubrations: Consisting of Essays, Reveries, &c. in Prose and Verse* (London: J. Dodsley).

Hale, Matthew (1667). *The Primitive Origination of Mankind, Considered and Examined According to the Light of Nature* (London: William Godbid).

Harris, George (1752). *Observations upon the English Language. In a Letter to a Friend* (London: Edward Withers).

[Hawkesworth, John] (1755). 'Some Account of a Dictionary of the ENGLISH LANGUAGE, by SAMUEL JOHNSON A.M.', *The Gentleman's Magazine* 25: 147–51.

Hawkins, John (2009). *The Life of Samuel Johnson, LL.D.,* (ed.) O. M. Brack, Jr. (Athens, Ga.: University of Georgia Press).

Hill, George Birkbeck (ed.) (1897). *Johnsonian Miscellanies*, 2 vols. (Oxford: Clarendon Press).

Hill, John (1751). *A History of the* Materia Medica. *Containing Descriptions of all the substances used in Medicine* (London: T. Longman, C. Hitch, and L. Hawes).

James, Robert (1743–45). *A Medicinal Dictionary, including Physic, Surgery, Anatomy, Chymistry and Botany, together with a History of Drugs*, 3 vols. (London: T. Osborne).

[Johnson, Samuel] (1742). 'Account of the Conduct of the Dutchess of Marlborough', *The Gentleman's Magazine* 12: 128–31.

[Johnson, Samuel] (1748). 'Life of the Earl of Roscommon', *The Gentleman's Magazine* 18: 214–17.

[Johnson, Samuel] (1755). *Account of an Attempt to Ascertain the Longitude at Sea, by an Exact Theory of the Variation of the Magnetical Needle* (London: R. Dodsley, 1755).

Johnson, Samuel (1755). *A Dictionary of the English Language; in which the words are deduced from their originals and illustrated in their different significations by examples from the best writers* (London: J. and

P. Knapton, T. and T. Longman, C. Hitch, and L. Hawes, A. Millar, and R. and J. Dodsley); 4th edn. (1773).

Johnson, Samuel (1756). *A Dictionary of the English Language... Abstracted from the Folio Edition*, 2nd edn., 2 vols. (London: J. Knapton, C. Hitch, and L. Hawes et al., 1756); corrected edn. (1760).

[Johnson, Samuel] (1756a). 'Review of *Memoirs of the Court of Augustus*', *Literary Magazine* 1: 41–2.

[Johnson, Samuel] (1756b). 'Review of "An Essay on Waters; in three Parts"', *Literary Magazine* 4: 167–8.

[Johnson, Samuel] (1756c). 'Preface'. In Rolt, Richard, *A New Dictionary of Trade and Commerce, compiled from the Information of the most Eminent Merchants, and from the Works of the Best Writers on Commercial Subjects* (London: T. Osborne and J. Shipton).

[Johnson, Samuel] (1757). 'A Reply to a Paper in the Gazetteer of May 26, 1757', *Literary Magazine* 14: 253–6.

Johnson, Samuel (1805). *An Account of the Life of Dr. Samuel Johnson, from his Birth to his Eleventh Year, Written by Himself. To which are added, Original Letters to Dr. Samuel Johnson by Miss Hill Boothby* (London: Richard Phillips).

Johnson, Samuel (1958–). *The Yale Edition of the Works of Samuel Johnson*, (eds.) John Middendorf et al. (New Haven, Conn. and London: Yale University Press). [*Yale*]

I. *Diaries, Prayers, and Annals*, (ed.) E. L. McAdam, Jr., with Donald and Mary Hyde (1958).

II. *The Idler and The Adventurer*, (eds.) W. J. Bate, John M. Bullit, and L. F. Powell, 2nd edn. (1970).

III–V. *The Rambler*, (ed.) W. J. Bate and Albrecht B. Strauss (1969).

VI. *Poems*, (ed.) E. L. McAdam, Jr., with George Milne (1964; repr. 1975).

VII. *Johnson on Shakespeare*, (ed.) Arthur Sherbo (1969).

XIV. *Sermons*, (eds.) Jean Hagstrum and James Gray (1978).

XVI. *Rasselas and Other Tales*, (ed.) Gwin J. Kolb (1990).

XVIII. *Johnson on the English Language*, (eds.) Gwin J. Kolb and Robert DeMaria, Jr. (2005).

XXI–XXIII. *The Lives of the Poets*, (ed.) John H. Middendorf (2010).

Johnson, Samuel (1973). *Early Biographical Writings of Dr. Johnson*, (ed.) J. D. Fleeman (Farnborough: Gregg International).

Johnson, Samuel (1992–94). *The Letters of Samuel Johnson*, (ed.) Bruce Redford, 5 vols. (Oxford: Oxford University Press).

K[ersey], J[ohn] (1702). *A New English Dictionary: or, a Compleat Collection of the Most Proper and Significant Words Commonly Used in the Language* (London: Henry Bonwicke and Robert Knaplock).

Kersey, John (1708). *Dictionarium Anglo-Britannicum: Or, a General English Dictionary.* (London: J. Wilde).

Locke, John (1824). *The Works of John Locke*, 12th edn., 13 vols. (London: C. and J. Rivington).

Locke, John (1975) *An Essay Concerning Human Understanding*, (ed.) Peter Nidditch (Oxford: Oxford University Press).

Lowth, Robert (1762). *A Short Introduction to English Grammar, with Critical Notes* (London: A. Millar; R. and J. Dodsley).

Lucas, Charles (1756). *An Essay on Waters* (London: A. Millar).

Mallet, David (1747). *Amyntor and Theodora: or, the Hermit* (London: Paul Vaillant).

Martin, Benjamin (1749). *Lingua Britannica Reformata: or, A New English Dictionary* (London: J. Hodges).

Murphy, Arthur (1792). *An Essay upon the Life and Genius of Samuel Johnson. LL.D.* (London: T. Longman, B. White).

Murray, James. *Murray Papers* (Bodleian Library, Oxford).

Murray, James A. H., Bradley, Henry, Craigie, William A., and Onions, Charles T. (eds.) (1884–1928). *A New English Dictionary on Historical Principles* (Oxford: Clarendon Press) [cited as *OED1*].

Nares, Robert (1784). *Elements of Orthoepy: Containing a Distinct View of the Whole Analogy of the English Language so far as it relates to Pronunciation, Accent, and Quantity* (London: T. Payne).

[Newbery, John] (1759–61). *The World Displayed: or, A Curious Collection of Voyages and Travels Selected from the Writers of all Nations*, 20 vols. (London: J. Newbery).

Pemberton, Henry (1746). *The Dispensatory of the Royal College of Physicians* (London: T. Longman and T. Sherwell).

Phillips, Edward (1658). *The New World of English Words, or, A General Dictionary* (London: Nath. Brooke).

Pope, Alexander and Warburton, William (eds.), (1747). *The Works of Shakespeare*, 8 vols. (London: J. and P. Knapton, S. Birt, et al).

Richardson, Samuel (1964). *Selected Letters of Samuel Richardson*, (ed.) John Carroll (Oxford: Clarendon Press).

S., W. (1749). 'The Signification of Words now Varied', *The Gentleman's Magazine* 19: 65–6.

Shaw, William, and Piozzi, Hester Lynch (1974). *William Shaw, Memoirs of the Life and Writings of the Late Dr. Samuel Johnson; Hester Lynch Piozzi, Anecdotes of the Late Samuel Johnson, LL.D.*, (ed.) Arthur Sherbo (London: Oxford University Press).

Sheridan, Thomas (1756). *British Education or, the Source of the Disorders of Great Britain* (London: J. and R. Dodsley).

Sheridan, Thomas (1762). *A Course of Lectures on Elocution: together with Two Dissertations on Language* (London: W. Strahan).

[Skinner, Stephen] (1659). *Gazophylacium Anglicanum: Containing the Derivation of English Words* (London: E. H. and W. H.).

Smart, Christopher (1756). 'Some Thoughts on the English Language', *The Universal Visiter and Memorialist*: 4–9.

[Smith, Adam] (1755). 'Review of *A Dictionary of the English Language* by Samuel Johnson', *The Edinburgh Review* 1: 61–73.

Smith, Simon and Munn, Richard (1746). *The Danger of Great Britain and Ireland Becoming Provinces to France* (London: J. Roberts and R. Davis).

Smythe, James (1727). *The Rival Modes. A Comedy* (London: Bernard Lintot).

Snell, George (1649). *The Right Teaching of Useful Knowledg, to Fit Scholars for Som Honest Profession* (London: John Stephenson).

Spence, Joseph (1966). *Observations, Anecdotes, and Characters of Books and Men*, (ed.) James M. Osborn, 2 vols. (Oxford: Clarendon Press 6).

Sprat, Thomas (1667). *The History of the Royal-Society of London, for the Improving of Natural Knowledge* (London: J. Martyn).

Stackhouse, Thomas (1731). *Reflections on the Nature and Property of Languages in General, and on the Advantages, Defects, and Manner of Improving the English Tongue in Particular* (London: J. Batley).

[Stanhope, Philip Dormer, Lord Chesterfield] (1754a). Letter to *The World* No. 100 (28 November): 599–604.

[Stanhope, Philip Dormer, Lord Chesterfield] (1754b). Letter to *The World* No. 101 (5 December): 605–10.

Stanhope, Philip Dormer [Lord Chesterfield] (1774). *Letters Written by the Earl of Chesterfield to his Son*, 5th edn., 4 vols. (London: Eugenia Stanhope).

Swift, Jonathan (1712). *A Proposal for Correcting, Improving and Ascertaining the English Tongue; In a letter to the Most Honourable Robert Earl of Oxford and Mortimer, Lord High Treasurer of Great Britain* (London: Benjamin Tooke).

Swift, Jonathan (2012). *Gulliver's Travels*, (ed.) David Womersley (Cambridge: Cambridge University Press).

Thrale, Hester Lynch (1951). *Thraliana: The Diary of Mrs. Hester Lynch Thrale, Later Mrs. Piozzi, 1776–1809*, (ed.) Katherine C. Balderston, 2nd edn., 2 vols. (Oxford: Clarendon Press).

Tickell, Thomas (1713). *A Poem to His Excellency the Lord Privy-Seal, on the Prospect of Peace* (London: Jacob Tonson).

Walter, Richard and Robins, Benjamin (1974). *A Voyage Round the World in the Years MDCCXL, I, II, II, IV by George Anson*, (ed.) Glyndwr Williams (London: Oxford University Press).

Warton, Thomas (1754). *Observations on the* Faerie Queene *of Spenser* (London: R. and J. Dodsley).

Watts, Isaac (1745). *Logick: or, The Right Use of Reason in the Enquiry after Truth*, 8th edn. (London: T. Longman, and T. Shewell).

Wilkins, John (1668). *An Essay towards a Real Character, and a Philosophical Language* (London: Samuel Gellibrand).

[Wilson, Thomas] (1724). *The Many Advantages of a Good Language to any Nation: with an Examination of the Present State of our Own: as also, an Essay towards Correcting Some Things that are Wrong in it* (London: J. Knapton, R. Knaplock, J. Sprint, D. Midwinter, R. Robinson, W. Innys, and J. Osborne).

Secondary sources

Abbott, J. L. (1967). 'No "Dialect of France": Samuel Johnson's Translations from the French', *University of Toronto Quarterly* 35: 129–40.

Aikon, Paul (1988). 'Johnson and Time Criticism', *Modern Philology* 85: 543–57.

Allen, Harold (1979). 'Samuel Johnson: Originator of Usage Labels'. In Mohammad A. Jazayery (ed.), *Linguistics and Literature/Sociolinguistics and Applied Linguistics* IV (The Hague: Mouton): 193–200.

Auden, W. H. (1951). *The Enchafèd Flood, or, The Romantic Iconography of the Sea* (London: Faber and Faber).

Balteiro, Isabel (2011). 'Prescriptivism and Descriptivism in the Treatment of Anglicisms in a Series of Spanish-English Dictionaries', *International Journal of Lexicography* 24: 277–305.

Barnbrook, Geoff (2005a). 'Johnson the Prescriptivist? The Case for the Prosecution'. In Jack Lynch and Anne McDermott (eds.), *Anniversary Essays on Johnson's* Dictionary (Cambridge: Cambridge University Press, 2005): 92–112.

Barnbrook, Geoff (2005b). 'Usage notes in Johnson's *Dictionary*', *International Journal of Lexicography* 18: 189–201.

Barrell, John (1983). *English Literature in History, 1730–80: An Equal, Wide Survey* (London: Hutchinson).

Basker, James (1984). 'Minim and the Great Cham: Smollett and Johnson on the Prospect of an English Academy'. In J. Engell (ed.), *Johnson and his Age* (Cambridge, Mass: Harvard University Press, Harvard English Studies vol. 12): 137–61.

Basker, James (1997). 'Myth upon Myth: Johnson, Gender, and the Misogyny Question', *Age of Johnson* 8: 175–88.

Basker, James (2000). '"To the Next Insurrection of the Negroes": Johnson, Race, and Rebellion', *Age of Johnson* 11: 17–51.

Bate, Walter Jackson (1955). *The Achievement of Samuel Johnson* (New York: Oxford University Press).

Batten, Charles (1974). 'Samuel Johnson's Sources for "The Life of Roscommon"', *Modern Philology* 72: 185–9.

Beach, Adam (2001). 'Standardizing English, Cultural Imperialism, and the Future of the Literary Canon', *Texas Studies in Literature and Language* 43: 117–41.

Beal, Joan (2004). *English in Modern Times 1700–1945* (London: Arnold).

Beal, Joan (2012). '"À la Mode de Paris": Linguistic Patriotism and Francophobia in 18th-Century Britain'. In Carol Percy and Mary Catherine Davidson (eds.), *The Languages of Nation: Attitudes and Norms* (Bristol: Multilingual Matters): 141–54.

Béjoint, Henri (1994). *Tradition and Innovation in Modern English Dictionaries* (Oxford: Clarendon Press).

Béjoint, Henri (2010). *The Lexicography of English* (Oxford: Oxford University Press).

Bingham, Tom (2010). *Dr. Johnson and the Law, and Other Essays on Johnson* (London: Inner Temple and Johnson's House Trust).

Black, Jeremy (1988). *Natural and Necessary Enemies, Anglo-French Relations in the Eighteenth Century* (London: Duckworth).

Black, Jeremy (2003a). *The British Abroad: The Grand Tour in the Eighteenth Century* (Stroud: Sutton).

Black, Jeremy (2003b). *France and the Grand Tour* (Basingstoke: Palsgrave Macmillan).

Boulton, James T. (ed.) (1971). *Samuel Johnson: The Critical Heritage* (London: Routledge).

Brack, O. M. and Kaminski, T. (1984). 'Johnson, James, and the *Medicinal Dictionary*', *Modern Philology* 81: 378–400.

Brack, O. M. and Kelley, Robert E. (eds.) (1974). *The Early Biographies of Samuel Johnson* (Iowa City: University of Iowa Press).

Brewer, Charlotte (2012). '"A Goose-Quill or a Gander's"? Female writers in Johnson's *Dictionary*'. In Freya Johnston and Lynda Mugglestone (eds.), *Samuel Johnson. The Arc of the Pendulum* (Oxford: Oxford University Press, 2012): 120–39.

Canfield, J. Douglas (1989). *Rhetorics of Order/Ordering Rhetorics in English Neoclassical Literature* (Newark: University of Delaware Press).

Cannon, John (1994). *Samuel Johnson and the Politics of Hanoverian England* (Oxford: Oxford University Press).

Carey, Daniel (1997). 'Compiling Nature's History: Travellers and Travel Narratives in the Early Royal Society', *Annals of Science* 54: 269–92.

Carey, John (ed.) (1999). *The Faber Book of Utopias* (London: Faber).

Carlson, Carl L. (1938). *The First Magazine; a History of the Gentleman's Magazine, with an Account of Dr. Johnson's Editorial Activity and of the Notice given America in the Magazine* (Providence, R.I.: Brown University).

Clifford, James L. (1980). *Dictionary Johnson: Samuel Johnson's Middle Years* (London: Heinemann).

Coleman, Julie (2004). *A History of Cant and Slang Dictionaries. Vol. I: 1557–1784* (Oxford: Oxford University Press).

Colley, Linda (2003). *Britons: Forging the Nation, 1707–1837* (London: Pimlico).

Considine, John (2010). *Adventuring in Dictionaries: New Studies in the History of Lexicography* (Newcastle: Cambridge Scholars Publishing).

Considine, John (2013). 'Ambrose Philips and *Little Preston*', *Notes and Queries* 60(1): 70–1.

Cowie, Anthony (2002). 'Examples and Collocations in the French *Dictionnaire de langue*'. In Marie-Hélène Corréard (ed.), *Lexicography and Natural Language Processing: A Festschrift in Honour of B. T. S. Atkins* (Grenoble: Euralex): 73–90.

Croker, John Wilson (1842). *Johnsoniana, or, Supplement to Boswell* (Philadelphia: Carey and Hart).

Cromartie, Alan (2004). 'Hale, Sir Mathew (1609–1676)'. In *Oxford Dictionary of National Biography* (Oxford: Oxford University Press).

Crystal, David (2012). *Spell it Out: the Singular Story of English Spelling* (London: Profile Books).

Curley, Thomas (1976). *Samuel Johnson and the Age of Travel* (Athens, Ga.: University of Georgia Press).

DeMaria, Jr., Robert (1986a). *Johnson's Dictionary and the Language of Learning* (Oxford: Oxford University Press).

DeMaria, Jr., Robert (1986b). 'The Theory of Language in Johnson's *Dictionary*'. In *Johnson after Two Hundred Years*, (ed.) Paul Korshin (Philadelphia: University of Pennsylvania Press): 159–74.

DeMaria, Jr., Robert (1997). *Samuel Johnson and the Life of Reading* (Baltimore: London: Johns Hopkins University Press).

DeMaria, Jr., Robert (2005). 'Johnson's Extempore History and Grammar of the English Language'. In Jack Lynch and Anne McDermott (eds.), *Anniversary Essays on Johnson's* Dictionary (Cambridge: Cambridge University Press): 77–91.

DeMaria, Jr., Robert (2006). 'North and South in Johnson's *Dictionary*', *Textus. English Studies in Italy* (Issue: *Samuel Johnson's* Dictionary *and the Eighteenth-Century World of Words*, (eds.) Giovanni Iamartino and Robert DeMaria, Jr.), 19: 11–32.

Dille, Catherine (2005). 'The *Dictionary* in Abstract: Johnson's Abridgements of the *Dictionary of the English Language* for the Common Reader'. In Jack Lynch and Anne McDermott (eds.), *Anniversary Essays on Johnson's* Dictionary (Cambridge: Cambridge University Press): 198–211.

Donaldson, Ian (1986). 'Samuel Johnson and the Art of Observation', *ELH* 53: 779–99.

Dossena, Marina (2006). '"The Cinic Scotomastic"? Johnson, His Commentators, Scots, French, and the Story of English', *Textus. English Studies in Italy* (Issue: *Samuel Johnson's* Dictionary *and the Eighteenth-Century World of Words*, (eds.) Giovanni Iamartino and Robert DeMaria, Jr.), 19: 51–68.

Durkin, Philip (2014). *Borrowed Words. A History of Loanwords in English* (Oxford: Oxford University Press).

Edinger, William (1997). *Johnson and Detailed Representation: The Significance of Classical Sources* (Victoria, B.C.: University of Victoria).

Fleeman, David (1984). 'Dr. Johnson's *Dictionary*, 1755'. In Kai Kin Yung (ed.), *Samuel Johnson 1709–84* (London: The Herbert Press): 37–46.

Fussell, Paul (1972). *Samuel Johnson and the Life of Writing* (London: Chatto & Windus).

Gascoigne, John (1994). *Joseph Banks and the English Enlightenment: Useful Knowledge and Polite Culture* (Cambridge: Cambridge University Press).

Geller, Jaclyn (2001). 'The Unnarrated Life: Samuel Johnson, Female Friendship, and the Rise of the Novel Revisited'. In Philip Smallwood (ed.), *Johnson Revisioned. Looking Before and After* (Cranbury, N.J.: Rosemont Publishing, 2001): 80–98.

Gilbert, Vedder M. (1952). 'The Altercations of Thomas Edwards with Samuel Johnson', *JEGP* 11: 326–5.

Gilmore, Thomas (1981). 'Johnson's Attitudes Towards French Influence on the English Language', *Modern Philology* 78: 243–60.

Görlach, Manfred (2003). 'A New Text Type: Exercises in Bad English', *Paradigm* (Issue: *The Teaching of English in the Eighteenth and Nineteenth Centuries. Essays for Ian Michael on his 88th Birthday*, (ed.) F. Austin and C. Stray) 2: 5–14.

Gove, Philip (1938). 'Notes on Serialization and Competitive Publishing: Johnson and Bailey's Dictionaries, 1755', *Proceedings of the Oxford Bibliographical Society* 5: 305–22.

Gray, James and Murray, T. J. (1996). 'Dr. Johnson and Dr. James', *Age of Johnson* 7: 213–45.

Greene, Donald J. (1965). 'Pictures to the Mind: Johnson and Imagery'. In *Johnson, Boswell and Their Circle: Essays presented to Laurence Fitzroy Powell in Honour of his Eighty-Fourth Birthday* (Oxford: Clarendon Press): 137–58.

Greene, Donald J. (1990). *The Politics of Samuel Johnson*, 2nd edn. (Athens, Ga. and London: University of Georgia Press).

Grieg, Hannah (2013). *The Beau Monde: Fashionable Society in Georgian London* (Oxford: Oxford University Press).

Grundy, Isabel (1987). 'Samuel Johnson as Patron of Women', *Age of Johnson* 1: 59–77.

Hanks, Patrick (2005). 'Johnson and Modern Lexicography', *International Journal of Lexicography* 18: 243–66.

Hanley, Brian (2001). *Samuel Johnson as Book Reviewer: A Duty to Examine the Labors of the Learned* (Newark, N.J.: University of Delaware Press; London: Associated University Presses).

Hart, Francis R. (1969). 'Johnson as Philosophic Traveler: The Perfecting of an Idea', *ELH* 36: 679–95.

Hart, Kevin (1999). *Samuel Johnson and the Culture of Property* (Cambridge: Cambridge University Press).

Hartmann, R. K. K. (1979). 'Who Needs Dictionaries?'. In R. K. K. Hartmann (ed.) *Dictionaries and Their Users* (Exeter: University of Exeter): 1–12.

Hawes, Clement (2001). 'Johnson's Cosmopolitan Nationalism'. In Philip Smallwood (ed.), *Johnson Revisioned. Looking Before and After* (Cranbury, N.J.: Rosemont Publishing, 2001): 37–63.

Hayden, Judy (2012). *Travel Narratives, the New Science, and Literary Discourse, 1569–1750* (Burlington, Vt.: Ashgate).

Hazen, Allen T. (1936). 'Samuel Johnson and Dr. Robert James', *Bulletin of the Institute of the History of Medicine* 4: 456–7.

Hedrick, Elizabeth (1987). 'Locke's Theory of Language and Johnson's *Dictionary*', *Eighteenth-Century Studies* 20: 422–44.

Hedrick, Elizabeth (1988). 'Fixing the Language: Johnson, Chesterfield, and the Plan of a Dictionary', *ELH* 55 (1988): 421–42.

Hodgart, Matthew (1962). *Samuel Johnson and his Times* (London: B. T. Batsford).

Iamartino, Giovanni (2000). 'Pragmatically Speaking in Early Modern English: Usage Notes and Labels in Johnson's *Dictionary*'. In Gabriella Di Martino and Maria Lima (eds.). *English Diachronic Pragmatics* (Naples: CUEN): 263–82.

Jemielity, Thomas (1972). 'Dr. Johnson and the Uses of Travel', *Philological Quarterly* 31 (1972): 488–59.

Johnston, Freya and Mugglestone, Lynda (eds.) (2012). *Samuel Johnson: The Arc of the Pendulum* (Oxford: Oxford University Press).

Justice, George (2002). *The Manufacturers of Literature. Writing and the Literary Marketplace in Eighteenth-Century England* (Newark, N.J.: The University of Delaware Press).

Kaminski, Thomas (1987). *The Early Career of Samuel Johnson* (New York: Oxford University Press).

Keast, W. R. (1957). 'The two *Clarissas* in Johnson's *Dictionary*', *Studies in Philology* 54: 429–39.

Kernan, Alvin (1987). *Printing Technology, Letters, & Samuel Johnson* (Princeton, N.J.: Princeton University Press).

Kolb, Gwin and DeMaria, Jr., Robert (1995). 'Thomas Warton's Observations on the *Faerie Queene* of Spenser, Samuel Johnson's *History of the English Language*, and Warton's History of English Poetry: Reciprocal Indebtedness?', *Philological Quarterly* 74(3): 327–35.

Kolb, Gwin and DeMaria, Jr., Robert, 'The Preliminaries to Dr. Johnson's *Dictionary*: Authorial Revisions and the Establishment of the Texts', *Studies in Bibliography*, 48 (1995), 121–34.

Kolb, Gwin J. (1970). 'Establishing the text of Dr. Johnson's *Plan of a Dictionary of the English Language*'. In W. H. Bond (ed.), *Eighteenth-Century Studies In Honor of Donald F. Hyde* (New York: The Grolier Club): 81–7.

Kolb, Gwin J. and Sledd, James H. (1953). 'Johnson's *Dictionary* and Lexicographical Tradition', *Modern Philology* 50: 171–94.

Korshin, Paul (1970). 'The Johnson–Chesterfield Relationship: A New Hypothesis', *PMLA* 85 (1970): 247–59.

Korshin, Paul (1974). 'Johnson and the Renaissance Dictionary', *Journal of the History of Ideas* 35: 300–12.

Lancashire, Ian (2005). 'Johnson and the Seventeenth-Century Glossographers', *International Journal of Lexicography* 18: 157–71.

Landau, Sidney (2001). *Dictionaries: The Art and Craft of Lexicography*, 2nd edn. (Cambridge: Cambridge University Press).

Lass, Roger (2000). 'Introduction'. In Roger Lass (ed.), *The Cambridge History of the English Language*. Vol. III: *1476–1776* (Cambridge: Cambridge University Press): 1–12.

Leapman, Michael (2012). 'What's so Funny about gout?', *The Daily Telegraph* (2 October 2012).

Le Rougetel, Hazel (2004). 'Miller, Philip (1691–1771)'. In *Oxford Dictionary of National Biography* (Oxford: Oxford University Press, 2004).

Life, Page (2004). 'Brereton, Thomas (1690/91–1722)'. In *Oxford Dictionary of National Biography* (Oxford: Oxford University Press).

Lipking, Lawrence (1970). *The Ordering of the Arts in Eighteenth-Century England* (Princeton, N.J.: Princeton University Press)

Lipking, Lawrence (1998). *Samuel Johnson: the Life of an Author* (Cambridge, Mass.: Harvard University Press).

Lowenthal, David (1995). *The Past is a Foreign Country* (Cambridge: Cambridge University Press).

Lynch, Deidre (1990). '"Beating the track of the Alphabet": Samuel Johnson, Tourism, and the ABCs of Modern Authority', *ELH* 57 (1990): 357–405.

Lynch, Jack (1996). 'The Ground-Work of Style: Use, Elegance, and National Identity in Johnson's *Dictionary*', Unpublished paper delivered 29 September 1996 at NEASECS in Worcester, Mass. Available at <http://andromeda.rutgers.edu/~jlynch/Papers/dict.html>.

Lynch, Jack (2000). '"The Ground-Work of Stile": Johnson on the History of the Language', *Studies in Philology* 97: 454–72.

Lynch, Jack (2005). 'Johnson's Encyclopaedia'. In Jack Lynch and Anne McDermott (eds.), *Anniversary Essays on Johnson's Dictionary* (Cambridge: Cambridge University Press): 129–46.

Lynch, Jack (2006). 'Disgraced by Miscarriage: Four and a Half Centuries of Lexicographical Belligerence', *The Journal of the Rutgers University Libraries* 62: 35–50.

Lynch, Jack and McDermott, Anne (eds.) (2005). *Anniversary Essays on Johnson's Dictionary* (Cambridge: Cambridge University Press).

Lynn, Steven (1992). *Samuel Johnson After Deconstruction: Rhetoric and the Rambler* (Carbondale, Ill.: Southern Illinois University Press).

McAdam, Edward (1951). *Dr. Johnson and the English Law* (Syracuse, N.Y.: Syracuse University Press).

McDermott, Anne (2005). 'The Compilation Methods of Johnson's Dictionary', *Age of Johnson* 16: 1–20.

McDermott, Anne (2005). 'Johnson the Prescriptivist? The Case for the Defence'. In Lynch and McDermott (eds.), *Anniversary Essays on Johnson's Dictionary* (Cambridge: Cambridge University Press): 113–28.

McGrade, A. S. (2004). 'Hooker, Richard (1554–1600)'. In *Oxford Dictionary of National Biography* (Oxford: Oxford University Press, 2004).

McMahon, April (1999). *Understanding Language Change* (Cambridge: Cambridge University Press).

Middendorf, John H. (1960). 'Dr. Johnson and Mercantilism', *Journal of the History of Ideas* 21: 63–83.

Minaeva, Ludmilla (2002). 'Quotations in the Dictionary: The Pros and Cons', in Anna Braasch and Claus Povlsen (eds.), *Proceedings of the Tenth Euralex International Congress* (Copenhagen: Center for Sprogteknologi): 623–7.

Monroe, B. S. (1910). 'An English Academy', *Modern Philology* 8: 107–22.

Moore, Thursten Maxwell (1966). *Samuel Johnson and the Literature of Travel* (Unpublished Ph.D. Dissertation, Ann Arbor: University of Michigan).

Mugglestone, Lynda (2005). *Lost for Words. The Hidden History of the Oxford English Dictionary* (London and New York: Yale University Press, 2005).

Mugglestone, Lynda (2008). 'The Dictionary as Watch', *The New Rambler. Journal of the Johnson Society of London* 2007–8 (2010): 70–7.

Mugglestone, Lynda (2010). 'Registering the Language—Dictionaries, Diction, and the Art of Elocution'. In Raymond Hickey (ed.), *Eighteenth-*

Century English: Ideology and Change (Cambridge: Cambridge University Press, 2010): 309–38.

Mugglestone, Lynda (2012). 'The Battle of the Word-Books: Competition, the "Common Reader", and Johnson's *Dictionary*'. In Freya Johnston and Lynda Mugglestone (eds.), *Samuel Johnson: The Arc of the Pendulum* (Oxford: Oxford University Press, 2012): 140–53.

Mugglestone, Lynda (2013). ' "Life-Writing": The Lexicographer as Biographer in the *Oxford English Dictionary*'. In R. W. McConchie, Teo Juvonen, Mark Kaunisto, Minna Nevala, and Jukka Tyrkkö (eds.), *Selected Proceedings of the 2012 Symposium on New Approaches in English Historical Lexis (HEL-LEX 3)* (Somerville, Mass.: Cascadilla Proceedings Project): 14–26.

Mugglestone, Lynda (2014a). 'Writing the *Dictionary of the English* Language: Johnson's Journey into Words'. In Howard D. Weinbrot and William Freeman Vilas (eds.), *Samuel Johnson: New Contexts For a New Century* (San Marino, Ca.: Huntington Library Press and University of California Press): 131–42.

Mugglestone, Lynda (2014b). 'Ranging Knowledge by the Alphabet: The Literature of Categorization and Organization 1700–1830'. In Robert DeMaria, Jr., Heesok Chang, and Samantha Zachar (eds.), *A Companion to British Literature.* Vol III: *Long Eighteenth-Century Literature 1660–1835* (Chichester: Wiley-Blackwell): 207–22.

Mugglestone, Lynda (forthcoming 2015). 'Prescription and Description in Dictionaries'. In Philip Durkin (ed.), *The Oxford Handbook of Lexicography* (Oxford: Oxford University Press).

Murray, James A. H. (1884). 'Thirteenth Annual Address of the President to the Philological Society'. *Transactions of the Philological Society* 19: 501–31.

Murray, James A. H. (1900). *The Evolution of English Lexicography* (Oxford: Clarendon Press).

Nagashima, Daisuke (1988). *Johnson the Philologist* (Osaka: Kansai University).

Nagashima, Daisuke (1996). 'How Johnson read Hale's *Origination* for his Dictionary; A Linguistic View', *Age of Johnson* 7: 247–90.

Neimeyer, Carl (1934). 'The Earl of Roscommon's Academy', *Modern Language Notes* 49: 432–7.

Nicholls, Graham (1975). ' "The Race with Death". Samuel Johnson and the Sense of an Ending', *Transactions of the Johnson Society*: 17–25.

Osselton, Noel (1983). 'On the History of Dictionaries'. In R. K. K. Hartmann (ed.), *Lexicography; Principles and Practice* (London: Academic Press, 1983): 13–21.

Osselton, Noel (1984). 'Informal Spelling Systems in Early Modern English: 1500–1800'. In N. F. Blake and Charles Jones (eds.), *English Historical Linguistics: Studies in Development* (Sheffield: CECTAL, University of Sheffield, 1984): 123–37.

Osselton, Noel (2006). 'Usage Guidance in Early Dictionaries of English'. *International Journal of Lexicography* 19: 99–105.

Parke, Catherine (1991). *Samuel Johnson and Biographical Thinking* (Columbia, Mo.: University of Missouri Press).

Parker, Fred (2003). *Scepticism and Literature: An Essay on Pope, Hume, Sterne, and Johnson* (Oxford: Oxford University Press).

Pearce, Chris (2006). 'Recovering the "Rigour of Interpretative Lexicography": Border Crossings in Johnson's *Dictionary*', *Textus. English Studies in Italy* (Issue: *Samuel Johnson's* Dictionary *and the Eighteenth-Century World of Words*, (eds.) Giovanni Iamartino and Robert DeMaria, Jr.) 19: 33–51.

Pittock, Murray (1997). *Inventing and Resisting Britain: Cultural Identities in Britain and Ireland, 1685–1789* (Basingstoke: Macmillan).

Poole, Robert (1998). *Calendar Reform in Early Modern England* (London: University College London Press).

Rastell, Paul (2003). 'What Do We Mean by *We*?', *English Today* 19: 50–63.

Read, Allen Walker (1935). 'The Contemporary Quotations in Johnson's Dictionary', *ELH* 2: 261–51.

Reddick, Allen, (1996). *The Making of Johnson's Dictionary, 1746–1773*, rev. edn. (Cambridge: Cambridge University Press).

Reddick, Allen (1997). 'Johnson beyond Jacobitism: Signs of Polemic in the "Dictionary" and the "Life of Milton"', *ELH* 64: 983–1005.

Reddick, Allen (ed.) (2006). *Samuel Johnson's Unpublished Revisions to the Dictionary of the English Language* (Cambridge: Cambridge University Press).

Reddick, Allen (2013). 'So What's Wrong with "Buxom"? Samuel Johnson, Poetical language, and Semantics'. In R. W. McConchie et al. (eds.), *Selected Proceedings of the 2012 Symposium on New Approaches in English Historical Lexis (HEL-LEX 3)* (Somerville, Mass.: Cascadilla Proceedings Project): 159–65.

Riddell, J. A. (1974). 'The Beginning: English Dictionaries of the First Half of the Seventeenth Century', *Leeds Studies in English* 7: 117–53.

Rogers, Pat (1972). *Grub Street; Studies in a Subculture* (London: Methuen).

Rogers, Pat (1996). *The Samuel Johnson Encyclopedia* (Westport, Conn.: Greenwood Press).

Romaine, Suzanne (1998). 'Introduction'. In Suzanne Romaine (ed.), *The Cambridge History of the English Language*. Vol. IV: *1776-1997* (Cambridge: Cambridge University Press, 1998): 7-8.

Sabor, Peter (2012). 'Women Reading and Writing for *The Rambler*'. In Tiffany Potter (ed.), *Women, Popular Culture, and the Eighteenth Century* (Toronto: University of Toronto Press, 2012): 167-84.

Salmon, Vivian (2000). 'Orthography and Punctuation'. In Roger Lass (ed.), *The Cambridge History of the English Language*. Vol. III: *1476-1776* (Cambridge: Cambridge University Press): 332-458.

Scanlan, J. T. (2006). 'Johnson's *Dictionary* and Legal Dictionaries'. In Iamartino and DeMaria (2006): 87-106.

Schwartz, Richard B. (1971). *Samuel Johnson and the New Science* (Madison, Wis.: University of Wisconsin Press).

Segar, Mary (1931). 'Dictionary-making in the Early Eighteenth Century', *Review of English Studies* 7: 210-13.

Siebert, Donald (1986). '*Bubbled, Bamboozled*, and *Bit*: "Low Bad" Words in Johnson's *Dictionary*', *Studies in English Literature, 1500-1900*, 26: 485-96.

Sledd, James (1946). 'Baret's *Alvearie*, an Elizabethan Reference Book', *Studies in Philology* 43: 147-63.

Sledd, James and Kolb, Gwin (1955). *Dr. Johnson's Dictionary: Essays in the Biography of a Book* (Chicago: University of Chicago Press).

Smallwood, Philip (2004). *Johnson's Critical Presence: Image, History, Judgement* (Aldershot: Ashgate).

Solomon, Harry M. (1996). *The Rise of Robert Dodsley: Creating the New Age of Print* (Carbondale, Ill.: Southern Illinois University Press).

Sorensen, Janet (2000). *The Grammar of Empire in Eighteenth-Century British Writing* (Cambridge: Cambridge University Press).

Spector, Robert D. (1997). *Samuel Johnson and the Essay* (London: Greenwood Press).

Spencer, Lois (1977). 'Robert Dodsley and the Johnsonian Connexion', *The New Rambler* 18: 1-18.

Starnes, DeWitt T. and Noyes, Gertrude E. (1991). *The English Dictionary from Cawdrey to Johnson, 1604-1755*, 2nd edn. (Amsterdam and Philadelphia: J. Benjamin).

REFERENCES

Straaijer, Robin (2009). 'Deontic and Epistemic Modals as Indicators of Prescriptive and Descriptive Language in the Grammars by Joseph Priestley and Robert Lowth'. In Ingrid Tieken Boon van Ostade and Wim van der Wurff (eds.), *Current Issues in Late Modern English* (Bern: Peter Lang): 57–88.

Straus, Ralph (1910). *Robert Dodsley: Poet, Publisher & Playwright* (London: John Lane).

Sweet, Rosemary (2004). *Antiquaries: The Discovery of the Past in Eighteenth-Century Britain* (London: Hambleden).

Thomas, Eugene (1974a). 'Dr. Johnson and his Amanuenses', *Transactions of the Johnson Society* (1974): 20–30.

Thomas, Eugene (1974b). *A Bibliographical and Critical Analysis of Johnson's Dictionary* (Unpublished dissertation, University of Wales).

Tieken Boon van Ostade, Ingrid (1991). 'Samuel Richardson's Role as Linguistic Innovator; A Sociolinguistic Analysis'. In Ingrid Tieken Boon van Ostade and John Frankis (eds.), *Language Usage and Description: Studies Presented to N. E. Osselton on the Occasion of his Retirement* (Amsterdam: Rodopi): 47–58.

Tieken Boon van Ostade, Ingrid (2009). *An Introduction to Late Modern English* (Edinburgh: Edinburgh University Press).

Tieken Boon van Ostade, Ingrid (2011). *The Bishop's Grammar: Robert Lowth and the Rise of Prescriptivism in English* (Oxford: Oxford University Press).

'To the Admirers of Shakespeare' (1757). *The London Chronicle: Or, Universal Evening Post* (12–14 April): 358–9.

Vance, John A. (1984). *Samuel Johnson and the Sense of History* (Athens, Ga.: University of Georgia Press).

Vance, John A. (1987). 'Johnson's Historical Reviews'. In Prem Nath (ed.), *Fresh Reflections on Samuel Johnson* (Troy, N.Y.: Whitston): 63–84.

Varney, Andrew (1998). *Eighteenth-Century Writers in their World. A Might Maze* (Basingstoke: Macmillan).

Vilmar, Christopher (2009). 'The Authoritative Samuel Johnson', *The Cambridge Quarterly* 38: 164–77.

Weinbrot, Howard (1971). 'Johnson's *Dictionary* and *The World*: The Papers of Lord Chesterfield and Richard Owen Cambridge', *Philological Quarterly* 50: 663–9.

Weinbrot, Howard (2005). *Aspects of Samuel Johnson: Essays on his Arts, Mind, Afterlife, and Politics* (Newark, N.J.: University of Delaware Press).

Wild, Kate (2008). 'Vulgar and Popular in Johnson, Webster and the OED'. In Eliswndra Bernal and Janet DeCesaris (eds.), *Proceedings of the XIII Euralex International Congress* (Barcelona: Documenta Universitaria): 1209–14.

Williams, Glyndwr (1999). *The Prize of all the Oceans: the Triumph and Tragedy of Anson's Voyage Round the World* (London: Harper Collins).

Wimsatt, W. K. Jr. (1951). 'Samuel Johnson and Dryden's "Du Fresnoy"', *Studies in Philology* 48 (1951): 26–39.

Wimsatt, W. K. Jr. (1959). 'Johnson's Dictionary'. In Frederick W. Hilles (ed.), *New Light on Dr. Johnson* (New Haven, Conn.: Yale University Press): 65–90.

Wimsatt, W. K. Jr. and Wimsatt, Margaret H. (1948). 'Self-Quotations and Anonymous Quotations in Johnson's Dictionary', *ELH* 15: 60–8.

Electronic resources

Oxford English Dictionary Online, available at <http://www.oed.com/> [cited as *OED Online*].

Oxford Dictionary of National Biography, available at <http://www.oxforddnb.com> [cited as *ODNB Online*].

Index

Dictionary of the English Language
  (1773) *(cont.)*
 and conservatism 212–13, 259 n.8
 correction of errors in 209–10,
  239 n.46, 259 n.6
 and prescription 212–13
disannul 120
Dodsley, Robert 30–1, 32, 35, 40, 49,
  50, 58, 172, 200, 226 n.30, 228 n.47,
  228 n.48, 230 n.61, 253 n.12
Donne, John 57, 58, 67
doubt viii, 14, 15, 48, 52, 100–11, 111,
  112–13, 115, 116, 129–32,
  254 n.20
Dryden, John 30, 57, 58, 62, 73, 74,
  76, 77, 80, 103, 112, 114, 124,
  125, 143, 149–50, 170, 174, 179,
  180–1, 183, 206, 248 n.26, 252
  n.7, 255 n.31
 criticism of 74, 124, 150, 152, 157–9,
  163, 171, 248 n.28

Edwards, Oliver 31
Edwards, Thomas ix, 13, 207–8, 258 n.23
empiricism viii, 22, 38, 39, 46, 54, 56–7,
  60–75, 115, 120–1
 flaws in 64, 119–21, *see also*
  citations; reading for the
  Dictionary
English 13, 14, 16, 36, 49, 87, 92, 126,
  142–3, 146–8, 150, 154, 159, 161,
  165, 166, 169, 175–6, 196, 198,
  250 n.52, 254 n.26
 comparison with French 29, 35–6, 145
 earlier history of 170, 172–4, *see also*
  Middle English; Old English
 lexical diversity of 160–1, 166
 as living language 165, 166, 167–8,
  170–2, 174, 191–3, 198, 202–4
 as modern language 170, 174, 184–8
 epistemic modality 20, 55–6, 103–5,
  129–30, 223 n.67
 etymology 3, 24, 44, 67–8, 83, 98, 101,
  103, 105, 115, 175–9, 181, 195, 233
  n.50, 244 n.35, 251 n.61, 254 n.20,
  255 n.27
Evelyn, John 28–9

expectation viii, 12, 13, 14, 19–20, 34,
  47, 48, 50, 51, 59, 91, 168, 170, 176,
  192, 198, 205, 253 n.8
 experience 21, 24, 25, 50, 51, 60, 86,
  150, 203
 importance of 20, 176, 184, 192, 201

falsify 158–9, 163, 250
fancy 46, 60, 61, 122, 126–7, 169, 173,
  197, 254 n.20
fashion, in language 25, 146, 147, 184,
  235 n.78, 247 n.17
Fenton, Elijah 96, 238 n.31
Fielding, Henry 111–12
finesse 152, 163
Fisher, Anne 12, 219
fixing the language vi–vii, 12–17, 21,
  28–31, 35, 40, 45, 49, 97, 113, 116,
  152, 168–9, 179, 185, 190, 200, 206,
  255 n.33, *see also* obsolescence;
  prescriptivism
 and impossibility of 16–17, 46, 47, 50,
  51–2, 159, 164–5, 168–70, 183–4,
  185, 189, 192, 196–8, 199–200
Florio, John 6–8, 9, 10, 11, 14, 16, 205,
  218 n.17
folk-linguistics 79, 85
Ford, Samuel 31, 226 n.27
fraischeur 149–50, 152, 159, 163, 171,
  248 n.26
France 27, 29, 30, 39, 142, 143, 145–6,
  196, 246 n.12, 246 n.13, 246 n.14,
  247 n.16
French 23, 44, 68, 143–4, 150–7, 160–1,
  162–3, 178, 250 n.52, 250 n.57,
  252 n.66
 influence on English 143, 146–7, 175
 and loanwords 143, 145–57, *see also*
  Gallicisms
 as site of change 164–5, 198
Frenchify 146
frugality 113, 114, 115

Gallicisms 148–9, 150–5, 156–7, 160,
  165, 247 n.21, 249 n.4, 250 n.47,
  251 n.68, 252 n.69, *see also* French
gaol 103, 239 n.47

Garrick, David 2, 50–1, 79, 205–6
gender and language 79, 85–6,
    235 n.77, 235 n.78
Gentleman's Magazine 15, 49, 55, 79,
    186, 190, 206, 227 n.43
Gil, Alexander 108
Gough Square 3, 216 n.5, 251 n.65
gout 146, 165
Gray, Thomas 123
Greene, Donald 21, 92, 95
Grubstreet 9, 50

Hale, Matthew 62–6, 68–9, 70, 74, 89,
    101, 232 n.36, 233 n.52.
Hall, John 3, 4
Hawkesworth, John 206
Hawkins, John 30, 31–2, 60, 62, 121,
    219–20
Hayward, Eliza 79
head 118, 125
headwords 21, 62, 64, 70, 87, 88, 99,
    101, 104–5, 107, 229
hedging 104, 130–2, 156, 177–8, 244 n.44
history 24, 143, 154, 156, 167, 170–1,
    173, 178, 184–5, 186–7, 198,
    255 n.28, *see also* time
engagement with in
    Dictionary 170–3, 174–6, 179–86
Hobbes, Thomas 72
Holder William 74
Hooker, Richard 57, 69, 73, 100, 196,
    233 n.53
hope viii, 14–15, 47, 96, 167–70, 189,
    201, 205
Horace 129, 167, 244 n.37
humour 134–5, *see also* ludicrous
hurly-burly 177
hyperbole 19, 197

-ick, and variation 99, 201, 240 n.53
Idler 121
ignore 159–60
imagination 20, 46, 47, 61, 96, 167,
    173, 184. 200, 228 n.54,
    254 n.20
innovation 29, 127, 147, 150, 159,
    170–1, 182, 185, 186–8, 192,

202–3, 252 n.7, 256 n.35, *see also*
    language change
condemnation of 127–8, 147, 150,
    212–13, 248 n.28,
Irene 93, 94, 226 n.30
Italian 159, 162

James, Robert 55, 230 n.5
Jervas, Charles 74, 155
Johnson, Samuel 3, 13, 15, 31–2, 33, 36,
    79, 84–5, 91–2, 98, 115, 127, 139,
    141, 144, 147, 154, 158, 160. 169,
    173, 184, 190, 216, 219, 246 n.12,
    252 n.66, *see also* Dictionary;
    lexicographer; lexicography
and Chesterfield 40, 42, 44, 47,
    49–50, 69, 91–2, 97, 144, 147,
    172, 196, 229 n.65, *see also*
    Chesterfield, Lord
and critical practice 120–7
as 'father of the dictionary' 25
as guardian of the language viii, 23,
    118–20, 138–9, 142, 144, 147,
    150, 152, 155, 163–4
interest in usage 31, 75, 93, 98–9,
    120–2, 171, 180–3, 185–6, 208,
    241 n.61, *see also* custom
and other languages 162–3, 165,
    248 n.28, 251 n.62, n.63, n.65
and patriotism 15, 95, 145, 146–7, 160
and political models of
    language 91–6, 102, 122, 127–8,
    238 n.28
and pragmatism 46, 47, 51, 52, 86,
    133, 152, 164, 253 n.8
and prescriptive ambitions vi–vii,
    17–18, 122, 168, 175,
    180–1, 188–9, *see also*
    prescriptivism
and private spelling 106–7, 227 n.44,
    238 n.34, 240 n.52, 240 n.54,
    see also spelling
reputation of 115–16
as reviewer 19, 79, 235 n.75, 241 n.61
and tolerance of variation 37–9,
    43–4, 97–8, 102–6, 129, 156,
    198, *see also* doubt; uncertainty

INDEX

uncertainty 15, 29, 40, 97, 99, 100,
103–4, 129, 131, 176–8, 179, 195,
204, 239, 254 n.20, *see also* doubt
utopias 169, 198–200, 257 n.13

variation 20, 21, 23, 28, 37,
39–40, 101–4, 129–30,
155–6, 168, 198, 227 n.39,
see also spelling; meaning
Voyage to Abyssinia 19, 162
vulgar words 137–8

Warburton, William 8, 11, 111,
112–13, 114–15, 249 n.43
Warton, Thomas vii, 3, 8, 11, 52, 57,
172, 173, 205

Watts, Isaac 66, 69, 77, 84, 89, 90, 98,
152, 185, 203
whence 119–20, 129
Wilkins, John 142–3
Wilson, Thomas 57, 74
Wiseman, Richard 74, 75, 76
with 211–12
witticism 170–1, 252 n.7
women writers 78–81, 86, 235 n.75
as authorities for language 79–80,
235 n.80, 236 n.81, *see also*
gender and language

Xerxes 17, 21, 69, 94, 233 n.51

yet 155

Printed and bound by CPI Group (UK) Ltd, Croydon, CR0 4YY